Gospel of the Kingdom

Not the Gospel of the Church

Robert J Cottle

Gospel of the Kingdom

Copyright © 2019 by the **Bellbird Trust**

Published by:

Revival Waves of Glory Books & Publishing

PO Box 596

Litchfield, IL 62056,

United States of America.

ISBN (pbk) 978-1-0878-1496-4

Gospel of the Kingdom

Robert J Cottle

Special thanks:

- To: Bruce for his time-consuming efforts in editing this book.

- To: David Nathan, Bread of Life Ministries, Johannesburg, South Africa. This book is primarily based on transcripts of the audio of 2010 recordings of teachings by David Nathan specifically given for his church and used with permission.

CONTENTS

Introduction

Much of this book is based on transcripts of recordings of teachings by David Nathan specifically given for his church in 2010 and used with permission. David is a Bible teacher, elder and leader of Bread of Life Ministries based in Gauteng, South Africa. Born into an orthodox Jewish family David came to faith in Jesus in his early twenties. This upbringing enables David to teach from the Scripture through a unique Hebraic understanding. Robert is a writer and published author of Christian books, living in Nelson New Zealand.

The Chapters which are based on the recorded teachings by David on the Kingdom of God have been modified as necessary to convert the oral address to a written media while still retaining the underlying message but be comprehendible. The remaining portions are original works especially written for this book by Robert.

The Kingdom of God is a subject that is not spoken about much, in context, in the Church. We tend to talk a lot about the Kingdom of God but we don't really understand what the Kingdom of God actually is. This is because the Church is busy with the gospel of the Church. The Church is about the Church and not about the Kingdom – generally speaking.

David recalls a time during which they meet a couple of times each week to pray and intercede to seek God's face for His will at his church. One evening someone shared a portion of scripture from Matthew 11 which was the first time he'd heard that particular verse accurately translated into Afrikaans. That translation gave the passage a more distinct understanding when compared to English. A question asked regarding that Scripture is what inspired David to give a series of teachings on the Kingdom of God that has now morphed into this book.

It's very important that we, as a Church, understand about the Kingdom of God. The King is returning to this earth very soon to set up His Kingdom, yet it is a subject seldom discussed in the wider body of Christ. The words of Jesus declare, *"And this gospel of the kingdom will be preached in all the world as a witness to all the nations, and then the end will come.*" Clearly at the conclusion of the Church Age the Gospel of the Kingdom will be widely discussed.

What then is a clear definition of the Kingdom? What are the characteristics of a citizen of the Kingdom? What is our part in the eternal Kingdom? What is the Power of the Kingdom and how is that seen now? What is the work of the Kingdom, now in this life, so that the Kingdom is advanced? What is the Gospel of the Kingdom as opposed to the Gospel of salvation? This book endeavours to provide definitive answers to these questions and many others. Entering and inhabiting the Kingdom is our divine inheritance. Just understanding about the Kingdom is not enough, we must use passion to enter it, experience it and work for its advancement.

Unfortunately, the devil through clever deception has successfully diverted the attention of many in the Church away from the true concept and purpose of the Kingdom of God. Instead, many leaders today are solely focused on numerical statistics and how to grow church membership with little concern for the state of those members. Their gospel preaching contains a strong bias towards what Jesus can do for my life now and not on how I can serve the King, advancing the Kingdom of God.

In this book the intention is to allow the Word to speak for itself and not instil any personal bias. Please read carefully and ask for understanding by the Holy Spirit. Also, don't only take the writer's word for it. Please personally check out all the Bible references given.

Finally, I believe that God has a sense of humour so I've incorporated meaningful but ambiguous quotes from various Church signs around the world at the start of each Chapter.

"Do you know what Hell is?

Come and listen to our preacher"

Chapter 1

The Kingdom of God

◆

I want to explore with you, by God's grace something that's really, really important for every Christian to fully comprehend.

Recently, I've been examining the subject of the reformation of the Church and the undeniable conclusion is that the present-day Church is not as the Bible describes it. It is therefore absolutely imperative for the Church to transform. Generally, what we currently understand as Christianity is nothing more than tradition. And tradition is completely devoid of any biblical roots. I know that may be very upsetting to hear but it's important we do get challenged because God is taking His Church into an area of restoration. God is coming back for a spotless bride for a bride without flaw or blemish. A bride that will reflect what Jesus died to accomplish – to establish the Kingdom of God.

Turn with me, if you would, to the Book of Daniel, Chapter 2. Here we find Daniel together with the remnant of the nation of Israel, and specifically Judah, in captivity under the Babylonians. Nebuchadnezzar, the Emperor of this Empire, one night had a dream, a nightmare; therefore, he calls all his wise men, magicians and sages together. He says "I had this dream and I want you to tell me its interpretation but before you tell me its interpretation I want you to tell me what I dreamed." Of course they cried, foul. "That's unfair, how can you expect us to interpret a dream that we haven't even heard." Nebuchadnezzar however, was in no mood to put up with their excuses and assigned one of his captains to begin executing all the wise men of Babylon. This news quickly reached Daniel who told the captain that had been assigned with the task of executing all of the wise men, to hold on for a bit as he, Shadrach, Meshach, and

Abednego were going to pray and seek God's face and get the dream from God together with its interpretation. This is exactly what happened and Daniel came before Nebuchadnezzar not only with the dream but also the interpretation.

So now we know the setting I want to just focus on verse 34. You probably are very familiar already with Nebuchadnezzar's dream. He saw a large statue with a head of gold, shoulders and chest of silver, a belly of bronze and thighs of iron and clay. So in verse 34 we read *"You watched while a stone was cut out without hands, which struck the image on its feet of iron and clay, and broke them in pieces. Then the iron, the clay, the bronze, the silver, and the gold were crushed together, and became like chaff from the summer threshing floors; the wind carried them away so that no trace of them was found. And the stone that struck the image became a great mountain and filled the whole earth."*

In the dream Nebuchadnezzar sees a statue and while he's looking at the statue a small stone is cut out without hands, it then strikes the statue at its feet. The whole statue doesn't just break; it literally disintegrates so that nothing is left but dust and powder. This dust and powder then gets blown into oblivion. Now, the interpretation of the dream we see in verse 44. Daniel begins to speak about the various kingdoms explaining that the golden head represents, Babylon, and that the chest of silver represents the next kingdom coming after Babylon. A further kingdom follows after which is the kingdom of iron and clay which we know represents Rome. The details about those kingdoms are covered in my teachings on eschatology; I don't want to revisit all that now as that's another subject.

So, in verse 44 it says *"And in the days of these kings the God of heaven will set up a kingdom"* [Part verse]. Now we know that in the vision the legs and feet of iron mixed with clay represent the Roman Empire. Eschatology is very clear on that. Here Daniel, speaking by the Spirit of God, says that at the time of 'that' Kingdom (the legs and feet of iron mixed with clay) that the God of heaven will set up His Kingdom. The dream is about the kingdoms of men but it also reveals the Kingdom of God. It says the Kingdom of God is going to strike the kingdoms of men. This Kingdom, it tells us in rest of verse 44 *"which shall never be destroyed; and the kingdom shall not be left to other people; it shall break in pieces and consume all these kingdoms, and it shall stand forever."* [Part verse]

4

The Kingdom that God will establish at the time of the kingdoms of men, this Kingdom, that God establishes, will not be left to the people of the world and the kingdoms of men will we be remembered no more. So, let's just conclude Daniels interpretation before we move on. Verse 45 continues *"Inasmuch as you saw that the stone was cut out of the mountain without hands, and that it broke in pieces the iron, the bronze, the clay, the silver, and the gold--the great God has made known to the king what will come to pass after this. The dream is certain, and its interpretation is sure."*

Saints, this seems like an unimportant portion of Scripture. But this is the beginning of God's revelation of His Kingdom. It informs us that the Kingdom of God will come and that it will begin during the times of the kingdoms of men. The Roman Empire, the kingdom of Rome, is symbolized in Daniel Chapter 2 as the part of the statue with legs of iron mixed with clay. The kingdom of Rome abides in some form even today as we've understood from our study of eschatology. The Kingdom of God will begin at the time of the Roman Empire but the end result is that the Kingdom of God will utterly destroy, obliterate and leave without trace, the kingdoms of men. The kingdoms of men will be extinct and remembered no more.

All that is absolute truth, it's undeniably certain, it will happen but what on earth does it mean to you and me? Well I'm so pleased you asked that question. The answer is; everything. That leads us on to Matthew Chapter 11. It's so important, when we speak about restoration, that we understand the Kingdom of heaven, because right now the Church is not busy with the Kingdom of heaven. The Church is not busy with the Kingdom of God the Church is busy with the gospel of the Church. The gospel of the Church is completely different to the gospel of the Kingdom. In fact, the gospel of the Church opposes the gospel of the Kingdom. My goodness, that's a bold statement so if you're new to Church please don't run of screaming "a heretic, a heretic"! One of my endearing idiosyncrasies is that I like to make outrageous statements but then systematically prove them scripturally. So, let's begin.

Saints, we've got to move from the gospel of the Church to the gospel of the Kingdom. Jesus made one promise, actually he made many promises, but one that's particularly important to what we're discussing and it's in the book of Matthew Chapter 24 verse 14. Jesus is speaking about the end times when he makes a most amazing statement. He says and this gospel of the Kingdom; let's check out the verse to ensure I'm quoting correctly. It says *"And this gospel of the Kingdom"* [Part verse], note, not "this gospel of salvation," not "the gospel of the Church." Jesus says; *"And this gospel of the kingdom will be preached in **all the world** as a witness to all the nations, **and then** the end will come."* [Emphasis added] Saints that is a very, very important prophecy. Jesus has promised the Church that before His return and before the end-time plays out, there is going to be a dramatic event and that event is that the gospel of the Kingdom will be preached to every single nation throughout the world – every man, woman and child will be exposed to the gospel of the Kingdom. However as long as we, the Church, are busy with the gospel of the Church, the gospel the Kingdom is not being preached, therefore there has to be a restoration. We can't continue in doing what Christ has not commanded the Church to do. We are not called to preach the gospel of the Church. I suspect that right now you may be asking, "Well what is the gospel of the Church?"

Thank you, I'm so pleased you asked that question. You should never be afraid to put your hand up in Church and say, "I have no idea what you're talking about; can you please explain what you've just said?" Do you know about the chap called John the Baptist? What did John the Baptist do? Yes, he preached repentance, but why did he preach repentance? He preached repentance because the Kingdom of God is at hand. Interesting isn't it. The New Testament begins with the forerunner of the Messiah, the Prophet John, and his message is repent for the Kingdom of God is at hand. In other words, it's *about* to come. The Kingdom of heaven is about to come, it had not yet come it, was *about* to come.

In Matthew Chapter 11 verse 1 the Bible says *"Now it came to pass, when Jesus finished commanding His twelve disciples, that He departed from there to teach and to preach in their cities."* In Matthew Chapter 10, Jesus sends out his disciples and He tells them, in verse 5 to 7, *"These twelve Jesus sent out and commanded them, saying: "Do not go into the way of the Gentiles, and do not enter a city of the Samaritans. But go rather to the lost sheep of the house of Israel. And as you go, preach, saying, 'The kingdom of heaven is at hand.'"* This is the instruction Jesus gave to his disciples before Chapter 11. He told them to go and preach to the nation of Israel that *"The Kingdom of heaven is at hand"*, it's about to come – that it is imminent. Then he goes on to say in verse 8, *"Heal the sick,"* the Kingdom of God is at hand. Go preach that message; *"Heal the sick, cleanse the lepers, raise the dead, cast out demons. Freely you have received, freely give."* Interesting, isn't it.

Okay, I'm laying the foundations and right now all you can see is scattered bricks everywhere, but we will bring them together. Matthew Chapter 11, Jesus sends out his twelve disciples and in verse 2 and 3 we read, *"And when John had heard in prison about the works of Christ, he sent two of his disciples and said to Him, "Are You the Coming One, or do we look for another?"* That's incredible, when you think about this. John the Baptist finds himself in prison and he sends two of his disciples to ask Jesus are you really the Messiah? "Have I blown it because not many years ago probably two at the most three years ago I proclaimed before everybody, "Behold the Lamb of God who takes away the sins of the world"? I baptized this man, I knew he was the Messiah then but now, just a few years later, I'm now questioning is this The Messiah?"

Saints what happened to John? Why did John doubt that Jesus was the Messiah? This is crucial if you want to understand the Kingdom of God. We need to look at why John fell into confusion. The Church is also in confusion because we don't understand the gospel of the Kingdom. John was in confusion but at one stage in his life he was absolutely one hundred per cent convinced that Jesus was 'The Messiah', that Jesus was 'The Christ', that Jesus was 'The coming King' of this Kingdom. But now a very short time later, actually a very, very short time later, we're talking at the most three years - that's a very short time, that we see John sending some of his disciples to ask Jesus are you truly the Messiah? Why did John fall into confusion? It was his expectancy! John fell into confusion because of expectancy. His expectation of the Messiah was not in line with the word of the Living God.

Saints, do you get that? This is very important. John the Baptist fell into error because of his incorrect perception of the King of the Kingdom. John's expectancy was that Jesus would increase and he would decrease but what John really expected was that Jesus would begin to rally the Nation of Israel with God's supernatural enabling, to overthrow the Roman Empire. Not only to deliver the nation of Israel but begin to take over the nations of the world – because, that is the promise of the Messiah.

Those of you are familiar with the Old Testament know that all the nations will serve the Lord Jesus Christ. It tells us so in Psalm 2 *"Why do the nation's rage and the people plot a vein thing?"....* *"Against the Lord and his Anointed". "He who sits in the heavens shall laugh; The Lord shall hold them in derision." The nations will bow down and kiss the prince."* The Old Testament teaches that when the Messiah comes, when the King of Israel comes, He will bring the nations under His authority and rule. This was the expectation of John the Baptist. So why is that incorrect? Why was John's expectation of the Messiah wrong? His expectation is biblical, yet erroneous at the same time. The Bible also teaches in Isaiah Chapter 53 that the Messiah will be executed for the sins of the nation. (Verse 8 *"For He was cut off from the land of the living; For the transgressions of My people, He was stricken."*) Psalm 22 tells us that He'll be crucified. Verse 16, *"They pierced My hands and My feet;"* ... Verse 18, *"And for My clothing they cast lots."* In Chapter 9 of the Book of Daniel verse 26 speaks about the Messiah being (kârath in Hebrew) cut-off, executed. *"And after the sixty-two weeks Messiah shall be cut off,"* [Part of verse]

The very same Old Testament that teaches about a glorious King who will take over the nations of the earth also speaks about a suffering servant, who will die for the sins of His people. The Old Testament teaches one Messiah, two comings – one King two comings. The first as a servant to pay the price for man's Redemption, the second to set up His Kingdom. John fell into error not understanding that there were two comings of the Messiah. That the first was for redemption and the second was to set up an eternal Kingdom. That's why John got confused and in the same manner Christians in the Church are falling into misunderstanding, into strife, into division, of backsliding because we don't understand the Kingdom.

We have expectations which aren't being met, so we are starting to question God and His Kingdom. We're starting to fight with each other, to destroy each other because we've lost sight of, or have never seen what the Kingdom of God is supposed to be. John blew it, he, who we read, was the greatest of all Old Testament Saints. Likewise, the Church has fumbled today for the very same reason. We don't understand the Kingdom but by God's grace we are going to learn about this glorious Kingdom.

In verse 3 of Matthew 11, John's disciples ask Jesus "Are You the Coming One, or do we look for another?" Jesus answered and said to them, "Go and tell John the things which you hear and see: The blind see and the lame walk; the lepers are cleansed and the deaf hear; the dead are raised up and the poor have the gospel preached to them. And blessed is he who is not offended because of Me.'"" Go, tell John. Look at what's being done, the blind are seeing, the deaf are hearing, the oppressed are going free and the Gospels is being preached to the poor. Why do you ask if I'm the Messiah or not? Look at the fruit of the Kingdom being established.

Jesus response to John's disciple is; "Look at what is being done. Look at the power of God being manifested. That is all the evidence you need that I am the Messiah and the Kingdom is at hand." He told these disciples in an earlier Chapter to go, preached the gospel of the Kingdom, tell the folk that the gospel the Kingdom is at hand, heal the sick raise the dead. It says in 1 Corinthians Chapter 4, verse 20 "For the Kingdom of God is not in word, but in power." The Kingdom of God is not a theology; the Kingdom of God is not a system or a doctrine. The Kingdom of God is God's power, manifest amongst men. Until we are seeing God's power manifest amongst men we are not busy with the Kingdom of God, we're just busy with the kingdom of the gospel of the Church.

The gospel the Church concerns itself with doctrine and disputes. The Kingdom of God answers all disputes by the manifest presence and power of God. One does not need to have a seminar about the baptism of the Holy Spirit; you simply need the presence of God present to baptize people in the Holy Spirit. You don't need the books the tapes or the DVDs. Do you see the difference, saints? The Kingdom of God is not in word but in power. The Church has no power, but much word. One is the gospel of the Church; the other is the gospel the Kingdom.

Now I am a staunch, staunch believer in sound doctrine, in fact I'm an advocate of flawless doctrine. However, I'm also just as fanatical about the power of God being manifest as I am about unblemished doctrine. One without the other is not the Kingdom of God. One without the other is not right.

So let's explore this Kingdom of God. Matthew Chapter 11, verse 6 says; "*And blessed is he who is not offended because of Me.*" Saints, the problem with the Church today is that there is so much offense. We are so offended one with another. It doesn't take much for Christians, who once loved each other, the next day to hate one another, with a vicious hatred. Where does this come from? Obviously not from God. That's not the Kingdom of God being manifest because the Kingdom of God speaks of brotherly love. The attributes Kingdom of God, the Bible tells us, are gentleness, meekness, lowliness of heart, self-control with each esteeming others better than themselves. We obviously are not in the Kingdom of God because we're not seeing those things in the Church.

If the characteristics of the Kingdom were manifest in the Church, then the Church would be behaving like Christ expects us to behave. But we're not, and in fact we sometimes act terribly then wake up the next morning, have our quiet time with God and think we're okay. That's the depth of our delusion. I'm not speaking of any particular individual; I'm speaking about the Church universally. I'm speaking about the Church of Jesus Christ, about the Church of Jesus universally. I know it sounds like I'm waffling but I'm going to move on and by God's grace this will all start to make sense soon.

Let's read Matthew 11: 7-11 *"As they departed, Jesus began to say to the multitudes concerning John: "What did you go out into the wilderness to see? A reed shaken by the wind? But what did you go out to see? A man clothed in soft garments? Indeed, those who wear soft clothing are in kings' houses. But what did you go out to see? A prophet? Yes, I say to you, and more than a prophet. For this is he of whom it is written: 'Behold, I send My messenger before Your face, Who will prepare Your way before You.'"*

Now, take note of verse 11 *"Assuredly, I say to you, among those born of women there has not risen one greater than John the Baptist; but he who is least in the kingdom of heaven is greater than he."* I can guarantee you that very few Christians today actually believe that's true. No, don't "Amen", say "Oh my, oh goodness!" Did you just hear what Jesus said? "Of all those born of woman," that's Moses, David, Samuel, Miriam, Esther, Ruth and Deborah, (so the ladies don't feel excluded), Elisha and Elijah. None of those are greater than John the Baptist. What Jesus is saying is that John the Baptist was the greatest prophet that ever lived, until that day. That means John the Baptist, according to Jesus, the words of the LORD, was greater than Moses in his spiritual authority and in his relationship with the Father. He was greater than King David, greater than any individual who ever lived, up until that moment. Saints, John was not just some insignificant prophet, he is, by the account of the actual words our Lord Jesus Christ, the greatest prophet that ever lived. Now, here comes a great truth that many of us refused to believe. Jesus says, "But he or, she, who is least in the Kingdom of heaven, is greater than he." Of those born of women none has been greater than John the Baptist but the least in the Kingdom of heaven is greater than John. This means that you potentially, according to the will of God, are greater in terms of the spiritual authority, your access to God and the power of God flowing through you, then Moses ever was.

After all I mean what did Moses do? He only split the Red Sea. He only called down ten plagues, struck a rock and a fountain of water gushed out. You know, he only prayed then God opened the earth and swallowed 250 people. I mean, after all Moses didn't do much, did he? Clearly, you obviously knew that you were greater than Moses so what is all the confusion about! You see Saints, the problem is that we look at what Moses did and then think that this scripture (Matthew 11:11) can't be true. That's because we don't understand the Kingdom of heaven.

Before I go on I do need to make some clarification, so please read carefully. At this point in Scripture round about AD 25 or 26, Moses was not in the Kingdom of heaven. Neither was John the Baptist in the Kingdom of heaven because the Kingdom of heaven hadn't come yet. The Kingdom of heaven was at hand but Moses never lived under the Kingdom of heaven. John the Baptist never lived under the Kingdom of heaven. King David never lived under the Kingdom of heaven. No, they all lived under the Old Covenant, under the Mosaic Law. They never tasted or experienced the Kingdom of heaven until the resurrection of Jesus. They ministered under the Law of Moses and never had the opportunity to minister under the power of the Kingdom of heaven which you and I have the awesome privilege of ministering under. Spiritually because of what Jesus has done, not because you and I are anything special but only because of the work of Jesus Christ on the cross of Calvary. It is because of what He did that we have the privilege of access to the Father, the baptism in the Holy Spirit – the Living God dwelling within our being – which makes us greater than any Old Testament Saints.

11

It's time then that we start believing that. Not because I am anything, actually it's quite the opposite, it's because God is everything. It's only because of God's love that I have the potential to do great works because the Kingdom of God is within me. It's only through God's enabling that can I do greater works than any of the Old Testament Saints. What a struggle for us, ah? How hard it is, to have the Word of God and not being able to believe it. Dear Saints, that's the problem with the Church. We have the Word, we might even know the Word, but we don't believe the Word. Many of say I can't deny what I read in that verse in Matthew. I can't deny what it says, because it's in the Bible. Jesus said it, so I know it's true but I cannot find faith to believe it. Is that where you are? Do you say "I can't find faith to believe that I am in a better position spiritually and have the potential to be more effective than any of the Old Testament Saints?" Unfortunately, that's where the Church finds itself today.

Anyway, moving on, Mathew 11 verse 12, *"And from the days of John the Baptist until now the kingdom of heaven suffers violence, and the violent take it by force."* Now if you've got an English translation that verse makes absolutely no sense. If you've got a new American Study Bible, then you can look at the footnote. Then perhaps it begins to make sense, but you probably don't have such a Bible in which case you're completely in the dark. So what does this verse 12 footnote say? It gives the literal translation. *"The Kingdom of heaven is forcibly entered and the violent seizes it for themselves."* That begins to sheds light on the meaning but only partially.

The verse begins, *"from the days of John the Baptist until now."* Let me ask you a question, how long had the Kingdom of heaven been suffering violence for? I'll give you a clue, *"from the days of John the Baptist until now the Kingdom of heaven suffers violence,"* How long had the Kingdom of heaven been exposed to violence? *"From the days of John the Baptist until now the Kingdom of Heaven..."* Saints this calls for comprehension. That's a wonderful tool to use, when reading the Bible! *"From the days until John the Baptist,"* so when did the Kingdom of heaven start suffering violence? From the days of John, that is what Jesus said. From the days of John, he didn't say from days of Moses. How long had John been ministering? "From the days until John the Baptist until now," We know that Jesus only ministered for three and a half years so, all right, let's assume that this account is taking place in the second or third year of Jesus' ministry. John probably started ministering at the age what about twenty. Jesus was baptized at the age of thirty. John was six months older than Jesus. Mary goes to visit Elizabeth and the Bible says Elizabeth was six months pregnant. Mary had just conceived, by the Holy Spirit, but it says that the babe in Elizabeth's womb leaped for joy. There were six months between Jesus and John. So let's assume that John started ministering at 20 and he baptized Jesus when Jesus was about 30. Let's say this verse takes place in the second or third year of Christ's ministry so we're looking at a period of 12 of 13 years. Or perhaps John started ministering at 18 in which case it was 15 years.

The point is the Kingdom heaven began to be reality when John the Baptist started ministering. Up until the time of John the Father had not introduced the Kingdom to earth. What does that mean? It means that the Old Testament has nothing to do with the Kingdom of God. The prophecies, however, in the Old Testament speak more about the Kingdom of God than the New Testament does but the Law of Moses has nothing to do with the Kingdom of God. The various foods that you can or can't eat have got nothing to do with the Kingdom of God. The way you worship, wearing certain clothing has got nothing to do the Kingdom of God. Anyway that's by the bye.

John's message was to repent for the Kingdom of God is at hand - the King of heaven is "*at hand.*" That is the message that he preached. The Kingdom of heaven, from the time of the preaching of John until now, the Kingdom of Heaven suffers violence. That word 'violence' in the Greek is biazō." Biazō actually doesn't mean violence, as a showing aggression towards somebody; it means energy to press in. For example, in a place like India when the train stops at a station and 300 people try to squeeze into a carriage that's only meant to accommodate a hundred then you will see biazo; you'll see energy being expended, to press in. You're going to see effort. to provide a more traditional explanation, it's like a department store's red-hangar sale, where there's one garment and ten ladies who want that garment. Who gets the garment? The one who expresses 'biazō'; the passion to press in, to seize hold of, to obtain, gets the garment. Biazō; it is a passion to obtain, a passion to press in, a passion to hold and have ownership of.

Now, understanding Greek a bit better we'll read the scripture again, "From the time of John the Baptist until now" – over the last fifteen years or so, since Jesus. Not 2000 years, not a century, it's just 15 years. From John to now, the Kingdom of heaven is seized by the passionate. It is seized by those who thirst to obtain the Kingdom. And the Kingdom has been seized by the passionate, and the 'biastēs', (the violent) those are the energetic the passionate, they take it by force.

Now what on earth does that mean? Why am I so excited about all this? Well, let me help you. Under the Law of Moses, you did not need to be biazō, you don't need to be energetic or passionate you just needed to be obedient. Please Saints, hear this. Under the Law of Moses and serving God prior to the resurrection of Christ you could have God's favour without passion. If you study the Law of Moses, you'll come to the conclusion that the law indeed is good. It's good, it's fair, there's nothing that God requires that is unreasonable. What God requires through the Old Covenant under the Law of Moses is that you obey the Law. When you mess it up, which you will then you go and sacrifice, you make it right with God.

The reward for your obedience is the following;

- God's blessing and favour will be upon you, upon your family, upon your body.
- You'll have no sickness; you'll be in perfect health.
- Blessing will be upon your offspring and upon your children; they'll be born healthy without defects.
- Blessing will be on your animals, which will reproduce healthy offspring every year.
- God's blessing will be upon your crops; you will have abundance in everything.
- God will keep your enemies away from your nation so that you'll not experience war.
- There'll be no need to defend yourself because God will fight for you. If in the event that your enemy does arise against you, five of you will put ten thousand of flight - so you'd never have to worry about your enemy.

All you needed to do was to obey the Law of Moses and God's goodness, God's blessings, God's grace and God's favour would abound toward you. That's the law, how much passion does that require? It doesn't, it just requires blind obedience. It doesn't require passion because I've got nothing really to lose. The rewards are too great. I can gain so much and lose nothing. It doesn't cost me my life. I've got no foes that are going to kill me. Nobody's going to hate me for wanting to serve God. God's goodness and God's protection will be upon me and my family and my nation.

Then, along comes Jesus and He begins this nonsense about the Kingdom. They hate Me; they're going to hate you. You're going to be hated by all nations for My name's sake. They're going to persecute you and blessed are you when you're persecuted. Don't lay up for yourselves treasures on earth where thief breaks in to steal and moth and rust destroy but lay up for yourselves treasure in heaven – follow Me. You'll have nowhere to lay your head; the Son of Man has nowhere to lay His head

That's a very different from the gospel of Moses or the Law of Moses. The Law of Moses promised wealth and protection. Jesus promised persecutions and hardship. What is the Church preaching? It's peaching Moses. The Churches are preaching Moses – God wants you wealthy, God wants you Blessed, God wants you're rich. God wants you to be overcomers, God wants you have to have no enemies. That's not the gospel of the Kingdom, Saints. If you want to enter into the Kingdom of heaven, it's going to cost you everything. Jesus says that he who wants to enter the Kingdom of heaven is likened to a man who's about to go to war. He needs to weigh the cost, has he got enough men to defeat his enemy. Or the man who wants to build a tower does he have enough resources to finish the project.

The Kingdom of heaven isn't entered into lightly. Why does it say to sit down and count the cost? Because this is going to cost you, it's going to cost you everything. Under Moses it didn't cost you anything, you just had to obey. Those rewards and the benefits were unbelievable, incredible. However, in the Kingdom it's going to cost you your very life. It's only by laying down your life that you can enter the Kingdom. You need to sit down and say am I prepared to pay the price to enter the Kingdom? It's not like the Law of Moses. Within the Kingdom of heaven one has to love one's enemy, one has to make oneself of no reputation, one has to deny oneself, one has to be broken – it's a high cost.

What then is the reward of the Kingdom, if the cost is so high? What is the benefit with the Kingdom of God? Well, the Bible says the Kingdom of heaven will abide forever and that the Kingdom of heaven will rule over God's new creation. Jesus died on a cross Saints, so that man might be forgiven, so that man could be adopted, so that man could be transformed, so that man could become sons and daughters of the Most High God – to be co-heirs of the Kingdom of heaven. Jesus said in the Gospel of Luke Chapter 12, verse 32, *"It is your Father's good pleasure to give you the kingdom."* [Part Verse] Jesus died so that you and I could be co-heirs of the Kingdom, we will rule for all eternity. Unfortunately, the Church is busy with a kingdom that is earth-bound that has no promise of the future, where power isn't important. You can have Church without having the power God manifest but you can't have the Kingdom of heaven present without having the King of the Kingdom presence in power.

The Law of Moses says we inherit the things of this life, the things of this earth and the blessings of Earth. In the Kingdom of heaven, we receive the blessing of the King; an inheritance of the King which is an eternal inheritance. The Kingdom of heaven requires passion. You enter into the Kingdom of heaven and begin to tastes of the fruit for the Kingdom of heaven by passion – by a passion to press in.

This Chapter is just laying the foundations and I believe we've done that. However, I need to share a bit more about passion. How does it affect you and me? Saints, the problem with the Church today is generally most Christians are apathetic. A simpler word for that is lazy, content, an attitude of who cares really. Yes, indifferent, content or apathetic. There is very little passion in the Church – very, very little. If God doesn't move when we come together that's okay, for most of us, for almost all of us. At least the word was good, the praise and worship was nice, I got to speak to somebody who hadn't really connected with for a while and of course the tea and coffee afterwards was particularly well served. But Saints, this is the state of the Church, am I wrong, am I? Am I right, am I? Of course I'm right, because the Church is so apathetic. Generally, we really don't care if God doesn't pitch up. It's okay if nobody gets healed, as nobody has ever been healed in our Church anyway! It's okay if we're Pentecostal Charismatic and nobody gets full of the Holy Spirit, that's all right. It's okay if the gifts of the Spirit don't function amongst us, because, you know, hey, they functioned two years ago. We know we're Pentecostal, based on what happened, oh, you know, three decades back! That is apathy in the Church because we don't understand the

Kingdom. The Kingdom of heaven is a Kingdom of power. The Kingdom of heaven is a Kingdom of glory. In another scripture the Apostle Paul says in Romans Chapter 14 verse 17 *"for the kingdom of God is not eating and drinking, but righteousness and peace and joy in the Holy Spirit."* The Kingdom of God Saints, when the Kingdom of God is present then the evidence of God's presence is on display.

If I'm in the Kingdom, then I won't be worrying about what I can or can't eat. Those of you that know me can see I'm on a see-food diet. I see food, I eat it. I don't eat pork or things like that that's because of my culture. I grew up not eating the stuff and I still think it's crazy to eat it but that's culture. You welcome to have your pork pie and that's great, just give me some smoked salmon and cream cheese while you're you doing it. Saints, if the Church is busy with stuff – food, drink, holidays, Sabbaths, this and that, where's the peace of God? Where's the joy of the Holy Spirit? Where's the power of God? Are souls coming into His presence and being convicted of sin by the presence of the Holy Spirit in your life? Does your testimony have power because you are in the Kingdom? The sad truth for many in the Church the answer is no. No, I do not walk in power. I do not walk in the joy of the Spirit. I do not walk in the love of Christ or in the contentment of Christ or the Passion of Christ.

Saints, from the time of John until Jesus the only way you could enter the Kingdom of heaven was with passion. Think about those who listened to the message of John the Baptist. In Israel you had one religion, called Judaism. Everyone went to synagogue and every synagogue was related. The Jews were all Jews so if you met at Capernaum or you met at Bethlehem, it didn't matter where you met you were all part of one religion, of one religious body. Then along comes John the Baptist and he starts upsetting the applecart. He says you need to repent of your sins. Don't say that you're, sons of Abraham. Don't get your identity from your heritage. Don't get your identity in God because of your tradition. Don't get your identity because of your religion. Don't say I'm a child of Abraham. John told them that God can raise up sons from these stones. They protested, "I'm Jewish, my father was Jewish, my grandfather was Jewish, I'm a child of the Covenant." "No," John says, "you need to repent. You need to love your enemy. You need to show the character of God in your life." All of a sudden he'd raised the bar, from blind obedience to responding to God. Now I am obliged to respond. If you see yourself as a sinner, you need to get baptized. So as people were being baptized word got out to the religious leaders and they began to send out some of their own to listen to John. These Pharisees and Sadducees would stand and look and see who was being baptized and those people were immediately ostracized from the community, immediately cut off. If you were in a nation where all believed in the one thing and now you've been cut off, it does certainly affect your life doesn't it? It certainly does create hardship. It has a cost to it. Am I willing to sacrifice my relationship with my loved ones, with my family and with my friends? I'm willing to suffer in the business world because now my contacts are going to have a problem with me. It began at the time of John. Entering the Kingdom began to have a high price and only those who were passionate, who were willing to pay the price, could enter the Kingdom. Mathew 11 verse 12, *"And from the days of John the Baptist until now the kingdom of heaven suffers violence, and the violent take it by force."*

The Kingdom of heaven is entered when one understands the value of the Kingdom in conjunction with one's absolute need and desire to obtain it. Many of Jesus' parables speak about the value of the Kingdom and what an individual is prepared to sacrifice to obtain it. Jesus on one occasion says the Kingdom of heaven is like a treasure in a field which, when a man finds he sells everything he has to purchase the field that he may obtain the treasure. The Kingdom of heaven is so valuable that I will give up everything, everything that I may obtain it. That's its value to me. It is more precious to have than anything and I will gladly, willingly sell everything so that I may obtain the Kingdom.

In another place he says that Kingdom of heaven is like a merchant going out to seek a pearl of great price and finding one he sells everything that he may obtain it. Jesus spoke a lot about the value of the Kingdom. Now, think about this Saints, the value of the Kingdom is beyond price because it is beyond anything that we can understand, comprehend or relate to.

God, the Almighty, our Creator has purposed for man, through Christ, to obtain the rulership of His Own Kingdom. The father has given Jesus rule and the Bible says we will be co-rulers with him. The cost, the price to obtain the Kingdom was paid for by the blood of God, that's how valuable the Kingdom is. That God, the Lord Jesus Christ, died on a cross to pay the entry fee. The value of the Kingdom is beyond anything because the Kingdom of God will rule for eternity. An offer has been made to men, by that I mean men and women, to obtain a place in the Kingdom. However, it will cost you everything, absolutely everything.

To enter the Kingdom, one has to be prepared to live by the laws and the rules of the Kingdom. Now, this is where the Church misses it. The gospel of the Church is a gospel of distorted grace. I repeat; the gospel of the Church is the gospel of distorted grace. What do I mean by that? Well, God knows we're all sinners. God knows we're all useless and pathetic, that's why the blood of Jesus cleanses us. Just live as you like, it's okay, God will forgive you – "Amazing Grace, how sweet the sound." ... I can live as I want to, - that's garbage! Jesus says in Matthew Chapter 7 verses 21-23 *""Not everyone who says to Me, 'Lord, Lord,' shall enter the kingdom of heaven, but he who does the will of My Father in heaven. Many will say to Me in that day, 'Lord, Lord, have we not prophesied in Your name, cast out demons in Your name, and done many wonders in Your name?' And then I will declare to them, 'I never knew you; depart from Me, you who practice lawlessness!'"* He's saying, "You live by another law, a law that is foreign to My Kingdom." See Saints, there is one; there's only one set of laws in the Kingdom of God, the Kingdom of heaven. It's the laws that Jesus taught in the Gospels and what the Apostles taught to the early Church. If you want to be part of the Kingdom you need to count the cost. Am I prepared to walk in love? Now, I'm talking about Godly love. You see I've been accused of being the most loveless, uncaring Minister, ever. I don't believe that besides me and Satan that anybody has ever had a worse rap. That's because people, who have been angered with me, say, "You have no love." Now, what does that mean? Well, they understand the gospel of the Church. They say you don't come and drink tea with me. You don't come and mourn and attend the wake when my pet budgie dies. No, quite right, I don't. I'm sorry, I'm just not pastoral. I don't remember birthdays; I seldom put much emphasis on mine. Here's the thing, that's not love. It's got nothing to do with love – that's pampering.

Real love is that I care about your eternal state. I care about you as Christians. I care that you would know God. My passion, that keeps me awake at night, is that you would know God in fullness. Knowing that everything is done for you. That you would live in it, walk in it, be part of it, - that's my love. That's Kingdom love. I'll tell you when you're in error. I'll tell you nicely the first time, I'd tell you not so nicely the second time and the third time if you won't repent, I'll ask you to leave the Church. But I will walk with you if there's repentance and that's called godly love. It's actually nicer that Jesus. Jesus said that if they won't listen to you, walk away.

Saints, the laws of the Kingdom are not the current laws of the Church. The Church has distorted the laws of the Kingdom and we devised our own form of Christianity. We require our Pastor to be a weak willy-nilly male. I'm sorry but many Christian Pastors pray feebly, "Dear Lord Jesus...." Listen, sorry I'm a man. I'm sorry, I have hair on my chest and I'm a man. I'm a guy and I'm not going be some nancy–pansy pushover just because that's supposed to be love. Love, is a genuine caring for an individual. If I have to slap you on the side of the head to get the nonsense out of you so that God can come into you, I'll do it. And you say, "You don't love me, you're a bigot." But I do love you, you just don't understand love.

Saints, this is what I want to say to you. To enter the Kingdom of heaven there are a set of rules to live by, they're the rules of Jesus. I'm telling you the problem the Church today is that it's not prepared to live by those rules. Genuinely, I mean. Will you love unconditionally? When somebody offends you, will you go to them to make it right? Or, are you going to have a pity-party and try to bring people in and attempt to stir up division and strife. When your enemy misuses or abuses you, will you cry out to God that he's unfair and unjust to allow this person to prosper ahead of you. Or, will you get on your knees and pray God's blessing for them, like Jesus taught. Will we do what Jesus did? You remember that old bracelets that some of the Christians used to wear, WWJD (what would Jesus do)? The truth was that people were wearing the bracelets but not living the life.

The Kingdom of heaven, Saints, requires your entire life. It is worth obtaining more than anything else. We need to be passionate, we need to lay-hold of God and say, "My God I want to know you." Passion says, I'm going press in and I'm going get to know God even if it costs me everything. Not just to wake up in the morning and say: "Our Father who art in heaven, hallowed be thy name. Thy Kingdom come, thy will be done etc., etc. Amen." – I got to go to work!

We need to have a passion to know God, declaring that "I would rather die than not know you". That is what needs to change in the

Church. An absolute passion to know him and if I don't know him I don't want to wake up tomorrow morning. That's the only thing that counts with God. It's just not okay otherwise. The Kingdom of heaven is pressed in by the passionate, by those who want to obtain it. I want to get on that train. I want to get that garment. I want that last BBQ steak. I'm going fight for it. That's the passion that we need. That's what Jesus was meaning and we'll explore this in further Chapters.

I haven't expounded too much about the gospel of the Church or the gospel of the Kingdom but we will expand on that later. I need to make a quick comment now regarding the "Word of Faith" belief, in the Church. The Bible says (Psalm 82:6) *"You are gods"* and even Jesus quoted the scripture (John 10:34). That doesn't mean we are gods in deity terms. Jesus will always be the King of kings and the Lord of Glory. He will always have the Name above every other name, we will never be gods, never, ever, ever - that is Mormonism. We do not have the power to create – at all. But we can have the nature of Jesus; we can have the fruit of the Spirit, abiding in us. The Apostle John writes in his first epistle, "Now we are children of God." That is your position, if Christ is the Lord of your life. If you have yielded yourself to the Lordship of Jesus and you have passionately surrendered your life to Him. Right now, as you stand, your spiritual position is that you're a son or a daughter of God Most High. Moses didn't have that position, John didn't nor did King David. *"Now we are children of God but it is not yet made known what we shall be."* Exactly how things are going to work out in eternity we don't know but we do know that God will share his glory with no man. The first commandment is still the first commandment – You love God. The second commandment is "there are no other gods but Him. God's not about to change that, all right, we will not be gods. This all spills out of the whole 'dominionism" theology, which is what gives rise to that sort of bad doctrine.

"The fact songs say that

there's a highway to Hell and

a stairway to heaven says a lot about traffic numbers"

Chapter 2

The Parable of the Sower

---◆---

In Matthew Chapter 11 Jesus turns to His disciples, in front of the disciples of John, and says that from the days of John the Baptist until now the Kingdom of Heaven suffers violence and the violent take it by force. We now know that that doesn't make much sense in the English. It makes a little bit better sense in the new Afrikaans translation but in the Greek it makes perfect sense. From the days of John, the Baptist till now, a period of only about 15 or 16 years, maybe less, Jesus says to His disciples that the Kingdom of Heaven suffers violence. That word violence there is Greek word biazō - suffers violence. Biazō means energy, the desire to press in, the desire to obtain, a passion to obtain. The Kingdom of heaven is at the mercy of the passionate. It's obtained by the passionate; it's obtained by those who will forsake everything to obtain it.

The Kingdom of heaven is not for half-hearted, lukewarm or indifferent people and that's where the Church is missing it. We have lowered the standard of salvation to such a minimal level that all you've got to do is believe in Jesus and you assume that you're born-again. The Bible reminds us, in the book of James, that even the demons believe in Jesus and they tremble. Faith in Jesus is not sufficient to get you into the Kingdom of heaven. The Kingdom of Heaven suffers violence; the Kingdom of Heaven is obtained by the passionate. The passionate, those who are willing to pay the price and commit themselves fully, gain entry. The violent, those who are passionate, take the Kingdom.

The Kingdom of God does not advance through being lukewarm. The Kingdom of God does not advance through being complacent. The Kingdom of God is not established through religion and tradition.

The Kingdom of God is a Kingdom of power. It is advanced by the King, who is Jesus, and by those who are willingly subject to His Lordship. I don't want to regurgitate the previous chapter, however it is really important you understand this because the Church generally needs to embark on a completely different course – the course of the Kingdom of God. The gospel of the Church does not advance the Kingdom. The gospel the Church builds kingdoms of men; it builds strife, division, contention and does not further the desires of the Almighty God.

In this chapter we are going to look at *the* most important parable ever spoken by the Lord Jesus Christ concerning the Kingdom of God. If we don't understand this parable we will not understand any of the parables of Jesus or any of the teachings of the Bible. Why is it that Christians can know what the Bible says and then willingly, without having their conscience bothering them do the complete opposite? I'm not trying to identify anyone specifically; I'm generalizing about the Church globally. I mean, just look at what happened in 2011 when many were saying that 21st of May was going to be the end of the world (*Harold Camping's fabricated prediction*). How can any Bible believing Christian have believed that, One who knows that the Antichrist must first come, that the 70th week of Daniel must be played out, that the rapture must take place, that the bride of Jesus Christ must come to perfection, that a temple in Jerusalem must be rebuilt and the thousand-year reign of Jesus must take place before the end of the world comes. The gospel of the Church, Saints, does not make Christians.

Please turn with me in your Bible to the book of Matthew Chapter 13. It's extraordinary that this one parable, this one portion of Scripture, if not understood will hinder us from ever apprehending the purpose of the life, death, resurrection and return of Jesus Christ. The words of Jesus Himself, Matthew Chapter 13; verses 1-10 *"On the same day Jesus went out of the house and sat by the sea. And great multitudes were gathered together to Him, so that He got into a boat and sat; and the whole multitude stood on the shore. Then He spoke many things to them in parables, saying: "Behold, a sower went out to sow."* Interesting it says *"He spoke many things to them in parables"* but we're only given this one parable. He told many parables but all we are told here is one of the many parables – the parable of the sower. So, continuing in verse 4 *"And as he sowed, some seed fell by the wayside; and the birds came and devoured them. Some fell on stony places, where they did not have much earth; and they immediately sprang up because they had no depth of earth. But when the sun was up they were scorched, and because they had no root they withered away. And some fell among thorns, and the thorns sprang up and choked them. But others fell on good ground and yielded a crop: some a hundredfold, some sixty, some thirty. He who has ears to hear, let him hear!"* – Then Jesus went back home. Interesting, Jesus did not explain the parable. He simply says "Let him, who has an ear, let *him* hear."

We then read in verse 10, *"And the disciples came and said to Him, "Why do You speak to them in parables?" He answered and said to them, "Because it has been given to you to know the mysteries of the kingdom of heaven, but to them it has not been given."* Think about this for a second. Jesus speaks many things to the multitudes in parables and He concludes with this final parable of the sower. Then he says to the multitudes, "Let him who has an ear let him hear," and departs. The disciples later asked Him, "Why do you speak to *them* in parables?" Interestingly, they were a bit puffed up weren't they? because they never understood a word He had just said. Why do you speak to *them* in parables? Don't assume that they knew what He was saying because we see they were also clueless. Jesus answered and says, 'It has been given to you, my disciples, to know the mysteries of the Kingdom of Heaven'. Notice this; the parable was not given so you would know the 'gospel of the Church' or 'the gospel of salvation,' no it's given to you so you would know the mysteries of the Kingdom.

Jesus said to Nicodemus, 'unless a man is born-again, he cannot *see* the Kingdom'. Being born-again, coming to salvation through faith in Jesus Christ and laying down your life to His Lordship is the very first step a person makes to enter the Kingdom. But salvation is not the Kingdom. The gospel message of salvation is not the gospel message of the Kingdom. It is a part of the Kingdom, but it's not the fullness of the Kingdom. Unless you are born-again you cannot enter the Kingdom. There's much more to the Kingdom than simply being born-again. The Church occupies itself with the message of salvation and not the message of the Kingdom. That message has little else to offer people other than a hope of eternal life; it is not the full revelation of what the Almighty God did through His Son Jesus Christ as a gift to humanity.

Isn't Jesus being a little bit unfair here though when He turns around to His disciples and says, "Only you have been reserved to understand the mysteries of the Kingdom of Heaven, to them it has not been given." Isn't Jesus unfair? Isn't that God showing partiality? A God desiring some to be saved, some to fully understand, others to be naive and others to be ignorant. Doesn't that sound like prejudice? Well, if you say 'no' you're going to have to explain why. It certainly does sound prejudicial, but for those who say, "No, it's not prejudicial," why is it not? Okay let scripture interpret scripture, - *"He that has ears to hear let him hear."* *"It has been given to you to know the mysteries of the kingdom of heaven, but to them it has not been given."* Saints, we need to understand scripture, through what scripture says.

It is pivotal. I know this might not sound very interesting but this is very important. Why wasn't it granted to crowds to understand the mysteries? Let's look at verses 12-17 of Matthew 13. *"For whoever has, to him more will be given, and he will have abundance; but whoever does not have, even what he has will be taken away from him. Therefore I speak to them in parables, because seeing they do not see, and hearing they do not hear, nor do they understand. And in them the prophecy of Isaiah is fulfilled, which says: 'Hearing you will hear and shall not understand, and seeing you will see and not perceive; for the hearts of this people have grown dull. Their ears are hard of hearing, and their eyes they have closed, Lest they should see with their eyes and hear with their ears, Lest they should understand with their hearts and turn, So that I should heal them.' But blessed are your eyes for they see, and your ears for they hear; for assuredly, I say to you that many prophets and righteous men desired to see what you see, and did not see it, and to hear what you hear, and did not hear it."*

So, blessed are their eyes for they see and their ears for they hear but the truth of the matter is the disciples didn't understand a word that Jesus was saying even then. How do we know that? Because in Mark's account of this parable, Mark adds something that Jesus said which Matthew omits. In Mark's Gospel chapter 4 verse 13 the Bible says, *"And He said to them, "Do you not understand this parable? How then will you understand all the parables?""* The disciples did not understand a word Jesus had spoken. In fact, even when Jesus quoted Isaiah they still did not understand what He was talking about. Because if you look in Mark's Gospel Jesus speaks to them about not understanding that parable *after* he quotes Isaiah. So, does that give you a whole lot more understanding or are you even more confused?

We know that the law is impartial. Why do we know that? Why do we know that God is impartial? Because the Bible says God is not a respecter of persons. The Bible says God shows no partiality. God says that He desires all to be saved and all to come to repentance. The Bible says that God is a fair God, that God loves everybody equally. How do I know that God is impartial just? Because the Bible says so. The Bible reveals the character of God. So, why is it not granted to the people to understand the mysteries of the Kingdom, but only to the disciples, who did not understand what Jesus had just taught? Why is it granted to them, to know the mysteries? I'll give you a clue. Matthew 13 verse 9, *"He who has ears to hear, let him hear!"*- Those who want to hear. You see, the disciples were no different to the multitudes to whom Jesus had just addressed. They were both clueless about what Jesus said. However, the difference between the disciples and the multitudes is that the disciples came to Jesus and said, "What on earth have you just said? We want to know. We want to understand the Kingdom. We want to understand what you have come to do. We want to understand what God's will is and what God's purposes are. We want to know God's ways so we can walk in them. We want to know. We don't know but we have ears to hear, we want to hear."

This is why this is the first and greatest parable because when Jesus begins to expound this parable and you don't understand it, it's because you don't have an ear to understand. You don't want to understand. Now, I'm not saying 'you' as individuals, I'm saying humanity. The person who does not understand scripture is the person who does not wish to understand scripture. God has given teachers in His body; He's given us the Holy Spirit to expound Scripture. Jesus said, if you seek God you'll find Him. If you ask it will be given you. If you want to know, God will make sure you know. If you have an ear to hear you will hear what you want to hear from God. That is the mystery of the Kingdom – if you want to know the heart of God and the ways of God you will learn because God will make sure you know, He will reveal it to you. But there has to be a desire. You see, the Kingdom of heaven is pressed into by the passionate; those who want to possess it, to take it fervently. The Kingdom of heaven is not received by the indifferent, by the complacent, by those who are unwilling to yield and learn. You cannot be a citizen of the Kingdom without a broken heart. You must have humility to understand the ways of God and not put your own thoughts or your own perceptions above God's. There is no place for self-opinion in the Kingdom. Your opinion or my opinion does not count in the Kingdom. He who has an ear, he who wishes, or she who wishes, to know God and know his Kingdom and is passionate enough to press in to seek the face of God, not accepting their current position or the status quo; they will hear.

All right, that was a bit of a side track. I don't want to go too far down that road. Suffice to say, Jesus showed no partiality. The multitudes weren't too concerned about understanding, they just enjoyed the concert. They enjoyed being in the proximity of Jesus and watching the great things He did. They weren't really passionate about the Kingdom. It was just cool being there.

A Pastor friend of mine told me that they've recently lost a whole lot of their youth to another church. Another person I was chatting to the other day said that a lot of his pastoral friends are losing a lot of the youth to a particular church denomination, or rather I should say Church grouping. You know why they're losing the youth? It's because this other church group puts on great concerts. I tell you; they've got the wildest praise and worship, with lights and smoke machines – it's just a cool place to be. I mean heck, you can just let loose and you know, worship Jesus. But that crowd doesn't have ears to hear. They want an external relationship they want an experience, "Look what Jesus just did? What's he going to do next? Let's follow him, who knows?" That's why they never understood a word Jesus said because they weren't trying to connect with the heart of God. They were looking at the outward. It's so nice to be part of the group. It's so nice that Jesus can heal everybody here. It's so nice that if we're hungry He just divides the food and we eat this amazing heavenly fish – it's great. However, they weren't passionate about knowing God; they weren't passionate about understanding the ways of the Kingdom. Saints, that's what's happening in the Church today. Too many people go to church for the wrong reason. They go to church to belong. They go to church for relationships or because a parent tells them to go to church or their friends go to church or because it's a really nice place to be. That's not the reason that we come together.

Jesus says in Matthew 13 verse 16 to 17 "*But blessed are your eyes for they see, and your ears for they hear; for assuredly, I say to you that many prophets and righteous men desired to see what you see, and did not see it, and to hear what you hear, and did not hear it.*" Jesus here is speaking about the Old Testament Saints who prophesied about this new covenant dispensation when God through Jesus Christ will begin to build the Kingdom. That God will take sinful man, save him, pour His Spirit into him, change him and give him the Kingdom as an inheritance. We do not understand the privilege we have of living in this age. We saw in the previous chapter that Jesus turns around to His disciples and said, "*For I say to you, among those born of women there is not a greater prophet than John the Baptist; but he who is least in the kingdom of God is greater than he.*" This means that the least saint that is born-again, is spiritually in a better position than any of the Saints of the Old Testament. You're in a more favoured place, than Moses, David, Miriam and all those incredible men and women of the Old Testament that we read about. Those whose lives have been forever engraved in the Word of God but you, who are least in the Kingdom, are greater than even them.

Saints, there is so much that God has done through the cross of Christ that we need to comprehend, but that's for another time. Let's understand this parable because if we don't understand this parable, according to Jesus, we will not understand any of the other parables of Jesus. Therefore, in verse 18 Jesus begins to expound the parable. Do you still recall what the parable was about? A man went out to sow seed; some fell by the wayside and was eaten by birds. Some fell on stony places and because of not much root sprang up quickly and choked. Some fell among thorns, sprang up but the thorns choked them and some fell on good fertile soil and produced a crop, some, one hundredfold, some, sixty and some, thirty. So now, starting from verse 18, Jesus begins to expound this parable. Remember, He's sharing it with those who want to hear. "*Therefore hear the parable of the sower: When anyone hears the word of the kingdom, and does not understand it, then the wicked one comes and snatches away what was sown in his heart. This is he who received seed by the wayside.*"

The Bible says in Hebrews Chapter 4, verse 12, *"For the word of God is living and powerful, and sharper than any two-edged sword, piercing even to the division of soul and spirit, and of joints and marrow"* The Word of God says in Isaiah Chapter 55, verse 11, *"So shall My word be that goes forth from My mouth; It shall not return to Me void, But it shall accomplish what I please."* But here Jesus turns around and says "the seed that fell by the wayside is likened to a person who hears the Word of the Kingdom, but does not understand it, and the wicked one comes and snatches it from his heart." Interesting, the enemy snatches the word from the heart **because the soul did not understand**. Just think about what Jesus said; the enemy does not snatch the word from the man's heart, the enemy snatches the word from men's understanding. What's the deal with that, well? Why is that important? Listen to the scripture. It's very important that we read the scripture and comprehend. It says "when anyone hears the word of the Kingdom and does not understand it then the wicked one comes and snatches away what was sown in his heart." It's been sown in the heart. The Word of God had been sown in the heart.

Saints, that's exactly how God's Word works. When you heard the gospel of Jesus Christ the first time didn't something happen in your heart? You might have rejected the gospel. You might have said no, this is nonsense, but there was something that happened in your heart. There was a tinge and sparkle of something. I know because that what's happened to me. I never understood the gospel. I thought it was absolute nonsense and foolishness but something happened, there was a spark. The Word of God, the word of the Kingdom is sown into the heart. It is spirit calling out to spirit. We're created in the image of God, we are spirit beings and God speaks into our spirits. Your spirit will never reject God, your soul will but not your spirit. When we do not comprehend or understand and have a revelation in our soul of the Word of God then that word will be taken away immediately and will profit you nothing. It is imperative that we understand the Word of God. If we do not understand the word of the Kingdom then even though our hearts receive it, it will be lost to us because our souls have not comprehended it. That is why, in the Old Covenant, over and over again, God says to Moses tell My people to ponder on My word, to meditate on My word, to speak on it when they rise up, when they go out, when they come home, on the wayside and at work. Continue to ponder on it, meditate on it, get to understand My word because if you do not understand the Word of God, if the Word of God is not a revelation to you, it will be stolen and profits you nothing.

Now, think about the context in which Jesus is speaking this. He's just spoken to a multitude of people; they all smiled, nodded their heads and went off to buy the DVD. However, they didn't comprehend a word of what He'd just said. Therefore, it was meaningless to them. That is why in church we should ask questions. If you don't understand something you stop what we're doing and say, "Please explain?" It's infinitely more important for you to understand than for me to preach. It's more important for you to understand than for the Pastor to get through his sermon. If you don't understand then what God is desiring to sow in your heart, is taken away. That is why we need to ask questions. We need to create environments when we come together in fellowship where one can ask questions and have the questions answered, so that God's Word can be explained, so that when hearing you actually hear. That's the point of ministry; that you hear and understand.

Verse 20 and 21, *"But he who received the seed on stony places, this is he who hears the word and immediately receives it with joy; yet he has no root in himself, but endures only for a while. For when tribulation or persecution arises because of the word, **immediately** he stumbles."* [Emphasis added] The key words in these verses are that;

He receives the word with joy,

The most important key – he has no root in himself.

What is this insinuating? If you do not have a root, a deep root. What is this talking about? Character; if you have no character the Word of God will be quickly lost in your life. Let's take a deeper look at the parable. Jesus says, *"He receives the seed on stony places, this is he who hears the word and immediately receives it with joy;"* There's an excitement, there's an understanding of the word, there is a response to what they've heard. They understand the word, that's why they're full of joy. They understand what has just been spoken. The Word of God is indeed joyous; it is wonderful, therefore there is joy and excitement. However, it goes on in verse 21 *"Yet he has no root in himself."* There's no character, there's no depth of godliness, and they have not endured in faith. The Bible says that as a result of faith, Romans 5:3-4 *"that tribulation produces perseverance; and perseverance, character; and character, hope."* The end result is character, a godly character. Because he does not have a godly character he only endures for a while. As soon as tribulation comes, as soon as there's opposition to the word, as soon as there's hardship, as soon as there are tough times, then that person crumbles, that person falls away. How many like that have we met? The Word of God is so awesome – I love this church! But after only one offence, boom, it's gone. Let's go outside your church, how many Christians have we known in other churches. They received the Word of God and then there's opposition – because of the word.

Hear what verse 21 says, *"For when tribulation or persecution arises **because of the word**."* God will allow you to be tested in what you've just learned so that that word, that you've learnt, will become real. Knowledge is not knowledge until it has been tested. You don't know something until what you know has proved itself in testing. You don't know you love your wife until your marriage has been tested and you stay strong and faithful. You don't know what kind of person you are until you've been tested. You don't know if you've got patience, until your patience has been tested. You don't know if you walk in love until your love is tested. You do not know if you're a giving person until you're in a position where you can't give but yet you give. I'm not getting into tithes and offerings, I'm just talking about knowledge; that knowledge is not knowledge until knowledge has been tested. Truth is not truth until it has been tested. That's a basic principle of science; a scientific truth always, always gives the same result, in the same circumstances, all the time – it is truth.

The Word of God will profit you nothing unless you have got the character of God in your heart to endure tribulations, endure testing and stand when everything contrary to what you have just been taught comes against you. When having endured everything you stand true. There are too many folks in the church, who have listened to the gospel of the Church which says Jesus died that you might be rich, healthy, and prosperous. Healthy, wealthy and wise is what we used to call it in the old days. "I'm healthy, wealthy and wise, blessed and overcoming; I'm the head not the tail. I'm overcoming; every place on which my foot should tread God has given to me." – Oops I've just stood on a dog's mess!

The point of the matter is, Saints, you're not healthy until you've endured sickness and have seem the grace of God seeing you through it. You're not prosperous until you have gone through the loss of all things, held fast to God and God has seen you through it, by meeting your need. The problem of the Church today is that we preach an easy Christianity. People, of course, receive the Word of God with joy; He was rich, became poor that we might be rich in all things. Oh, we love that one, - until you lose everything. Now do you believe that I became poor that you might be rich? Saints, unless we've got character we will not endure. Too many in the Church today gladly received the word then trials and tribulations come and that's it, they backslide and go. Or perhaps they change denominations because they prayed for their baptism in Holy Spirit and didn't receive it. Now they're devout Baptists and assert that God doesn't baptise in the Holy Spirit anymore. Our experience has robbed us of the truth.

Saints, here is truth. Do you want to enter the Kingdom, do you want to remain in the Kingdom, do you want to grow in the Kingdom and do you want to see the Kingdom of God come alive in your life? Then let me share with you a very important truth. Everything that you learn about the Kingdom of God *will* be tested – every single thing. Jesus, so correctly, said, "Tribulation and persecution will come, because of the words' sake." His actual words are in verse 21 *"For when tribulation or persecution arises because of the word."*- Because of the word.

Every time God sows a word into you, God is going to allow that word to be tested – for sure. Saints, I'm telling you. You may have been walking with the Lord for a number of years and you'll agree with me and say, "Yes, it is true". Now, for the young Christians who are still in their honeymoon stage; that stage is going to end. Every single thing you've learnt, as sure as the sun will rise in the East tomorrow and go down in the West, everything you ever learn of the Kingdom of God is going to be tested by God. God will allow it to be tested; he'll allow the enemy to come in. He'll allow people to stand up against you and allow negative circumstances to arise. I'm telling you, as sure as my desk is made of solid wood, this is going to happen. Therefore, ask yourself this question; do you have roots within yourself? If not here's a wonderful opportunity to develop them as James 1:2-3 tells us, *"My brethren, count it all joy when you fall into various trials, knowing that the testing of your faith produces patience."* Add to that what Paul says in Romans 5:4 *"that tribulation produces perseverance; and perseverance, character; and character, hope."* We can rejoice in tribulation knowing that the word that you've learned is going to be tested. When you've endured testing, that word becomes undeniable truth. Many people don't produce fruit. Why? Because, firstly they don't understand the Word of God and secondly, because they understand and received with joy but have no roots in themselves. They have no character and stumble and fall.

Let's move on to verse 22 *"Now he who received seed among the thorns,"* Now Jesus is speaking about the third type of person. *"Is he who hears the word, and the cares of this world and the deceitfulness of riches choke the word, and he becomes unfruitful."* – Barren. In reality Jesus is validating Matthew chapter 6, verse 24, "*No one can serve two masters.... You cannot serve God and mammon*". You cannot live for the rewards of this life. I'm not saying we don't get educated, that we don't get a decent job, or that we don't plan for our retirement or for our future. No, I'm not saying that I'd be a fool to deny that these things are not important. But Saints, this world is not our hope. This world is not our 'everything'. There are too many in the Church whose lives revolve around this life, the deceitfulness of riches, to possess, to earn, to have, to aspire. Those are deadly aspirations because when we look to the world for our joy, for our happiness, for our comfort, for our security, for our peace, we have denied the Kingdom.

The Kingdom of God is *to come*. Although it is present tense, it is also future tense. The fullness of the Kingdom will only come when Christ reigns on earth. But, even then, it's not actually fully come. It is only fully, fully come when God recreates the heavens and the earth. This earth is bankrupt, this earth is falling away. When you go in to vote on Election Day, let me ask you a question. There is great euphoria leading up to the vote, but in four years' time will there be very much change? That's not meant as a slight against the ruling politicians. What I'm saying is that now there is only hope in the kingdoms of men. The Americas were all excited when Barack Obama became President but did he change their lives? No. Hope in this world is futile.

This world is bankrupt as the Apostle John tells us in chapter 2:16-17 *"For all that is in the world--the lust of the flesh, the lust of the eyes, and the pride of life--is not of the Father but is of the world. And the world is passing away, and the lust of it; but he who does the will of God abides forever."* Too many in the Church have backslidden and fallen away because of a lust for wealth. I can't go to

33

church, I can't be in fellowship, you know, I've got my business, my business, my business. Your business is to be involved with the Kingdom of God and to leave your business to God. Many Christians say, "God is Lord of my business." Yes, perhaps; but only when there is trouble. He's the head of the troubleshooting department. He's the director of problems, complaints and trouble. He has great access to those departments, but everything else is mine!

Saints, the world is not our desire. We are in the world but not of the world. We live in this world, we need to be educated, we need to obey the rules of the land, we need to pay taxes, to whom taxes are due, - but we are not of this world. We don't live by this world's standards, we do not crave for this world, we do not desire this world and we do not lust after this world. If you don't have something, it's okay. You don't need to drive the best or wear the best. If you can't afford it, that's fine. Those who can, God bless you; please take us for a ride one day. Our treasure is in Heaven. We seek what is above; we set our minds on things that are above. A Christian who is worldly is of no use to God; you're barren, you're unfruitful. The sad thing about being unfruitful is what Jesus speaks of twice. Once in the parable of the talents and the other in parable of the minas, "That he who does not bear fruit and buries his talent, is thrown into outer darkness." If you are lusting after the world, desiring the things of this world and you get your identity from the way the world responds to you then you are barren and fruitless. Not you, specifically as an individual, I mean the individual who falls in this category.

So, is there any good news? Well of course there is, of course there's good news. That's found in verse 23 about the seed that fell on good soil. Jesus says in verse 23 *"But he who received seed on the good ground is he who hears the word and understands it, who indeed bears fruit and produces: some a hundredfold, some sixty, some thirty."* Isn't that wonderful? He that hears the word and understands it will always be fruitful. Just one question, where's the fruit? If we hear the word and we understand the word where's the fruit? Jesus says we will be fruitful. Fruitful and not like producing nuts – there's plenty of nuts in the Church. Nuts are better in fruitcakes, not in the Church. No, we're talking about fruitful, in the sense of, of use to the Kingdom.

If Jesus says that he who hears the word and understands it will be fruitful, why is there so little fruit in the individual lives of Christians?

The answer is because we don't understand what the word 'understand' means. That's why there's so much fruitlessness in the body of Christ. We don't understand what it is, to understand. Does that sound confusing? Actually, it's quite simple. He who hears the word and understands it **will** be fruitful. So, if we hear the word, and understand the word, we'll be fruitful. If you're not being fruitful it's because we don't understand what we should understand.

What then does it mean to understand what you hear? That word to 'understand', means to comprehend, it means to grasp what is being taught, understand its significance and let that truth become part of who you are. The big difference is that I understand many things. There are a few things that I understand that you might not believe I understand. I understand that a slab of chocolate has close to thousand calories and I also understand that if I eat the slab of chocolate as opposed to say an apple, then I'm going to put on weight. I might look like I understand this reality, because I'm living proof that chocolate puts on weight, but I do not have the understanding I need to have. Well, actually I do, but I'm in rebellion. Let me show you how real I am and how I'm not perfected. The knowledge I have about diet, about nutrition, is useless to me. Believe it or not, I actually understand a lot about nutrition, a phenomenal amount about nutrition, from my youth. However, I do not apply what I know to be true. It's called hypocrisy. If I do not bear the fruit of the understanding I have of nutrition, there's no fruit. I certainly do not look like it; unless I was Japanese and I'm shaping up for the sumo wrestling championships!

Saints, my example is also true of the Word of God. Many of us know the word, we know the truths of the Kingdom of God but we do not live them. Why? because it's not part of our character. Your character is who you are. I heard a preacher once defined the difference between character and reputation. Reputation is who people say you are. Character is who you really are. People can easily have an incorrect perception of your character based on your reputation. But character is who you are.

Knowing the Word of God and not doing it means you don't understand it. Just like myself and dieting. I know I should lose weight; my wife wants me to lose weight. My children want me to lose weight. They desire for me to look after my health so that I can

35

be with them for a long time because they actually love me. It's a foreign concept but they do. My desire is also to be with them.

Here's the thing. When you analyse the Word of God; the Word of God is good, the laws of the Kingdom are good, they will give you a life, they'll give you hope, they'll give you a future. It will give you everything that you could possibly dream of. But we do not live it out because we don't comprehend *its value*. We do not comprehend the value of God's Kingdom because we do not understand its worth. We do not understand that it is critical as believers we must obey God. That is why there's no fruit because many in the Church are walking in wilful, premeditated disobedience to God. To know what to do and not to do it, the Bible says, is sin. If we don't understand this parable, we will not understand anything else that God has to say to us. Isn't that so true? If I do not receive the Word of God with my whole being and passionately hold on to it, by faith in God and through faith and patience make the truth real to myself, so that it becomes part of my character, then I won't receive anything from God.

It's no good just knowing, one has to have an absolute conviction that the truth I hear must become part of my life. It can't be brushed aside. I cannot compromise it. I cannot substitute it. I cannot say, well, it's not that important, God will forgive me. Yes, God will forgive you but you will be barren, you will be of no use to the Kingdom of God. You'll not experience the Kingdom. You'll not experience the King of the Kingdom. The modern church is all about the outward and doesn't place a high virtue on character. We should be mortified when we, as a congregation, do not show the character of Jesus.

Unfortunately, in this modern church era we do not have the parameters, all the barriers that the early church had. You get offended in one church; you just head off to a church down the road. If you tried that in the early church, say you left the church at Ephesus, which church would you go to? If you left the church at Rome which church would you go to? If we left the church at Corinth which church would you then go to? If you left for the Church of Colossae which church would you then go to? If you left the church of Lystra, Iconium, Antioch or Derbe, which church could you then go to? Nowadays, if you don't like this church, you go to that church. If you don't like that church, you go to the next church. You don't like this doctrine you go to that church. You know you can go all over the place because we're not forced to address issues. We just get up and go. Therefore, we don't learn to develop character. We're not forced to develop character by staying and dealing with things, growing with things and maturing in Christ.

Saints, it's impossible to force any person to be a doer of the word, to do what they know should be done. It is something that you have to work out between you and God as an individual. You have to say Lord, I'm either going to be obedient or I'm not going to be obedient. I don't like what you're saying so I'll go to another church but the facts are it doesn't matter where you go. The truth is, what I'm sharing with you today, is the Word of God. You can put your head in the sand and pretend that the world doesn't exist. You can go to another church where they do all sorts of other things but that won't absolve you from doing what is true.

Why is this one the most important parable? Because it teaches us about the character that the son and daughter the Kingdom of God must have. We've got to understand the word. There are four things that need to happen;

- We need to understand the word. Without understanding the enemy is going to steal it
- We needed to develop character. We need to know that God is going to test us; we need to know that. That doesn't mean he doesn't love you when He tests you. He tests you so that the word can be rooted in you, and so your character can develop.
- If you love this world and you desire to chase after the things that this world can offer, you will become fruitless and your salvation is at stake. In fact, according to Jesus, you will lose your salvation.
- When we hear the word, if we understand it, if we comprehend its' value and its' importance to us and by God's grace strive to make it a part of who we are. Then we will always be fruitful – always.

Did you understand all that? That's good because than you can continue learning about the Kingdom of God. If you understood this chapter then you can understand what we're going to continue with in the next chapter.

Chapter 3

Destined To Reign

I need to share a very unusual message with you in this chapter as part of this series of teachings on the Kingdom of God or the Kingdom of Heaven. It's very radical because the Church generally, is not involved with the Kingdom of God. The Church generally is involved with the gospel of the Church. We're busy building our churches and the empires of men and, by and large, the body of Christ around the globe is not busy with the Kingdom of God.

In the previous two chapters we've looked at some pretty radical things in the scripture that the Church doesn't often prioritize, or minister much on. We need to worship God, I want to worship the Lord, but I feel that we need to worship God with understanding. There are many Christians who don't actually know why they're Christians. There are many Christians who come to church and are ignorant of what the Church of Jesus Christ is all about. So now, I do believe by the Spirit of God, and by God's Holy Word, we are going to learn something about Christianity that we have not really considered before.

Let's commit this word to God in prayer. "Father, Lord in all things may you have supremacy through Christ. Let your Word be true, my God. Give me grace to teach, give us all grace to hear so that when we continue to worship you Father, we would worship you in spirit and in truth. The truth of what you have accomplished, what you have purposed through the incredible sacrifice of our Saviour Jesus."

Saints, this is so important. Our rituals in church are sometimes just a frustration and distraction. We need to know why we are Christians. Why is it that Jesus died on a cross and rose again? Why did He spend three-and-a-half years teaching and what did He teach?

What does the Bible actually speak of regarding the plan of God for Humanity?

What did Jesus speak about for three-and-a-half years before His crucifixion? He went about speaking and preaching about the Kingdom of God. That's what He spoke about. He spoke about the Kingdom of God, He preached about the Kingdom of God. He spoke about the God of the Kingdom. That the Kingdom of God needs to be entered into through faith and belief, that one has to be born-again. Unless one is born-again he cannot see the Kingdom. Everything that Jesus spoke about, everything Jesus taught was about the Kingdom of God. He was preparing His disciples to be equipped to take the message of the Kingdom to the nations. However, the Church is not busy with the Kingdom of God; the Church is busy with the gospel of the Church. Therefore, what we do in the Church, in general, is that we preach a gospel that gets people into our pews and onto our membership lists. As long as they're in our church being good Christian citizens, paying their tithes and giving offerings and generally behaving themselves the pastors believe that they have accomplished their job – that they have fulfilled the Great Commission.

That however, is not the Kingdom of God. The disciples and even their mothers knew the message of the Kingdom. Those who listened to Jesus and those who followed Jesus understood the message of Jesus. Yet the Church today, even though we have the fullness of the scripture, generally speaking, most Christians do not know the message that Jesus taught. But as I said just now, even the mothers of the disciples understood the message of Jesus. In Matthew Chapter 20 verses 20 -21, Matthew records and says. *"Then the mother of Zebedee's sons came to Him"* (came to Jesus) *"with her sons, kneeling down and asking something from Him. And He said to her, "What do you wish?" She said to Him, "Grant that these two sons of mine may sit, one on Your right hand and the other on the left, in Your Kingdom."*

For those of you not familiar with the Jewish culture, the Jews placed a very strong emphasis on giving their children the very best start in life. It was and still is really important in Jewish culture that the children are given every opportunity to excel and to succeed. Mrs Zebedee was a good Jewish mother. She wanted the very best for her two boys and so she asks a favour of Jesus. "If you're not too busy, and if you don't mind, I would like a small favour. For my little boy Johnny, if he can sit on your right and little Jamie he can sit on your left, when you come into your Kingdom." A small request! It was not a small request Saints, it was a monstrous request – it was huge!

What did Mrs Zebedee know? She understood something about the Kingdom. But what does it mean to sit at the right of Jesus and on the left of Jesus? What is it speaking about, a cosy place with the view or prime property in Heaven? No, it meant authority. Sitting at the right hand, or on the left hand of Christ – as close to Jesus as possible – speaks of authority. In the court of a king, those who sit nearest to the king have the greater authority, have the greater power and have the king's ear. She was asking Jesus that her children would have great authority in the Kingdom when the Kingdom of God comes. She wanted her sons to be second and third after Jesus. It wasn't a small thing.

But Saints, there's something that we need to learn from Mrs Zebedee. She understood the principles of the Kingdom. She understood what the Kingdom of God actually was. This is what the Church doesn't understand. We do not know what the Kingdom of God is. We think the Kingdom of God is the church on a Sunday morning. We think that maybe the Kingdom of God is; that when we go to Heaven that God is going to give us mansions, that there are parks, which we're going to walk in. Or perhaps, that we're going to have these wonderful times of fellowship and praise and worship for all eternity, or that we can ask God whatever you need to ask and He'll answer us, that we'll be able to eat this most wonderful food, without putting on weight, that we will never age – all that wonderful stuff. That's what we think the Kingdom of God is about. However, although all those things will happen it's not the Kingdom. It's not the reason Christ died and rose again, that we might be saved and enter the Kingdom.

The Kingdom of God is way more than enjoying eternity. The Church is robbing its' members of the blessing of God, because all we want is for people to be saved. We don't know and we do not teach what they're being saved for. Why are you saved Saints? What is the purpose of your salvation? To serve in the Kingdom, enjoy Kingdom life, to have fellowship with God? Yes, those things are true, but Saints, you are saved to rule. We are training for reigning.

That might not sound like a phenomenal revelation, but the truth is most Christians are content just to make it to Heaven. For most Christians, all they're trying to achieve, the goal of their existence is; "I hope I can get to Heaven." What a miserable empty, fruitless, waste of a life. Jesus did not die so that you could just get to Heaven. You are born-again to get to Heaven, to get started in what Christ has purposed for you to do. Salvation is the door to the Kingdom; but it is not the goal of the Kingdom. The Church is only offering salvation.

Let's go to the book of Revelation because there you'll see the purpose of our salvation through the Scriptures. I don't want to expound the whole book of Revelation, that's covered in the series on eschatology. Here we're looking at the moments before the Lord Jesus comes with His Church to dethrone the Antichrist and set up His Kingdom on earth. We're just going to be looking at a few events that happen very shortly before Christ returns. Revelation Chapter 19 and verses 6-9 says; *"And I heard, as it were, the voice of a great multitude, as the sound of many waters and as the sound of mighty thunderings, saying, "Alleluia! For the Lord God Omnipotent reigns! Let us be glad and rejoice and give Him glory, for the marriage of the Lamb has come, and His wife has made herself ready." And to her it was granted to be arrayed in fine linen, clean and bright, for the fine linen is the righteous acts of the saints. Then he said to me, "Write: 'Blessed are those who are called to the marriage supper of the Lamb!'"*

This event speaks of a great feast in the city of Heaven where all the Saints, who have come out of the tribulation, who have been raptured together with the Saints of old are feasting with Christ. You agree on that, right? This feasting is not for seven years. Actually, it doesn't say how long the marriage feast of the Lamb is. All we know is that there's a marriage feast of the Lamb. But notice verse eight, *"and to her"* this is the bride of Jesus, the Church of our Lord. That's you and I together with those who are saved around the earth and those who are still to be saved. *"To her it was granted to be arrayed in fine linen, clean and bright, for the fine linen is the righteous acts of the saints."* Alright, just bear in mind; fine linen, surf thermo washing powder, etc. got that? Let's go down and read from verse 11 *"Now I saw heaven opened,"* So, after the marriage feast the Lamb opens Heaven, *Now I saw heaven opened, and behold, a white horse. And He who sat on him was called Faithful and True, and in*

41

righteousness He judges and makes war. His eyes were like a flame of fire, and on His head were many crowns. He had a name written that no one knew except Himself. He was clothed with a robe dipped in blood, and His name is called The Word of God."- speaking of Jesus. Verse 14, this is what I want you to pay attention to. *"And the armies in heaven, clothed in fine linen, white and clean, followed Him on white horses."* Who is that? That's right, it's the Church.

How good are you at horse-riding? We're training for reigning so you'd better learn to ride a horse. That was humour! These are heavenly horses, I'm sure they'll not throw you off. Verse 15 *"Now out of His mouth goes a sharp sword, that with it He should strike the nations. And He Himself will rule them"* (that is the nations) *"with a rod of iron."* Jesus is returning to rule the nations with a rod of iron. Not soft and meek, not mild and gentle, not turning the other cheek, not blessing those who persecute, but punishing, bringing wrath, bringing order, bringing law and rule to a lawless world. And who's coming with him? - The Saints, the bride, the Church of Jesus Christ.

The rest of the chapter goes on to tells us that Jesus makes war with the Antichrist and with Lucifer. He casts the Antichrist and the false prophet into the lake of fire, Satan is bound for a thousand years. Then we get to verse 4 of Revelation Chapter 20. The Bible says, *"And I saw thrones,"* Notice the plural – I saw thrones. A throne is a seat of authority. John saw many thrones. *"And they sat on them,"* (who is they?) *"and judgment was committed to them."* Who are they to whom judgment is committed to, who sit on these many thrones? It's the Church. *"Then I saw the souls of those who had been beheaded for their witness to Jesus and for the word of God, who had not worshiped the beast or his image, and had not received his mark on their foreheads or on their hands. And they lived and reigned with Christ for a thousand years. But the rest of the dead did not live again until the thousand years were finished. This is the first resurrection."*

The first resurrection Saints, are those who literally returned from the dead. That is the first resurrection. For the Church that is the rapture. The Bible says in the book of 1 Thessalonians 4:15 when Christ comes *"that we who are alive and remain until the coming of the Lord will by no means precede those who are asleep."* Then we read in 1 Corinthians 15:52 *"in a moment, in the twinkling of an eye, at the last trumpet. For the trumpet will sound, and the dead will be raised incorruptible, and we shall be changed."* This is the first resurrection. So the 'they' here, who John refers to as the Saints who were beheaded and persecuted through the tribulation period, is the Church as a whole. The Church will rule and reign with Christ for a thousand years. Saints, there's work to be done. We are saved that we might be adopted, that we might be co-heirs with Christ, in His Kingdom. There's a real purpose to our salvation. It's not to make it to Heaven. That, of course, is one of the benefits of salvation but it's not the purpose of salvation.

Saints, unless we know what we're striving for, unless we know what God is trying to accomplish in our lives and through our lives, then our Christian experience is going to be confusing, mundane and at times seemingly pointless. Why am I a Christian, what is the point of all this stuff, why does God try me, and test me, and allow me to experience difficulties? What is the purpose of God's dealing with my life? Unless I can answer that question I will soon become discouraged with Christianity. Anything in life that has no purpose it's quickly forsaken. Without a vision a man perishes; without a purpose we wander aimlessly. And the Church is just that, we're this huge organization that wanders aimlessly, so full of activity, so full of programs but no goal. We're not trying to achieve anything concrete, all we want to do is get people into the church and get them saved. Just being saved is not sufficient because there's a longing in your heart, but you don't know what it is. We are destined to reign.

You and I are destined to rule. To varying degrees all of us will rule, all of us will have a function in the Kingdom of God. You have a function. That function is not predetermined. Let me say that again and expound on it. Whilst on earth, when we get saved, God places us in the body as He pleases. He gives us gifts to function; that's cast in stone. When God gifts you it's not negotiable, you can't squabble, you can't be jealous, you can't ask for something that God hasn't purposed for you. Whilst on earth, whilst in this flesh, God ordains the gifts He gives you. God determines through His own sovereignty where He wants you and how He wants you to function – that's non-negotiable. So, God calls you and all you've got to do is serve tea in the church, then be grateful, be the best tea server the church has ever known. Do not think yourself a lesser than the Evangelist who is called to turn a nation to Christ. That's irrelevant; your function is not to be measured. The great mistake of many Christians is we that compare our function with others. We think that if God hasn't called us to something great then we think we're lesser than someone else. In the Kingdom of God obedience is more important than function.

But, in the Kingdom of God, when we leave these mortal bodies, our function has not yet been determined. It is still to be seen where you'll function in eternity. The church by and large, and there are some wonderful exceptions, I'm just generalizing because I'm allowed to - the Church, it's just trying to get people saved, and once the people are saved, that's fine but they're not preparing them for eternity. If I tell you that you are now preparing for your eternal position in the Kingdom, will that change the way you live your Christian life? Every moment of your life is preparation for eternity and depending on your obedience, your willingness and your faithfulness to what God asks of you; it will determine where you end up in eternity. Right now, we have a blank canvas; the only person that can determine where you'll end up is you.

Let me just expound that. In the Gospel of Luke Chapter 19 Luke there's the parable of the minas. It's not about people who mine underground, the mina was a coin. Luke records a parable that Jesus taught about the purpose of Jesus Christ and His Kingdom. We'll read from verse 11 of the Gospel of Luke in the 19th chapter. The scripture says, *"Now as they heard these things, He spoke another parable, because He was near Jerusalem and because they thought the kingdom of God would appear immediately."* The Jews, as many of you know, believed that the Messiah would come and he would lead a revolt against the Roman Empire then set up the Jewish nation as the greatest Kingdom that the world has ever seen. This was the expectancy of the Jews and by and large they were correct, with one small exception. They didn't understand their own prophetic writings that there were two comings of the Messiah. The first as a suffering servant to pay the price of man's Redemption and salvation and the second as a King to set up a Kingdom. For this reason, Jesus wanted to put the Kingdom of God into perspective. As Jesus nears Jerusalem the capital city of Israel, the city from where all the kings of Israel reigned, they were believing and anticipating that Christ would now set up an earthly Kingdom. This was the anticipation. This is very relative today because there's a faction in the church and unfortunately, it's a very large faction, numbering millions of believers, who believe that just what the disciples believe, that Christ is busy establishing His Kingdom on earth, now. That the Kingdom of

Heaven is going to come to the earth, now. That's not going to happen Saints, there's too many events that need to take place. The Kingdom of heaven will come, but not now, not like that.

Jesus shares this parable to prepare the Church, His first disciples, to understand the purpose of the Kingdom and the timing of when the Kingdom will come in its' fullness. He says in verse 12 this is a parable. A parable is a story that illustrates the spiritual truths of the Kingdom of God. *"Therefore He said: "A certain nobleman went into a far country to receive for himself a kingdom and to return."* Doesn't that sound like Jesus? Jesus died, rose again, spent 40 days with His disciples then ascended to Heaven to receive a Kingdom and come back again. Verse 13 *"So he called ten of his servants, delivered to them ten minas, and said to them, 'Do business till I come.'"* Trade, make money: remember Jesus is Jewish. He gives them a mina which is about three months' salary. Verse 14 says *"But his citizens hated him, and sent a delegation after him, saying, 'We will not have this man to reign over us.'"* Ten of his faithful servants are given a mina each to keep his interests alive. He gives them all his earthly assets and says keep my assets alive, trade with them, bring increase, bring profits, grow what I've given you. But the rest of the people in his Kingdom hated him and refused to accept him as their Lord and as their master. That refers, of course, to those in the world, who still reject their King.

Verse 15 *"And so it was that when he returned, having received the kingdom,"* notice that; he returns when he has received the Kingdom. Jesus will return Saints, when God the Father gives Him the Kingdom. It's not for the Church to give Christ the Kingdom; it is for the Father to give Jesus the Kingdom. When the Father has given Jesus the Kingdom then Jesus will return. There are so many in the Church who are 'Kingdom-now,' Dominionists. They say that the Church is preparing the Kingdom for Jesus. No, the Father will give the Kingdom to Jesus. You and I are about the business of the Kingdom. It's the Father who gives the Kingdom to Jesus at the correct time.

"Having received the Kingdom," verse 15, *"he then commanded these servants, to whom he had given the money, to be called to him, that he might know how much every man had gained by trading."* He wanted to know what they had done with the money he had given them. That is just like the Church, to whom Christ has given gifts to

45

us as individuals. God expects a return on His investment. God has invested in every one of our lives; He has placed Himself in us, by the person of the Holy Spirit. God is in us, God has gifted us therefore God expects a return. The scripture continues as he now brings these men before him. Verse 16 and17 says, *"Then came the first, saying, 'Master, your mina has earned ten minas.'"* (So he had a tenfold return) *"And he said to him, 'Well done, good servant; because you were faithful in a very little, have authority over ten cities.'"* You see that? What is the reward of our labour in Christ? Well, what is the purpose of the Kingdom? To rule and reign over the works of God's hands.

The Bible tells us, very clearly, that there will be a thousand-year reign of Christ. Those who come through the tribulation, those of Israel who heed the message of the hundred and forty-four thousand, they will live on earth and we will rule over them in glorified bodies. We'll have the same bodies as Christ has. We will rule over them well. What do you think you're going to be doing? Ruling: not playing harps or picking berries in the fields of Heaven. You've got work to do Saints, there's graft to be done. You're being trained to reign. What was the reward of the first servant's faithfulness? – Ten cities.

Verse eighteen continues, *"And the second came, saying, 'Master, your mina has earned five minas.' Likewise, he said to him, 'You also be over five cities.'"* Saints, this is a parable illustrating the purpose of the Kingdom of God. This is the purpose of the crucifixion of Christ, to adopt unto to the Father as sons and daughters, who will share the heart of the Father and inherit with Christ the Kingdom of the Father. *"It is your Father's good pleasure,"* Jesus said in Like 12:32, *"to give you the Kingdom."* Not to get your blessed assurance on some pew so that you can sit in church every Sunday in the hope that you can go to Heaven. There's a greater purpose. That purpose is that you would align yourself with the purposes of God, to establish a Kingdom that will reign for eternity. You, with Jesus Christ, the Lord of all lords, the King of all kings, will be a ruler over His Kingdom. Working together with God for whatever purpose there is in eternity – which is not a hundred per cent clear right now. There's so much more to church then just doing church.

Let us continue with verse 20 to 26, *"Then another came, saying, 'Master, here is your mina, which I have kept put away in a handkerchief. For I feared you, because you are an austere man. You collect what you did not deposit, and reap what you did not sow.' And he said to him, 'Out of your own mouth I will judge you, you wicked servant. You knew that I was an austere man, collecting what I did not deposit and reaping what I did not sow. Why then did you not put my money in the bank, that at my coming I might have collected it with interest?' And he said to those who stood by, 'Take the mina from him, and give it to him who has ten minas.' (But they said to him, 'Master, he has ten minas.')"* (We've already received, how can we have more?) *"For I say to you, that to everyone who has will be given; and from him who does not have, even what he has will be taken away from him."* That sounds confusing. To him who has more will be given, we can understand that. But to him who does not have, what he has will be taken away. How can you take away nothing when you've got nothing? How do you take nothing away from somebody who has nothing so that he loses everything? How do you remove nothing from somebody and then he loses everything? What nothing did this man have to lose? He had something, he had the gift of salvation, he had the talents that God had given him, but it was nothing because he never used it. It was as though he had nothing. There are many Christians who are roaming around gifted of God with the Holy Spirit dwelling in them and they have nothing though they have everything. Sadly, that's the state of the Church. Generally speaking, about eighty per cent of Christians walk around with everything but have nothing because, that which they have, they do not use therefore that will be taken from them. They are unprofitable because they have not grasped the purpose of the Kingdom because the Church, the Church leadership are not teaching the Kingdom of God.

Effectively we're killing our sheep. We're slaughtering our very own sheep because we're not giving them a hope and a purpose. We're not explaining the purpose of the Kingdom. We're too busy talking about the politics of the Church and how to be good members of our church. We are not equipping Saints to function in the Kingdom of God so that they may have a place in the Kingdom in eternity. Being born-again is not the goal; it is the beginning of the journey. It is the first step of the journey to eternity, to functioning in the Kingdom. This is what Jesus is teaching.

Then it continues in verse 27, *"But bring here those enemies of mine, who did not want me to reign over them, and slay them before me."* The first coming of Jesus was a coming of grace, a coming of mercy, a coming of the expression of the love of God. However, the second coming of Christ will be God's coming in His wrath, in His judgment, in His fury, to judge the nations. Guess who's going to be functioning with Him? - You and I. That's why the Apostle Paul says in 1 Corinthians Chapter 6 verse 5, *"Is it so, that there is not a wise man among you, not even one, who will be able to judge between his brethren?"* Then in verse three he says *"Do you not know that we shall judge angels?"* But we the Church shout, "Oh you can't judge!" Says who? Who says you cannot judge? Actually, you're instructed to judge. Not to condemn, not to criticize, not to break down, not to destroy but to judge a matter in alignment with the Word of God. You are commanded to do that because as Paul says in 1 Corinthians 6:2, *"Do you not know that the saints will judge the world?"* Where do you think you're going to learn to judge? We're training for reigning Saints.

It's important you know that Luke's account is not a scripture out of context. Jesus says the very same thing to the Church of Thyatira in the book of Revelation. There He speaks about the reward of the faithful Saints and tells them that the reward is to govern over the cities and the nations of men. Jesus says in the Revelation Chapter 2 verse 26, speaking to the Church of Thyatira, *"And he who overcomes, and keeps My works until the end, to him I will give power over the nations."* That's interesting Saints. It says, to him whoever overcomes, to him who stays faithful to Christ, amidst the tribulation, amidst the hatred of the world and amidst the temptations of the things that Satan throws at us. He was faithful and overcomes. Jesus says *"and keeps My works."* I love that, 'who keeps my works,' not my word, my works. The Word of God, with our faith, without living it out, is empty. The works of God is the word of God in action. That's what the works are, the Word of God in action. He that overcomes and keeps my works until the end, to him I will give power over the nations. That's three times, now that we see this in God's Word and if you want more scriptures, I can give you many, many more scriptures where the Bible teaches that the Saints will rule with Jesus. We will have authority with Christ. Christ will be based in Jerusalem but some of you might find yourselves scattered over the world, in various cities or ruling over provinces of a nation. Therefore, isn't it time we learned the ways of the Kingdom? Because that is how we are going to rule. We're going to rule according to the works and the ways of the Kingdom.

How then do you learn to become a king? How do you learn to become a governor? How do you learn to become a ruler? Paul says of Jesus in Philippians 2 verse 6 "*Who, being in the form of God, did not consider it robbery to be equal with God, but made Himself of no reputation, taking the form of a bondservant,*" Paul says in the previous verse, verse 5 "*Let this mind be in you which was also in Christ Jesus,*" Paul states in his first letter to Timothy chapter 6 verse 15, when talking about Christ, he say that He is "*the King of kings and Lord of lords.*" Jesus is the supreme King yet the Bible says that He learned obedience through the things He suffered. (Philippians 2:8 says, "*He humbled Himself and became obedient to the point of death, even the death of the cross.*") He's King of kings because He is the Servant of servants. If that is how Jesus became the King of all glory, through servant-hood, therefore we too need to learn to become servants. That is the instrument that God uses to turn His children into rulers.

That's what Jesus says to Mrs Zebedee so we go back to Matthew Chapter 20 now. When the other disciples hear Mrs Zebedee's request, well, they get jealous. These great men of God, the likes of Peter and Matthew and that incredibly well-known apostle Thaddeus, they all get jealous. Of course, Christians today never get jealous of anybody, right? There are never any church splits or distinction in churches because we just love everybody, there's no jealousy! We're so much better than them. This is what Matthew records in Chapter 20 verse 24, "*And when the ten heard it, they were greatly displeased with the two brothers. But Jesus called them to Himself and said, "You know that the rulers of the Gentiles lord it over them, and those who are great exercise authority over them.*" The way of the world is that the strongest rules. Whether it's the strongest financially, intellectually or physically, that's the way the world works. "You listen to me because I'll sue you, throw you in prison, or rip your head off! That's the way the world rules, through fear, through power, through intimidation and through manipulation. But that is not the way of the Church. The fact that the Church, by and large, is ruled like the world, that many ministers act as mini dictators, is just an indictment against the Church.

The way that the Kingdom of God nurtures its' great leaders the way Jesus describes in verse 26, "*Yet it shall not be so among you; but whoever desires to become great among you, let him be your servant."* You want to be great in the Kingdom of Heaven? You want to have great authority in eternity? Then, be a servant. Serve; do not seek to be served. Bless; do not seek to be blessed. Give; do not seek to receive. Verse 27 continues *"And whoever desires to be first among you, let him be your slave"* Now, here's a distinction. If you want to be great be a servant. If you want to be first, if you want to have the spot that Mrs Zebedee was looking for, for her sons, if you want to be in the throne-room of Jesus, if you want to be one of the knights of the round table then you need to become a slave. You want to be great, be a servant. The servant still has rights. A servant still gets paid and rewarded for his service. A slave, however, gets no reward, no recognition and has no rights. You want to be the greatest in the Kingdom then give yourself totally in service, without requiring, requesting or hoping for anything. Verse 28 *"Just as the Son of Man did not come to be served, but to serve, and to give His life a ransom for many."* Christ again, is our example. You want to be great in the Kingdom, be a slave. For eternity Saints, we are going to function.

There are many examples in Scripture, but I'll just give you two examples of how God raises up kings and leaders. First example is of the journey of one of the greatest prime ministers of the Empire of Egypt, this Jewish kid named Joseph. Joseph starts off his life as a spoiled brat. He's daddy's blue-eyed boy. Pampered, favoured, an obnoxious young man – with the hand of God on him. That's God's grace! Joseph's character wasn't so good. What happens is, Joseph irritates his brothers with Godly visions, they sell him into slavery and he's bought as a slave by a man of great authority in the nation of Egypt, a man by the name of Potiphar. He starts off a lowly servant but soon because of his faithfulness, his willingness to serve, his willingness to yield he gets promoted to the head of the whole household. In fact, the scripture says of Joseph, that Potiphar, his master did not know what was in Joseph's hand. Joseph had complete control of Potiphar's assets and finances. He was so diligent and so faithful that Potiphar didn't even have to check up on him. How many of you would trust another person with all your financial affairs to the point that you didn't even worry about them. It speaks of a man of great integrity, through servant-hood. Joseph learned to be a man of integrity.

What was the great reward he received for serving Potiphar so faithfully? He gets thrown into the dungeon because of a little altercation with Mrs Potiphar. He goes from being a servant of great authority to the pit of a dungeon but he faithfully serves there, in the prison. Soon he is given charge of the entire prison, under the authority of the warden. Second time in his life this happens. First, the affairs of a household, then the affairs of a prison are placed in his hand. The person who's actually in charge goofs off, because Joseph is so competent. We read that from the prison he becomes prime minister of Egypt. But look at the pattern. He was faithful under a man, he was faithful under the warden and he was faithful under Pharaoh – but he served.

Next, we have David. David was an amazing young man. Not really considered by his parents because when the great prophet Samuel comes to town and he called for the sons of Jesse, all the sons line up except David. He was not considered or esteemed by his parents and he was left out in the field to tend his father's flock. So, it's clear that he was not his dad's blue-eyed boy. David was not part of the family and was excluded from all the good things. Yet he was so committed, to a seemingly absent father, that when a bear or a lion came to take the sheep David risked his own life for the sake of his father's flock. How many of us, if we feel that people aren't appreciating us, if we feel that people aren't respecting us, if we're not getting the recognition we deserve, would just say, "Well the hell with you," and we're off. If somebody kicks over your prized rose, well, they say, "You deserved it." But notice the heart of David. His family takes him for granted yet he's committed to that which belongs to his family.

When the brothers go off to war David takes them cheese and bread and suffers insults. Then, because he killed Goliath, he was promoted by King Saul to be captain of his armies and chief musician in his palace. Saul hates David's guts – hates him. He tries to kill him on a few occasions. So, David flees from Saul and finds himself in this cave of Adullam with four hundred of the biggest misfits in Israel. The worst down-and-outers, gripers, complainers and moaners join him. You know what David does? He began to serve them. He begins to give his life for them and from these four hundred misfits he creates an army that is undefeatable. Mighty men! One of these guys could take on a thousand people – just one of them. David had his three mighty men of valour and other men of valour. If you read the exploits, in the Bible, of these guys. I mean they made Rambo and

Arnold Schwarzenegger look like a city girl or like Mother Teresa. These guys were killing machines. David served them and turned those misfits into an army. Then you know what David does with this army? Does he hunt Saul? No. Saul was trying to kill him, trying to rid Israel of David. On two occasions David spares Saul's life and he declares "I will not raise my hand against the Lord's anointed." Even though King Saul had lost the plot years ago David remained faithful, even to his enemy because God had not yet taken the throne from Saul. So, David takes this army which he had raised and served and goes and fights the enemies of Saul – the very man who is trying to kill him. How's that for commitment to a master, even one who hates you. What was his reward? King of Israel and great, great, great, great, grandfather of Jesus.

Those are two examples of people who are willing to serve. Who were willing to go through hardship, to go through trials as God moulded their character, as God prepared them for rulership. Paul writes in the New Testament about the Old Testament saying that it was written for our instruction and our admonition. These are examples of how God deals with us, in preparing us to rule.

Saints you're not saved to be blessed, healthy and wise, to be overcomers and all the garbage which the word of faith preachers proclaim. You are saved and given the highest privilege, the highest call that any human being can have. You are called sons and daughters of the Almighty God, those to whom God has given the Kingdom with His son Jesus. So that with the King of kings and the Lord of glory and the Creator of all things you will rule and reign over the works of the hands of God. You are being equipped to reign. The purpose of your life is that God can build your character so that in eternity you can be found faithful and diligent in the things that God has purposed for you. You and I are determinants of our function in eternity.

This is Christianity, you are saved to serve. There's a purpose in our lives which is that we want people to come into the Kingdom of God. That's a slightly different perspective of the church isn't it? How many times do we fail to love our enemies? The thing is that until you learn to love your enemies God is going to make sure that you have many enemies. Pray for those who misuse you. If you stop praying for those who misuse and abuse you, God is going to make sure that there are plenty people who use and abused you. Until we learn the ways of the Kingdom God is going to keep putting these lessons before us. That's the problem with the Church. We go for there for inner-healing, outer-healing, deliverance, this and that and all the rubbish that's become part of the Church —oh, please deliver me! All we need to do is to simply learn the lessons.

"Gardening for God

brings Peas of mind"

Chapter 4

Beatitudes of Kingdom Living Part 1

A friend of mine shared recently that a church he was previously part of is very active doing wonderful work in the community. However, although it was a great church he left there and became involved with another church because he wanted more teaching, more doctrine. Unfortunately, his previous church now sees him as an enemy. Isn't that terrible! How that must break the heart of God when God's children do not walk in love one with another. What is the root of that, where does this come from?

It comes from what I've been teaching in the previous three chapters. The Church does not understand the Kingdom of God. The Church is busy with the gospel of the Church. Each church is busy trying to build itself. It's trying to protect its members, to keep its members. Doing what they believe God wants for their church in isolation with the rest of the body. Every church by and large is guilty. It's a terrible, terrible indictment against us as believers that the greatest command that Jesus gave His church, outside of loving the Father, is that we would love one another. That by this love, by the love and deep affection and care which we have for one another, the unsaved would know that we are the disciples of Jesus.

Isn't it amazing that the enemy has come into the Church and diminished the very area that is meant to be our greatest witness? The greatest witness of the Church is not the gospel of Jesus. The greatest witness of the Church is the fruit of the gospel. That fruit opens the door for the Church to share the gospel. The people in the world are looking for the love of God made manifest. They're looking for the reality of God in the life of another mortal human being like themselves. However, we, the Church, are not showing them this. Our behaviour is as bad as the world and at times far worse. Why is that?

It's because we don't understand the Kingdom. We are busy with our own agenda.

I want to expound a little bit more on what the behaviour of sons and daughters of the Kingdom must look like. We started off in the first chapter looking at what the Kingdom of God is about. How does it differ from the Church? Next, we looked at the great parable, the parable of the sower, where Jesus said to His disciples if you don't understand that parable, you'll not understand any other parable which teaches about the Kingdom of God. How true that is in the Church. If the Church is not producing fruit it's because we don't understand the concept of Kingdom.

What needs to take place within us to cause us to respond to the Word of God? Jesus said in the parable of the sower, that he who received the seed on good soil is he who hears the word and understands it. That word 'understand' means more than to just simply comprehend in your head what Jesus is saying. It means to have such a revelation of the truth that Jesus is sharing that that revelation changes your entire perception. It changes your understanding, your behaviour and the way you live out your life. It so grips your heart that you allow God to change you and you begin to live out that truth. There are so many in the Church who know what the Bible says but don't place high value on it, and therefore they don't do it. What do you value, what you put a price on? What is important to you, that you take hold of or you take ownership of? If the word of God was precious to us, we would live it out. Jesus said if you don't understand this parable, you won't understand anything. You won't produce fruit in your life until you have a revelation of the preciousness of the value of the Word of God which speaks about the Kingdom of God.

In the previous chapter we saw that our whole Christian life on earth is preparing us to reign with Christ. Everything in this earthly life is preparation. The things that God allows us to go through, our obedience to God, it's all preparation. Every single thing in the Christian church is preparation for us to reign in the Kingdom. We also saw that God expects us to be faithful in the small things which He calls us to do on earth. No matter how small the task is, that God requires of you, it will not reflect on your position in eternity. It's so important that Christians understand this because most Christians don't grasp it. Most Christians believe that the great evangelists and the great apostles and the wonderful men and women that have changed nations will automatically have places of great honour in the Kingdom. But us who, well you know, God doesn't give us much. We think that because on earth there has not been *much* fruit from the things that God has called us to do that by default we're not going to have any great authority in the Kingdom. That is the biggest lie of the devil.

God wants us to be faithful with what He's given us to do. If you have something that is seemingly unimportant – that word seemingly is important because nothing is unimportant in the Kingdom. Absolutely nothing is unimportant! A glass of cold water to a fellow Christian receives a reward. If that's all that God has called you to do, to serve people, make a meal here and there, pick up a phone once in a while and encourage the fellow brother and sister. If that's all God's called you to do and you do that faithfully you will receive a greater reward then the Evangelist who is called and gifted to win a million souls, but only wins 750,000. It's not the quantity of our obedience it's the quality.

All right, now I want to look at Matthew Chapter 4. We already know what the Kingdom is. By now we know that our lives on earth are training for the Kingdom. We know that we need to cherish the Word of God. But what are that characteristics of a child of the Kingdom. Many people are Christians but very few people are children of the Kingdom. There are a lot of people who have mouthed the word "Jesus is my lord" but they are not part of the Kingdom of God. That's what Jesus said in Matthew 7:22-23, *"Many will say to Me in that day, 'Lord, Lord... them I will declare to them I never knew you."* Saints, saying Jesus is Lord does not make you part of the Kingdom, Living by the laws of the Lord of the Kingdom is being a part of the Kingdom. Now when I talk about law I'm not talking about the Mosaic Law, please. I'm talking about the law of love and grace.

Today I want to share on the Beatitudes from a slightly different angle than usual. I'm not in any way side-lining what others have taught but I want to revisit this teaching in light of Kingdom understanding.

Let's look in Matthew Chapter 4. For context I'll read from verse 23. Matthew records and says, *"And Jesus went about all Galilee, teaching in their synagogues, preaching **the gospel of the kingdom**,"*

[Emphasis added]. As I've made clear in the previous chapters, Jesus preached the gospel of the Kingdom. He didn't preach about the church, do you know that? The church only came into existence after the resurrection of Jesus. Before that, when Jesus was busy with was the Kingdom of God or the Kingdom of Heaven, there was no church. This is why Jesus taught Israel, about the Kingdom. As I've said frequently, to be born-again is the way we enter the Kingdom, but being born-again is not the goal of the Kingdom. Jesus said to Nicodemus unless a man is born-again, he cannot enter the Kingdom. Therefore, unless you bow your life to the Lordship of Jesus, surrender yourself to His will and give yourself fully to Him, you cannot enter the Kingdom. Most Christians live their lives striving to give themselves fully to Jesus in order to get born-again and sadly that's their life's goal. "If only I can yield myself fully to Jesus." Isn't it ironic that because the goal of most Christians is just to make it into the Kingdom that they never learn how to live in the Kingdom, they'll never get to experience the Kingdom? Our aspirations are down way too low, God wants us to live up high but we're aiming down low. The sights of most Christians are way down low. God wants us to look up. That's why Paul says in Colossians 3:2 *"Set your mind on things above."* Seek where God wants you to be. Don't grovel down in the dirt.

Jesus is about the Kingdom, the Church is about the Church. It's about time the Church started being Kingdom-minded and not Church-minded. Being church minded brings division, hatred, envy, bitterness and suspicion. It does everything to turn unsaved people away from Jesus. How many of you want to bring an unsaved person to a church where every few years there is a split? I wouldn't! So back to Matthew Chapter 4, verse 23, *"And Jesus went about all Galilee, teaching in their synagogues, preaching the gospel of the kingdom, and healing all kinds of sickness and all kinds of disease among the people."* Okay, that's what Jesus was doing. It provides the context. In chapter 5, verse 1 -2, it says, *"And seeing the multitudes, He went up on a mountain, and when He was seated His disciples came to Him. Then He opened His mouth and taught them, saying:"* Jesus was preaching about the Kingdom but then He takes His disciples aside and begins to teach them. What does He begin to teach them about? He didn't teach them about the church because the church is supposed to be an expression of the Kingdom. The church is supposed to show the Kingdom of God, on earth – like an embassy. In fact, that's exactly how Paul describes it. He says we are His ambassadors and that we have the Ministry of reconciliation. 2 Corinthians Chapter 5, verse 20 says *"Now then, we are ambassadors for Christ, as though God were pleading through us:"* We are ambassadors; we are to reflect the nature of the King of the Kingdom, the laws of the King of the Kingdom in our coming together.

We're going to take our time going through this very short yet very profound teaching of Jesus that He taught His disciples in Matthew Chapter 5. Note, He did not teach this to the multitude. The verse is very clear, it says in verse 1, *"And seeing the multitudes, He went up on a mountain, and when He was seated His disciples came to Him."* He saw the multitudes then He withdrew. He did not share the Beatitudes with the masses. Why not? *"He that has an ear to hear let him hear,"* remember the parable of the sower. It says that *"To you it has been granted to know the mysteries of the Kingdom but to them it's not being granted."* To those who are just spectators in the things of God, God will never reveal the mysteries of His Kingdom. He only reveals His mysteries to those who are passionate. That's what Jesus said *"From John the Baptist until now the Kingdom of Heaven suffers violence and the violent take it by force."* We saw it's the Greek word "Biazo', those who are passionate, those who are energetic, those are willing to sacrifice everything to enter the Kingdom, do enter the Kingdom. If you are just a bit curious, you're probably not going to find God.

Jesus departs from the multitudes to be with His disciples and begins to teach them. The very first thing He says is recorded in verse 3, "*Blessed are the poor in spirit, for theirs is the kingdom of heaven.*" Did you notice that; "Blessed are the poor in spirit, for **theirs is the kingdom of heaven**." Not theirs is salvation, not theirs is a good standing in the church. Those who are poor in spirit are given the Kingdom. What does it mean to be poor in spirit? It's a reflection of who I am. To be poor in spirit is the opposite of being rich in spirit, to be puffed up, to be self-righteous. Keep your place in Matthew 5 and go with me to the Book of Isaiah.

There are two scriptures I want to share with you from Isaiah. The first is Isaiah 57 verse 15. As we go through these Beatitudes we're going to see what God's requirement is for His children and why, as a result of our disobedience, God is not that obviously present in His church. In verse 15 the prophet writing by the Spirit of God says,

"For thus says the High and Lofty One Who inhabits eternity, whose name is Holy: "I dwell in the high and holy place, With him who has a contrite and humble spirit," God says I will dwell, I will live with and I will live together with those who have a contrite and a humble spirit. Does anybody know what the word contrite means? Yes, it means broken. The word contrite in Hebrew is the word dakkâ'. It means to be something that is broken. Its root comes from the Hebrew word daka. Daka means something which is crushed. Contrite therefore means to be crushed or to be mortified by your state.

How many people come into church just because they've responded to the sinner's prayer? "God doesn't want you to go to hell, He sent Jesus to the cross for you. If you're poor or sick, make Jesus the Lord of your life and everything's going to be okay!" Hey sera, sera! How many folks say the sinner's prayer but have not been broken in spirit? They do not see themselves as wicked and deserving of God's wrath? Those who don't see themselves as spiritually bankrupt with nothing to offer God? How many of those coming in are completely overwhelmed and desperate to give their lives to God in response to this incredible love? If there are no tears of repentance, there is no salvation. Unless we are not only contrite but broken we can't become humble. Humility is as a result of brokenness. Humility, you might say, is an expression of brokenness. I am humble because I know my state, sorry I'm not addressing myself personally but a person who's truly humble is humble because they know their state. If I'm truly humble, I'll come broken before God knowing I've got nothing to offer God and that in my own self I deserve the full judgment of God. I deserve the punishments of God, I am bankrupt, and I'm destitute. I can't even beg God or plead with God to look at some sort of righteousness of my own. God says "a person who is understanding of his spiritual state before Me and humbly cries out to Me, I will dwell with that person now and in eternity".

Jesus said in the Gospel of John 14:21 *"He who has My commandments and keeps them, it is he who loves Me. And he who loves Me will be loved by My Father, and I will love him and manifest Myself to him."* In other words, God will dwell with us, if we are broken in heart, if we're humble, then we will have the fellowship of the Father and of the Son by the Holy Spirit. We will know God; we will have intimacy with God. The price, however, is brokenness, the price is humility.

In the last part of Isaiah 57 verse 15 God says, *"I dwell in the high and holy place, With him who has a contrite and humble spirit, To revive the spirit of the humble, And to revive the heart of the contrite ones."* Are we crying out for revival? For the life of God to once more flood us as individuals and to flood our churches. Are we screaming out, "God revive us"? Many churches are praying for revival and speaking about revival but why is revival being delayed? Well, look at the church I minister; we've been crying out for revival, praying for revival but there are splits, hatred, unforgiveness, bitterness, backbiting and gossip and it's actually a pretty good church. Everyone is asking, why isn't God present? Well our hearts are black. There's no humbleness, there's no contriteness, there's no brokenness. We think that we're so spiritually strong that we can point fingers at each other, that we can break each other and destroy reputations. We think we're righteous but we wonder, where's God? God is with the contrite and the humble, He's not with the proud, the arrogant or the backbiter. He's not with us because we are not with Him. Jesus said the Kingdom of God is given to those who are poor in spirit. Unless we're poor in spirit, guess what, we're not going to experience the Kingdom.

The thing is, if I'm not experiencing the Kingdom now what makes me believe I'm going to experience the Kingdom when I die. If I'm not experiencing the Kingdom now, if you're not experiencing the Kingdom now, what hope have we got of ever seeing the Kingdom? If we don't know the King now; He's not going to allow us to enter the Kingdom then. Matthew 7:23 *"I never knew you; depart from Me,"* said Jesus. But Lord, we prophesied in your name, we did mighty wonders in your name! Jesus relies, *"Depart from Me, you who practice lawlessness!"* I'm not interested in how many demons you've cast out. I'm not interested in how many times you prophesied. I'm not interested in what you've done. I'm interested in who you are! Saints, this is pretty hectic isn't it? Now let's be clear, this doesn't apply for all as many as are broken in heart. We are on the journey. But sadly there are some in the Church who call themselves Christians who are not contrite, who are not broken. They're proud; they're puffed up with a guise of humility.

Humility is not your posture. Humility is not the way you speak. Humility is not the clothes you wear. Humility is a state of the heart. It's an attitude of the heart. It's acknowledging your state before God.

Yet the funny thing about humility is that true humility brings incredible confidence. That's the irony about humility. If I'm completely broken, not trusting in myself, and I trust completely in God then my confidence is in God. I'm not questioning whether I'm right with God, or not right with God. When I'm completely broken and completely yielded I'm completely assured I'm with God, because God is with me. In contriteness and brokenness God Manifests Himself. God dwells with the contrite.

In Isaiah Chapter 66 verses 1 and 2, *"Thus says the Lord: "Heaven is My throne, And earth is My footstool. Where is the house that you will build Me?"* We can talk so lofty – "Well, we have come today to the House of the Lord, into the Sanctuary of the most holy and the most esteemed one!"- Saints, you can build the sanctuary, you can put steeples on it and put velvet pews in it; but, God does not dwell in buildings. Where is the place of my rest? Verse 2 *"For all those things My hand has made, And all those things exist," Says the Lord."* God is not looking for places to dwell he's looking for hearts to rule over. God is not interested in buildings. Don Francisco said "I don't care how steep your steeple is if it's sitting on a cemetery." *"For all those things My hand has made, And all those things exist," Says the Lord. "But on this one will I look: On him who is poor and of a contrite spirit, And who trembles at My word."*

There we see the parable of the sower. Jesus says, "it's not he that hears the word but he hears the word and understands the word." He that allows the Word of God to grip his heart, or her heart, to such a one who reveres my word so much so that when they read the Word of God and align their lives up with the word of God in fear and trembling, they repent and line their lives up with the Word of God. Saints, there are so many Christians who will read in the Word of God where it says to walk in grace, to pray for your enemies and not to be bitter. But they have bitterness and justify their bitterness, they justify their anger, justify their greed, justify their covetousness and justify their adulteries – because God knows, because God understands! The Bible is very clear. God is not going to dwell with us unless we tremble at His word, unless we fear Him, unless we are broken of spirit.

Saints, individually and corporately, as an expression of the body of Christ, we have no other option than to obey God. We must have a healthy fear of God in our hearts and we must humble ourselves to realize our absolute need for the grace and the mercy of God. There's coming a day when Jesus is going to turn around to many in His church and say, 'I never knew you'. That is why I am convinced, along with many other Christians, beyond any shadow of a doubt, that we will experience a revival. Why, because of the words of Jesus in Matthew 24 verse 14 where He says, "*And this gospel of the kingdom will be preached in all the world as a witness to all the nations, and then the end will come.*" Jesus said that the gospel of the Kingdom is once more going to be preached. That is the greatest encouragement I have in my soul, it's a thing that keeps me going in the ministry. When I wanted to run away the thing that burned in my spirit was these words of Jesus that the gospel of the Kingdom will once more be preached. God will restore His Church. God is going to make the Church like He wants the Church to be. And every single soul on the planet is going to hear the gospel of the Kingdom. That's exciting stuff. As many of us who yearn to serve God, God is going to work in our hearts to bring us low, to humble us, to give us a revelation of our need for Him. All we can offer God is a willingness to be dealt with, a willingness to be broken. The result is that we will experience the Kingdom. Saints, As many of us as are willing, not as many of us that are perfect because none of us are perfect. All of us need to grow, all of us need to allow God to change and mould us. Those of us, who are willing, will experience the Kingdom of God.

Matthew 5, verse 3, "*Blessed are the poor in spirit, for theirs is the kingdom of heaven.*" How many of you really, really, really want to have fellowship with God? How important is that to you, as an individual? Think about what I'm saying to you, really think about this. How many of you want to know Him, to really be able to communicate with God, to know His presence, to hear His voice, to experience Him? Not just merely hearing doctrines, hearing teachings, hearing other people's stories. As an individual, how many of you reading this right now are saying I want to know God? I want to hear God talking to me? We serve a loving Father who desires nothing more, absolutely nothing more, than to be in fellowship with you as individual. We serve a God who loves you as a person and wants to be intimate with you. He wants to pour himself into you He wants you to know His love for you. He wants to be actively involved in your life as an individual – this is the heart of the God. We serve a God who calls Himself Father, He calls Himself Daddy – the Hebrew word Abba. He gives Himself this title of 'Abba' because it expresses the very nature of God the Father.

Unfortunately, the majority of us in the Church don't passionately desire that relationship. There are so many Christians who say, "It's okay if I don't hear God's voice. It's okay if I don't have intimacy with the Father." Saints, that's not okay. The whole purpose of Jesus dying on a cross was to bring you into the same relationship He has with the Father. Do you know that? That's what the word co-heirs with Christ means, to be equal partakers in the Kingdom. God wants you to know Him as Jesus knows in. That's why Jesus came and took on the form of a man. Just as Jesus knew the Father in human form while He walked the earth, so God wants you to know Him, while in human form. This should be something that you and I should be passionately striving for.

I get so frustrated when we walk out of church and God hasn't revealed His presence. I can go home absolutely smitten because the whole nature and purpose of coming together is to communally have fellowship with the Father. To be in the presence of the Father is Church and anything less is not Church, anything less is an abomination, anything less is failure, anything less is not what Christ died for, it's not Christianity. Is anyone getting this? That's why Paul writes in Chapter 14 of 1 Corinthians, verse 26, *"How is it then, brethren? Whenever you come together, each of you has a psalm, has a teaching, has a tongue, has a revelation, has an interpretation."* That's natural Christianity, people fellowshipping with God, coming together with so much to share because they've been in the presence of God. Our coming together should be an expression of our experience with the Lord and as we hear each other sharing and ministering we'll be compelled to worship God, our very beings will be beyond restraint to give glory to God. At that point we worship in spirit and truth because our hearts are rejoicing.

If we come into church, dead, we present death to God therefore God is unresponsive and we wonder why. You see God dwells with those who have a broken and contrite heart. God dwells with those who want Him. All of us have a need to be wanted, isn't that true? It might surprise you but even I have a desire to be loved! For many of you that seems like a strange phenomenon. God wants to be loved by you. He doesn't need to be loved by you but He wants to be. He's waiting for us to love Him; He's waiting for us to submit ourselves to

Him. He's done everything He's going to do. He sent His Son – He crucified His own, Son, what more can God do? It's now up to us. If you want to press into the Kingdom, then you need to be crushed in your heart. We need to fight and war against pride and self-righteousness with every fibre of our beings.

Now to Luke Chapter 18, verse 9 which is our last scripture on this point. *"Also, He spoke this parable to some who trusted in themselves that they were righteous, and despised others:"* This parable was aimed at the self-righteous, those who thought that they were better than somebody else. He was speaking to the Jews. The religious Jews think they're better than the non-religious Jews. Jesus shares this story; verse 10, *"Two men went up to the temple to pray, one a Pharisee and the other a tax collector."* Wonderful choice of characters; a Pharisee; self-righteous, sitting in the seat of Moses, knowing the law, the esteemed of Israel and a tax collector; one who had sided with the Romans, one who was a traitor to his own people, a Jew by birth but a Gentile by nature, by choice. Two absolute opposites of life in Israel, at that time: A Pharisee committed in theory to the Law of Moses, to the independence of Israel and a sinful, wicked, greedy, covetous lowlife. Verse 11, *"The Pharisee stood and prayed thus with himself, 'God, I thank You that I am not like other men,"* (I'm so glad I'm me!), *"--extortioners, unjust, adulterers, or even as this tax collector."* Both of them go to the temple the Pharisee takes a look around and says, "Yeah, God thank you, I'm just so credible. I thank you I'm not like this guy." Verses 12, *"I fast twice a week; I give tithes of all that I possess."* "I've never missed a church meeting; I have quiet times, religiously." Verse 13, *"And the tax collector, standing afar off, would not so much as raise his eyes to heaven, but beat his breast, saying, 'God, be merciful to me a sinner!' I tell you, this man went down to his house justified rather than the other; for everyone who exalts himself will be humbled, and he who humbles himself will be exalted."* Saints, this is such a great truth. There are no heroes in Christianity. There are no great men and woman of God. There are only individuals who have a revelation of their brokenness, their barrenness and their absolute need for God.

The greater your revelation of your need for God, the greater the outcome of your salvation. . Jesus said these words, *"He who is forgiven much, loves much."* Now, let me ask you a question. Has anyone of us sinned more than the other? How do we quantify our sin? So how do I compare if I'm the greatest sinner than you? Human nature will say, "Well did you murder, have you committed adultery?" In our human nature we begin to list what we deemed to be the greater sins. But that's not how God sees sin. Sin is every act of disobedience to God, in thought, in word, in deed or in omission. By doing nothing you can sin. You need to have the revelation that while I might not have murdered somebody physically but I have once hated, therefore I am a murderer. When we see our state without Christ, the greater that revelation will be and we will say it is only by the grace of God that I stand. At that point our salvation will be great. Our love for God will be great.

When we are self-righteous like the Pharisee, "Oh God you really didn't have to die on a cross for me. I mean one or two stripes maybe, yeah. I don't know, perhaps just one thorn in a crown would have covered my sin." There are Christians like that. Many, many, many Christians, self-righteous "Oh Jesus didn't really bleed that much for me. He's shed all his blood for you." Consequently, these self-righteous Christians do not have the joy of the Lord, do not have the peace of the Lord, and are not used by God. There is no fruit of the Spirit in their lives, why? Because: they have not loved much, they have not been forgiven much nor do they see a need for forgiveness.

"*Blessed are the poor in spirit, For theirs is the kingdom of heaven.*" "Dear God, I need your grace." Isn't God good; He sends His Spirit to convict us of our sin so that the goodness of God, which leads us unto repentance, may open up our hearts for salvation through Christ? It's because of God's love we are saved. Every single one of us, no matter whom we are, no matter where we come from we're all utterly wicked before God. It is His love, it is His goodness, and it is His passionate desire to be our Father that took Jesus from heaven and put Him on a cross. Ultimately, Daddy wants you to be with Him for eternity. He wants to pour His love into you, He wants you to know Him, He wants to dote over you, He wants to swoon over you, and He wants to be absolutely everything to you. The only way that you'll know or ever experience that is by allowing God to show us our state before we came to Christ. To not think anything of ourselves and to know that without God I am nothing and, but by the grace of God, I am as deserving of Hell as the devil himself.

Saints, the Kingdom is possessed by those who do not think anything of themselves. Their hope, their trust, their thankfulness, their love, is for God their Father who so incredibly and willingly gave his Son to pay the price for their salvation. That through faith in that awesome work, and a willingness to surrender their lives to His Lordship, they will inherit the Kingdom of God. That's awesome! God is a God of incredible love.

This is the first thing that Jesus said to His disciples in preparation for them to take the message of the Kingdom to the Church that was to be formed after His resurrection. *"Blessed are the poor in spirit, for theirs is the kingdom of heaven."* Do you fully understand what is required? You and I cannot be saved if we believe that there is any virtue in ourselves. We think that we're okay and that somehow we are doing God a favour by giving our lives to Him. If that's the case, then the blood of Christ will profit us nothing. But if we realized that by His grace, by His goodness, by His love and by His Mercy He has given us an opportunity of salvation by embracing the sacrifice of His son, then you and I are sons and daughters of the Kingdom.

"God's Will is perfect

People make mistakes"

Chapter 5

Beatitudes of Kingdom Living Part 2

I want to continue to examine the attitudes of Kingdom living – the attitudes of the Christian. Unfortunately, many Christians do not have Kingdom attitudes. Many Christians do not behave like Christians. To be born-again is not an end of a journey, to be born-again is not a destination, it is a beginning. Jesus said unless a man is born-again he shall not see the Kingdom. Unfortunately, the Church has preached a very contrary gospel, a very different gospel to the gospel that Jesus preached. Jesus preached the gospel of the Kingdom but the Church preaches the gospel of the Church. The Church only wants people to be saved. As long as you're saved and if you're Pentecostal or charismatic and full of the Holy Spirit you're okay. However, most Churches place no emphasis on Kingdom living, therefore most Christians behave very badly and do not reflect the character of the Kingdom of God. The reason for that is because there has been very little emphasis placed in the Church on Kingdom attitudes. I'm sure you might be aware of some incidences where you've encountered un-Christ-like behaviour from Christians. Unfortunately, these are not rare but very common and the reason for that is because we do not preach the gospel of the Kingdom and insist that we become mature in Christ, that we begin to reflect the nature of Jesus.

In the previous Chapter we started looking at the Beatitudes or the beautiful attitudes of the Kingdom. We looked only at the first of these Beatitudes *"Blessed are the poor in spirit, For theirs is the kingdom of heaven."* Continuing in that theme I want to take up from verse 4 of Matthew Chapter 5. These attitudes are not the great suggestions. These characteristics, these character traits, these attitudes are essential for the Christian. They are not suggestions. These are not good traits and qualities that God wants us to perhaps, maybe, inherit and adopt. These are attitudes that God, by His Holy Spirit, through His Word and through circumstances that He brings into your life, wants to create in you and in me. It is essential we understand this – these are not options.

When you become a Christian we're not immediately presented with a number of pick or choose choices such as:

Remain a babe,

Inherit the earth,

Change your conduct,

All three.

We've not arrived at some sort of smorgasbord or buffet. The Christian buffet where you can choose what you want out of Christianity. Saints, the reason Christ died was so that we would become like Him. Romans Chapter 8, verse 29, *"For whom He foreknew, He also predestined to be conformed to the image of His Son, that He might be the firstborn among many brethren."* This is God's purpose. As we go through the Beatitudes there will be things that we need to look at, line our lives up with and if need be ask God to forgive us and give us grace to change.

Verse 4 of Matthew Chapter 5, *"Blessed are those who mourn, For they shall be comforted."* What on earth does that mean? Blessed are those who mourn, for they shall be comforted. What are we morning about? Yes, our sinful state, our condition before God. We mourn for our sinfulness, the sinful state of Man. We mourn for what we have become, fallen from the grace that God gave to Adam. We mourn our state without God. The Christian cannot live separated from God. We need to understand the fullness of what it means to be separated from God. To mourn that highest estate from which we are called. God created man to have rule over the works of His hand. God created man to have an intimate fellowship with Him. When we lose that intimacy with God, when we lose that right relationship with God, we should be devastated. When we mourn and realize what we have lost we shall be comforted. We shall come into the comfort of salvation, into the restoration of relationship. Saints, it is a tragedy for a man or a woman to be separated from God.

Verse 5 continues; *"Blessed are the meek, For they shall inherit the earth."* It doesn't say "Blessed are the weak," it says, *"Blessed are the meek, for they shall inherit the earth.*" What is meekness? The Greek word here means 'humble.' In Matthew 5 verse 5 "*Blessed are the meek, For they shall inherit the earth.*" That's the meek, the humble one, who will submit himself to God. We saw in the first beatitude, "*Blessed are the poor in spirit, For theirs is the kingdom of heaven.*" To be poor in spirit is to know your spiritual state before God. That without Jesus Christ you are separated from God, that you have no life, that you have no hope of eternal life and that you are separated by sin. The humble, those who acknowledge that state, those who know, that without God they have no future, that they have nothing. The humble will inherit the earth, because the humble person relies fully on the grace of God. Humility brings us to salvation. Salvation brings us into inheritance. Inheritance is; "*You shall inherit the earth.*"

Remember in Chapter three, Destined To Reign, I spoke about the fact that you and I are being disciplined by God to reign. The purpose of salvation is that we ultimately will be co-heirs with Christ, to reign in His Kingdom. Most Christians don't understand this they, think we're born-again so we can walk the streets of Heaven, sit in the parks and play harps on clouds just wafting away in eternity. Right now we are in training for reigning, we are training to reign. If you will humble yourself and continue to be humble you will inherit the earth. This is very interesting; notice it says "we will inherit the earth," literally God's creation." God the Father made the Creation for us. Jesus created all things, He's Lord of all things and He freely shares all things with those who surrender their lives to His Lordship. You are training for reigning. These attitudes that we are to adopt, these characteristics, are to enable us to reign with the same character, the same heart that Christ has.

Now, "You **will** inherit the earth," the only question is, when will you inherit the earth? "*Blessed are the meek, For they shall inherit the earth.*" We'll inherit it when Christ comes. Within the Church right now there are three schools of thought.

- There are some who believe that when Christ returns that's when we begin to inherit the earth.
- Others believe that we are right now inheriting the earth. And that before Christ comes, the wealth of the earth, the major business of the earth and the governments of the earth will all belong to the Church.

- The third group have no clue and aren't interested in inheriting anything.
- We'll ignore the third group.

The Bible says very clearly in two places that we will not inherit the earth before Christ comes. The first is in the book of James Chapter 5 verses 7 and 8 where James encourages the Church and says, *"Therefore be patient, brethren, until the coming of the Lord. See how the farmer waits for the precious fruit of the earth, waiting patiently for it until it receives the early and latter rain. You also be patient. Establish your hearts, for the coming of the Lord is at hand."* That is when we will inherit the earth; when the Lord returns. The other is in Psalm 37. The psalmist says the same thing in verses 9 to 11, *"For evildoers shall be cut off;"* (that word cut off is the Hebrew word "kaw-rath" which means to be destroyed.) *"But those who wait on the Lord, They shall inherit the earth. For yet a little while and the wicked shall be no more; Indeed, you will look carefully for his place, But it shall be no more. But the meek shall inherit the earth, And shall delight themselves in the abundance of peace."*

About a thousand years before Jesus came and took His disciples aside to say to them, "The meek shall inherit the earth," the Psalmist, by the Spirit of God says; when *"the wicked shall be no more"* when God has judged the nations and the wicked have been sent off to their eternal future in the flames of hell, that is when the Saints inherit the earth. Why is this important? Why is it important to know when the meek will inherit the earth? The thing is that if we believe we're going to inherit the earth now, it's going to change our theology. If you believe that God wants you, while the sinners are still around, while Satan still very much involved in the affairs of Man, if you believe contrary to Scripture, that God is wanting the Church to have dominion, that is to control and rule the of earth, it is going to drastically affect your theology. In what way, you ask? Well firstly you're expecting the wealth and the power that the world has to come to you, or certainly to come into the hands of the Church.

That thinking brings an expectation that God wants us successful in every facet of life and we begin to measure that success in worldly terms. Success then becomes having wealth, having great influence, having power, subjecting the unsaved under Christian dominion. Any sign of sickness or weakness, anytime there's adversity then one would see that as having God's disfavour. If you get sick that means it's because you're in rebellion to God, or you haven't got faith. If you're not filthy rich it's because you have no faith for finances, or there's sin in your life. So your entire Christian doctrine will be distorted. The Bible, however, is very clear, that until God judges the wicked, the Christian will not inherit the earth. We will inherit a Kingdom of peace and a Kingdom ruled by Christ. Until the Kingdoms of men have been destroyed the meek will not inherit the earth.

In the meantime, we will have adversity, we will have hardship, and we will have opposition. Our treasure is not on earth, it is in heaven; that's what Jesus taught. Jesus did not lie, He actually told the truth. I don't know if you're aware of that because I think the Church believes that Jesus is a liar. Jesus said accumulate for yourselves treasure in Heaven. Many in the Church say, "No you've got to be wealthy now." Until Christ returns we will not inherit the earth. What we are going to inherit is not a fallen world, what we're going to inherit is not what we see. The Bible is very clear that God will recreate the heavens and the earth. What we will inherit is a recreated earth. I don't know about you but I'm tired of driving pre-owned cars. If someone gave me a brand new one, out of the box that would be much better. Actually, I've never driven a second-hand car, a thirtieth-hand car, yes. Why do we want to inherit a broken, corrupt, distorted and perverted world?

Verse 6, *"Blessed are those who hunger and thirst for righteousness, For they shall be filled."* Oh yes! *"Blessed are those who hunger and thirst for righteousness."* These are very, very strong adjectives. Not those who want righteousness but those *"who hunger and thirst for righteousness."* Hunger and thirst for the righteous ways of God to be established in their hearts, in their lives, in the communities and on earth. How many of us, and this is a question you need to ask yourself right now, how many of us are satisfied with the state of the world and the state of our lives? How many are so passionate to see the unsaved coming to the knowledge of the truth? How many lives are moved by a passion to see righteousness established on the earth? The answer will be clearly shown in what occupies us. If I thirst and hunger for righteousness and for the establishing of the things of God in the hearts of men and on the earth, then I will be busy with that labour. The time I devote to the Kingdom of God and the things of God are a direct reflection of the importance I placed on it. Ouch, I sense that cut deep!

Do we hunger and thirst for righteousness? Do we hunger and thirst that we be righteous? Do we hunger and thirst that our lives are holy and that our lives are pleasing to God? Do we hunger and thirst so we can be instruments in the hands of God? When we hunger and thirst for righteousness for ourselves we will be filled with the righteousness of Jesus. When we're in right standing with God, which is what Jesus is speaking about here, we will be filled. Paul writes in 2 Corinthians Chapter 5, verse 21 *"For He made Him who knew no sin to be sin for us, that we might become the righteousness of God in Him."* In Christ, we are righteous, as righteous as God is. If you hunger and thirst for righteousness, then that hunger and thirsting will cause you to humble yourself. Under the Lordship of Jesus, making Him Lord and Saviour of your life, and then you will be righteous, through His righteousness.

But then, Saints, but then, we should become passionate to see others coming into righteousness. When we hear Jesus speaking about those who want righteousness for themselves, they thirst to be in right standing with God, which is a fantastic attitude to have. We should passionately seek right standing with God, which we get through faith in Jesus. However, that righteousness goes a bit deeper. You see, without holiness you won't see God. It is one thing to be righteous through the blood of Jesus, but it's another thing to be holy. Righteousness through the blood of Jesus is a gift of God to us, which is called Grace. When we believe on Jesus and we surrender our life to Jesus, then the grace of God, the goodness of God, the mercy of God, floods over us and God forgives us, and God restores us to Himself. That is grace; it is unmerited favour – we do nothing to deserve it. It is God's goodness poured out, it's God's love given to us. That's awesome but that's not the same as holiness. Don't ever confuse righteousness with holiness.

Righteousness is a grace from God; holiness comes as a response to God's grace. What do I mean by that? Well, if I experience the goodness of God, the forgiveness of God, the cleansing of God and the mercy of God then I should desire to live a life that honours God, which pleases God, a life in obedience to God. That is called holiness – to live according to the will of the Father. There are many Christians who have feasted on the grace of God, on the mercy of

God, but they have not responded to God, in holiness. Without holiness you'll not see God. Isn't it amazing how we're not seeing God as we want to see God, in our lives, in our congregation, as we share the gospel with others?

We need to hunger and thirst for God's righteousness. We must hunger and thirst for His Holiness. It's not good enough to just be saved. This is the essence of what I'm trying to share. The Church has made salvation its end goal, but that's not the preaching of Jesus. The goal, or the aim, is to become Christ-like, by entering the door of salvation and being baptized in the Holy Spirit. Jesus said to His disciples *"But you shall receive power when the Holy Spirit has come upon you; and you shall be witnesses to Me."* That why it's important to be baptized in the Holy Spirit. These, however, are all just steps in a journey and the ultimate fulfilment of that journey is to be like Christ.

If you hunger and thirst for righteousness you will be filled. Not just forgiven, but filled, with the righteousness of God, full of the presence of God. Saints, thirst, hunger, and have passion for Jesus. Verse 7, *"Blessed are the merciful, For they shall obtain mercy."* Once you have received the righteousness of God, once you've tasted the goodness of God, the grace of God, then God wants us to be merciful to others. All of us who are saved have received great mercy, haven't we? All of us who are born-again and have given our lives to the Lordship of Jesus have received incredible mercy. None of us deserve God's grace. There's not one of us who deserved that incredible goodness and love of God. It is God's love that has saved us. Therefore, God wants us to be merciful with the mercy that we have received. Why is it that Christians are the most unmerciful people in the world, generally speaking? You'll often receive more grace from the unsaved then you will from a fellow Christian. Do you know that? As a Christian you can walk with somebody for years showing love and friendship and caring but one mistake *"Hasta la vista hombre,"* "See you later Man, it's over." I mean, "You and your friend, aren't brothers anymore."

What is it with Christians, where is the mercy? When a brother or sister falls, instead of us being gracious, in love, in quietness we rent a bill-board and display this sin for the world to see. Why don't we show mercy? Paul says in Galatians Chapter 6 verse 1 *"Brethren, if a man is overtaken in any trespass, you who are spiritual restore such a one in a spirit of gentleness."* What do we, as Christians, do when we see our brother or sister falling, the first thing we do is not to go to them but, you know, phone as many people as you can! Where is the mercy in the Church, Saints? Where is the mercy that we have received in abundance from God and do receive in abundance from God? The same mercy that we have received, we are to show to others in the same magnitude. Of course, if that person doesn't receive the love of correction then we need to go through the Church discipline. But, how about trying to be merciful? *"Blessed are the merciful, For they shall obtain mercy."*

There is a very scary teaching of Jesus, a frightening, frightening teaching of Jesus. There's not much spoken about it in the Church and it's found in the Bible, just in case you're wondering, in Matthew Chapter 7. It's such an important teaching that is neglected by and large. There are those who teach it, but by and large it's neglected. Jesus in Matthew Chapter 7, verse 1 says *"Judge not, that you be not judged."* Saints please hear me, there's a difference between judging and judging. You're allowed to judge but you're not allowed to judge! Do you understand that? You're allowed to judge. Paul says "Why don't you judge" but here it says to "Judge not." The Apostle Paul rebukes the Church at Corinth in 1 Corinthians Chapter 5, verse 12 and says *"Do you not judge those who are inside?"* He continues in Chapter 6, verse 3 and 4, *"Do you not know that we shall judge angels? How much more, things that pertain to this life? If then you have judgments concerning things pertaining to this life, do you appoint those who are least esteemed by the Church to judge?"* Paul says, "Are you not able to judge in this matter because God has given you this ministry to judge," but Jesus says, "Don't judge". Do you understand the difference? Matthew Chapter 7, verse 1, *"Judge not, that you be not judged. For with what judgment you judge, you will be judged; and with the measure you use, it will be measured back to you."* Saints, we're called to judge. If somebody is in sin, in the Church, we need to judge the matter. Is it okay that this person is a car thief? But Jesus said, "Don't judge." How am I supposed to judge him, then? There is a difference between the judging that Jesus speaking about and the judging that we're supposed to judge with. The matter is either right or wrong. It either honours God or it doesn't honour God. It either lines up with the Word of God or it doesn't line up with Word of God. It's either appropriate behaviour for a Christian or it's inappropriate. We ought to judge in those matters. We judge however, so that we can restore. This is what the Church is supposed to do.

You get these very spiritual, baby Christians who say, "You mustn't judge, Jesus said so." Yes, did Jesus say you mustn't judge and we're going to discuss that judgment, but, we in the Church are called to judge, the Bible says so in 1 Corinthians 5. That judgment is not to hurt, is not to destroy, and is not to destruct but is to construct, to bring correction, to bring life, to bring healing. That's what we're called to judge. When a matter is wrong we go and deal with it in a spirit of love, in a spirit of meekness and in a spirit of gentleness to bring restoration, to bring healing, to bring wholeness, to root out wickedness, to root out the darkness. The attitude of our judgement is one of love, mercy, grace and restoration.

What Jesus says *"Judge not, that you be not judged,"* is clarified in the following verse. He says in verses 2 and 3 of Chapter 7, *"For with what judgment you judge, you will be judged; and with the measure you use, it will be measured back to you. And why do you look at the speck in your brother's eye, but do not consider the plank in your own eye?"* Jesus is speaking about hypocrisy. He's speaking about judging people according to a human standard, judging people according to my sense of right and wrong, judging according to my morality. That's precisely what the world does and unfortunately that's what the Church frequently does. It's okay for us to lie, to speak falsehood but it's not okay for somebody to commit adultery! In our morality, in our sense of right and wrong, it's okay to lie but it's not okay to commit adultery. Jesus says, "Well, okay you want to judge like that, then I will judge you according to your sense of right and wrong. I will judge you according to your standard." We're not called to judge according to the worldly standard. We're not called to judge according to our own sense of morality. We're called to judge by God's standard, to show grace and to show mercy. That's why Jesus says, "All the while you try to remove the speck in your brother's eye you've got a plank in your own. Don't think that you're so great and so splendid that you're sinless and perfect. Look first at your own state because then, when you go to your brother, you'll have mercy. *"Blessed are the merciful, For they shall obtain mercy."* God wants us to be kindly affectionate, one to another. God wants us to love each other. Saints, the Church seems to find that so incredibly difficult. It's such a shame on us that we cannot genuinely love each other. We need to show mercy.

Can you imagine if God treated you or I the way we treat each other – how very empty and unpopulated Heaven would be. But with the grace that we have received or the mercy that we have received we need to show that mercy to others because this is the nature of Jesus. This is the character that Christ showed the world when He went to the cross and suffered excruciating pain and prayed to the Father saying, *"Father, forgive them for they know not what they do."* That is the example Saints. If Jesus could say those words with rusty nails through his wrists and his feet, with his back ripped open rubbing against a splintered cross, with thorns pressed into his skull, parched, humiliated, dehydrated, how much more can we show grace, we who have never suffered anything comparable to Jesus. We need to show mercy. We need to be a gracious people.

This brings us back to what I was saying in the previous Chapter. The greatest testimony the Church has is that we would love one another as Christ loved us. Jesus said those words to His disciples, he says, "By your love will all men know that you're my disciples." In the previous Chapter I said that the greatest test the Church has, the greatest message we have, is not the gospel of Jesus, - it really isn't. That sounds blasphemous, that sounds like a heresy. Of course, we say, it must be true that the gospel of Jesus would be the Church's greatest testimony but it's not. Not according to Jesus. He said that the greatest testimony that you have is the love that you have for your brothers and sisters in Christ. This is what John records in John 13:35, – the actual words of Jesus – *"By this all will know that you are My disciples, if you have love for one another."* People don't want to hear the gospel of Jesus when they see the heart of Christians, I'm generalizing of course. Some of you are wonderful, no, I say, most of you are wonderful. All of you are getting more and more wonderful, you're getting 'wonderfuller!' Saints, the sad and heart-breaking truth is that the Church, in general, is a most unloving a most dangerous place to be in. It is safer to be in the world. In fact, I think it's probably safer to be a hawker in Somalia with their Warlords than it is to be an active Christian in the Church. Yeah, at least you can see a gun, you can hear the explosion but in the Church, my goodness, the gun goes off and you only hear about it three weeks later when the devastation is complete and the destruction is over and the blood is everywhere. What an indictment against us as a Church. I'm not talking about a specific Church I'm talking about the global Church of Jesus. Why is this? Because we do not show mercy, we do not show grace, we don't show love, we do not show the character of Jesus.

We do this irrespective of the reaction of the other person. One needs to show grace, because all of us do things, we have actions that are ungodly. But the bottom line is we're just not willing to show grace. It comes back to what I was saying that we judge according to our understanding of morality. Whatever is wicked to me, I'm going to place a strong emphasis on. You forgot my birthday, some people say. Actually, I forget everyone's birthday; it's not high on my list of priorities. It doesn't mean it's right, it doesn't mean it's unjustified. If I was a good pastor, a loving pastor and a caring pastor I'd make birthdays a priority. So, I'm growing. Saints, we need to start showing the character of Jesus.

As soon as we enter strife, offence, bitterness, unforgiveness and anger then we're playing on the devil's turf. What is the root cause of it? It's a lack of love. You all know somebody whom you love greatly and it's very difficult for them to truly offend you. I've got a great friend, I mean really a very close friend, he's like a blood brother to me. But this guy is always late, always undependable. He says, "I'm going to meet you at three o'clock," but I may as well go camping for the next three months. If he says he's going to do something I may as well just forget it. If he does do it I'm going to be surprised, shocked, overwhelmed and probably going to need therapy. But the thing is I love this guy so much that it doesn't bother me. It just doesn't bother me. I don't take offence when he doesn't come through when he says he will, I can live with it. Why? It's because of Love. Love covers a multitude of sins.

Saints, if you're walking in love with somebody that person can't hurt you. Jesus' love is our example. In agony, bleeding on a cross, He says forgive them Father. How could He say that? How could He not hold the wickedness they'd done to Him, against them? How could He not pray, that God would smite them? Why did He not take offence? – Love. He loved the world so much that He willingly gave Himself. When you are filled with love for somebody, that person can't hurt you, they can't offend you. If that statement is true why is it that, when we reflect honestly on ourselves, we observe an attitude that demonstrates we are not in love. We allow things to offend us.

Sometimes 'ouch' is good, because it brings healing, it gives us a revelation of where we are in our spirit so then we can make necessary adjustments. If we truly love, we will not treat one another the way we do. We need to fall on our knees and ask God to help us change. *"Blessed are the pure in heart, For they shall see God."*

Verse 7, *"Blessed are the merciful, For they shall obtain mercy."* One can only be merciful when one has received mercy. All of us who are born-again have received the most incredible mercy from a loving God. Do you know that the potential, the ability to love, the ability to show mercy and ability to show grace is already in you, if you are born-again? Do you know that? The Bible says in the book of Romans Chapter 5, verse 5, through the apostle Paul *"Now hope does not disappoint, because the love of God has been poured out in our hearts by the Holy Spirit who was given to us."* The love of God has been shed abroad in our hearts by the Holy Spirit. When you are born-again God's love in-dwells you by his Spirit. The ability to love as God wants you to love is already in you. Just do it God's Way.

"Having trouble sleeping?

Come hear our sermons"

Chapter 6

Beatitudes of Kingdom Living Part 3

━━━━━━━━━━━━━━◆━━━━━━━━━━━━━━

It's important we continue looking at the Beatitudes or the blessed attitudes of the sons and daughters of the Kingdom. There have been countless sermons preached on the Beatitudes throughout history but unfortunately many Christians believe that these are only suggestions on how we should live. They do not understand that these are the characteristics and the attitudes that God desires, His children to adopt and to live out. In this Chapter we'll remain in Matthew Chapter 5 and start from verse 8.

We looked at *"Blessed are the merciful, For they shall obtain mercy,"* and we saw that, generally speaking in the Christian Church, it is very difficult to find mercy. Christians generally are not very merciful because generally Christians are not very loving. Mercy is an expression of love. We saw that Jesus commands us to be merciful as God has been merciful with us - a God, who is gracious and forgives us our transgressions; therefore, we in the Church are called to be merciful to others. Mercy does not mean we excuse sin. Mercy does not mean we do not deal with sins but mercy is the attitude that we have when relating one to another. Mercy does not mean we turn a blind eye. Mercy does not mean we use hyper grace – "Don't worry, God forgives everything." Mercy is an attitude of heart, that I love somebody enough to minister to them in Grace.

In Matthew Chapter 5, verse 8 Jesus says *"Blessed are the pure in heart, For they shall see God."* That means that if you're not pure in heart then you're not going to see God. It's quite interesting because Jesus is speaking to the disciples whose only reference to serving God comes through the Law of Moses. The Law of Moses begins with an outward observation. As long as you observe all the 613 commandments then you are in right standing with God. That was very external, but yet the Law was meant to go beyond the external, beyond just mere obedience, to a heart attitude. Yet Jesus is not saying anything that is not already written in the Old Testament. He's saying *"Blessed are the pure in heart,"* the heart of man needs to be pure. Unless the heart of man is pure we cannot see God. God is interested in the inward, not the outward. God is interested in who we are inside not what we exhibit to the world. This is so important because there are many in the Church who are busy outwardly, doing the things of the Kingdom, but inwardly, their hearts are not where they ought to be. *"Blessed are the pure in heart, For they shall see God."*

Turn with me to the Book of Jeremiah Chapter 17 and let's just look at the natural state of the heart. Why is it, that God wants our hearts to be pure? The Prophet Jeremiah writes by the Spirit of God in Jeremiah Chapter 17, verses 9 and 10. *"The heart is deceitful above all things."* Interesting! *"The heart is deceitful above all things, And desperately wicked; Who can know it?"* What a wonderfully encouraging portion of Scripture to begin our Chapter with. I'm sure we all get a warmth quiver down our spines when God turns to humanity and says, *"The heart is deceitful above all things."* That means it's deceitful above Satan, it's deceitful above anything in existence, and it is desperately wicked. Who can truly know what is in the heart of men? Saints, that is so true. That is the state of humanity. Without Jesus Christ the heart of men is desperately wicked, it is desperately deceitful. You can never truly know anyone. That is the state of the unsaved. Unfortunately, it is also the state of many who claim to be Christians!

Do we really know the heart of each other? Have we not sometimes been a little surprised at the behaviour of Christians? It comes as a shock; we think 'well where did that come from?' That is the state of the heart when Christ is not Lord of all. When Jesus does not rule sovereignly in our own hearts then our own hearts begin to express themselves. Our own hearts, left to our own devices, are exceedingly wicked. That is why we desperately need salvation. In fact, we desperately need to go beyond salvation. It's no good just being born-again, we need to surrender ourselves fully to the Lordship of Jesus. We need to die to everything that is not of God, because unless Christ is enthroned sovereignly and singularly upon our hearts then our hearts will express themselves. Every time we exclude

Christ's Lordship from a part of our heart, then our true self comes forward and that is wickedness. That is why Christians can sometimes do the most dreadful things because Christ is not truly enthroned over their heart.

Jeremiah says, *"The heart is deceitful above all things, And desperately wicked; Who can know it? I, the Lord, search the heart, I test the mind."* That is why Jesus now says to His disciples, *"Blessed are the pure in heart, For they shall see God."* If our hearts aren't pure then our hearts are full of sin. And wickedness cannot be in the presence of God. We cannot know God, we cannot have fellowship with God and we cannot have intimacy with God while there's wickedness in our spirit. God is searching our hearts. Isn't it amazing how God tests the hearts? That is why sometimes people behave in a very strange manner and the rest of us say well where did that come from? But it was just a failed test.

This is not about what is outward, Saints. Jesus says *"Blessed are the pure in heart,"* blessed are those who have been internally purified by God. We are so used to observing the outer appearance. Are they doing what we think is the right thing to do? We judge people according to our own standard of what we believe Christians should do. We believe we have understanding of how Christians should act, therefore when Christians do not behave according to our gospel, according to our standard then we say, "Well, they're wicked." But, not so with God, God looks at the heart and if the heart is right then the actions will be right, in the sight of God, not necessary in the sight of man.

Saints, the psalmist says in Psalm 32, verses 1 and 2, *"Blessed is he whose transgression is forgiven, Whose sin is covered. Blessed is the man to whom the Lord does not impute iniquity, And in whose spirit there is no deceit."* Blessed is the man, or the woman, who is forgiven. Blessed is the man, or woman, who has been cleansed and washed of the blood of Jesus. Blessed is the person whose sins have been forgiven in the sight of God. 'And' – There's an 'and' there, there's a conjunction in verse 2 – I love conjunctions. If you don't know what a conjunction is, it's a 'joining word'. That much I learnt in my early years at school. It joins a sentence together, it says whoever is speaking or whoever is writing is not finished – they are still talking. It's like going to a restaurant and the waiter says well our special delicacy today is hamburger and chips and.... But you chip in,

"I don't want the 'and', I just want the hamburger and chips." So you miss out on the free thick shake, you miss out on the free toy for the kids and you miss out on the trip to Mauritius! You see, God's not finished.

Blessed are those who are forgiven, Blessed are those whose sins have been washed away in Jesus, and... *"And in whose spirit there is no deceit."* Blessed are those who are forgiven *and* whose hearts have been cleansed by God. Only the Spirit of God, through faith in Jesus Christ can cleanse our spirit. This is the phenomenal work of the Cross, and I don't have time to go into that in detail just now. It Suffices to say that Christ has put to death the old man, the sin nature and unless we allow Christ to put to death our sin nature then the wickedness will remain in our heart. When we submit ourselves fully to the Lordship of Jesus and we allow Christ to be established as Lord, then He cleanses the spirit. No longer are we then just forgiven but our hearts have been purified.

As I've already said copiously, the Church preaches the gospel of the Church. The gospel of the Church is simply, 'just come to Jesus and everything is going to be alright.' 'Just come to Jesus and He'll forgive you. That's not why Jesus died. He didn't die just to forgive us. Christ died not to just forgive you. That wasn't the reason Jesus came to earth. God didn't have a meeting and say, "You know we need to get man sorted out, so Jesus, why don't you go to die for them and I'll forgive them their sins," and all three concurred saying that's a good idea, - let's just forgive them their sins. That wasn't in the heart of God, Saints. That is so far from the heart of God. God didn't send His Son to forgive you for your sins, but that's what the Church preaches. Thank God though; that the forgiveness of sins is very much a part of our salvation but it's not the major reason for it.

This is what the Church needs to understand; What was the reason for the Son of the Living God to come to Earth, to take on the form of a man, to die in a cross and to rise again? What was the reason, what was the purpose? If we don't understand the purpose we're not going to understand His ministry. If I don't understand the purpose of Christ, I won't understand the Ministry of Christ. Christ came to adopt unto the Father sons and daughters. That's the only reason that Jesus came to earth. The purpose was to adopt, unto the Father, sons and daughters. Now, the methodology, the way that this was accomplished, was that, first, Christ had to pay for the price for our

82

sins. He had to pay the ransom, that's the Cross, He had to shed his blood, that's the atonement, and He had to rise again, that's the justification. Through faith in what He did that we are forgiven, we are adopted and we become sons and daughters of God. God then begins to mould our character as we allow Him. Ultimately, God is not coming back for a Church; He's coming back for a family. That's why we call him Father. We need to have pure hearts.

All of us are very familiar with the scripture in Hebrews Chapter 12 that says, "without holiness we shall not see the Father." God is looking for worshipers and until we're ready to worship God we're not going to worship God. God wants us to worship in spirit and truth. He doesn't want us to just sing songs to Him. Trust me, God can listen to all the radio stations all over the world broadcasting Christian praise and worship. If God wanted to listen to songs, He can listen to them but He's not interested in songs, He's interested in worship. He wants to be worshipped by people who love Him. We need to get our hearts pure and then we can worship God.

Hebrews Chapter 12 verse 14 *"Pursue peace with all people,"* - chase after, run after, and hunt it down. Hunt peace down, pursue peace; be actively involved in being peacemakers. *"Pursue peace with all people, and holiness, without which no one will see the Lord:"* It's no good being holy and living in strife. It's no good being friends with everybody and being unholy. We have peacemakers and we have holy people but we have very few holy peacemakers. Do you see that? *"Pursue peace with all men and holiness."* There's that conjunction again, - The Bible is full of conjunctions. *"Pursue peace with all people, and holiness, without which no one will see the Lord:"* We, as children of the Living God need to have the same heart that Jesus had. Jesus pursued peace with all men. Jesus never sought to bring division. The fact that He did bring division was not His fault; it was the result of the heart of men, those who wickedly rejected him. Those who were willing to yield, received Him. We are called to chase after, run after and actively pursue peace and holiness, without which no one will see the Lord.

In verse 15 the writer of Hebrews continues saying *"Looking carefully lest anyone fall short of the grace of God; lest any root of bitterness springing up cause trouble, and by this many become defiled;"* If we are not pursuing peace and holiness, if you're not pursuing a clean heart; *"Blessed are the pure in heart, For they shall see God.*" If we are not pure in heart, then we cannot be peacemakers and then what is it going to be the end of that? If we're not peacemakers, then a root of bitterness is going to spring up in our own hearts. The problem with that is when this root of bitterness springs up in your heart many will fall. That's what the writer of Hebrews is saying, "*lest any root of bitterness springing up cause trouble, and by this many become defiled;*" Saints, we are called to be the light of the Earth, we are called to draw people to us. If there's bitterness in our heart, it's not going to just affect us; it's going to affect all those whom we are in relationship with. They will become defiled by our own bitterness.

That is why Jesus says that we need to be "*Pure in heart,*" because the pure in heart are the true sons and daughters of God. God is pure in heart, God is holy and He expects His children to be holy. These are not the great suggestions but unfortunately within the Church we think, "Well, okay, maybe, one day if I feel like it, I'll try to obey the Beatitudes of Jesus." This is the mentality of many in the Church. Saints, this is non-negotiable, this is not an option, it's not a choice, this is not, as I already said, a smorgasbord – a buffet. "I'll choose this, I have some of that, and I'll reject a bit of this." No, you've got to embrace everything! Christianity is not a pick-and-mix, you receive it all.

We are called to be pure in heart; we are called to have Christ as Lord over our hearts, to hate sin, to hate everything that Christ hates. Only then, will we see God. How many of us want to see God? I do, I can't wait to see God. I can't wait to run into Heaven fall at the feet of Jesus and jump on the Father's lap. But for me to get there it is not just a matter of me confessing Jesus as Lord. That's why He says later on in the book of Matthew Chapter 7 verses 22 and 23, "*Many will say to Me in that day, 'Lord, Lord, have we not prophesied in Your name, cast out demons in Your name, and done many wonders in Your name?' And then I will declare to them, 'I never knew you; depart from Me, you who practice lawlessness!*" It's not about saying that Jesus is Lord of my life, anybody can say that. I can say I'm the President the United States of America. I can say it all day long, but does that make me the President the United States? No. There's a difference between the pronouncement and the being. There's a huge difference between saying and being. We ought to be sons and daughters of God, not just say we are.

God wants us to be pure of heart. He's going to test us; He's going to put people in your life who are going to test you. The only way to learn patience is to have your patience tested. The only way to learn love is to have your love tested. The only way to be gracious is to have ungracious people come into your life. Saints, that's the way it works. Many years ago, and I know it's going to sound funny, but I used to do competitive bodybuilding. Now I'm an amateur bodybuilder, I'm just building a different body, using very different tools. But as a young man, I used to lift heavy weights, weights that were out of my comfort zone. You know what that did? It made me stronger. If I used light weights it wouldn't make me stronger because I was capable of handling them. It's exactly the same in the spiritual realm. If you want patience then you need things that are going to test your patience, to grow your patience, that are going to exercise your patience. Things are going to frustrate you. If they don't frustrate you, they're not going to grow you. Oh boy, where do we go for an easy Christianity? Hell – that's where you go with easy Christianity. *"Blessed are the pure in heart,"* Saints, we don't have a choice we need to be pure in heart. We need to live a holy life; we need to be holy as God is Holy.

Matthew Chapter 5, verse 9, *"Blessed are the peacemakers, For they shall be called sons of God."* This is an awesome portion of Scripture. *"Blessed are the peacemakers for,"* 'the peacemakers are the,' *"sons of God."* The Bible says in Romans 8:29 that *"He* (Jesus) *might be the firstborn among many brethren."* Isaiah 9:6 says, *"For unto us a Child is born, Unto us a Son is given;"* Christ the man. The 'man' Christ Jesus – It's not talking about Christ in His deity – was the firstborn of the sons of God. I won't go into that doctrine except to say that Jesus is God, Jesus is equal with God, but Jesus laid aside the power of His deity and took on the form of a man. When Jesus walked the earth, He was a perfect man and He was the first of the sons of God Outside the power of His deity. Now that I've confused you let me continue, just put that thought on the back-burner. It is very sound theology, I promise you.

Jesus came to reconcile man to God. He came to bring peace between man and God, didn't He? We have peace with God, through the Cross of Jesus. Through the Cross, through Christ's sacrifice, you and I are now in a right relationship with God. So our elder brother, Jesus showed the way. He was a peacemaker. He was the Son of God and that means that the children of God, those who follow Christ, are first-fruits. Those who follow after Him need to be peacemakers. Now you can begin to see how these Beatitudes follow each other. If I'm pure in heart, if my heart is right and there is no bitterness, there's no wickedness, no deceit in my heart, then there's going to be no division in my heart. Therefore, I can become a peacemaker. Only those who are peacemakers are sons and daughters. It follows then that those who sow strife, those who sow division, those who sow contention, those who destroy and divide, those who hate, are not sons of God they're not daughters of God.

In Matthew Chapter 5 in verses 43 to 45 Jesus continues and expands a little bit more about love. *"You have heard that it was said, 'You shall love your neighbour and hate your enemy.' But I say to you, love your enemies, bless those who curse you, do good to those who hate you, and pray for those who spitefully use you and persecute you,* ***that you may be sons of your Father in heaven;"*** [emphasis added]. It's not a suggestion, to love your enemies, to pray for those who spitefully use you, to love those who persecute you. It's not something that we have a choice about. If you want to be a son or daughter of God then we need to love our enemies, we are to bless those who curse us, we need to do good to those who hate us. We don't ignore them but actually bless them. You need to pray for those who spitefully use you and persecute you that you may be a son of your Father in heaven. I don't know very many Christians who obey this. It's strange that within the Christian community we can hate one another so quickly over things that are silly and irrelevant. Have you ever been actually persecuted by another Christian? Have you actually been spitefully used by another Christian? I've never been persecuted by another Christian nor have I ever been spitefully used by another Christian, I've never been hated in the true sense. I've been disliked but I've never actually been hated by another Christian. What I'm trying to say is most Christians do not act like the very wicked. Yet we find it hard to love our brothers and sisters. Jesus says that we are to love and He's not talking about those in the community of God He's talking that those who are outside! If we can't love those who are within, what chance have we got of loving those who are without?

We need to love that we may be sons of our Father in heaven. If I'm a peacemaker I'm not going to let things hinder my relationship with another person because a peacemaker seeks to keep or make peace. I mean, how hard is it? That's what a peacemaker is. A peacemaker, one who pursues peace, will not allow division or strife and will fight against anything that brings disunity. That's what the sons and daughters of God are called to do. We are called to be peacemakers. So let me ask a question, why are Christians not peacemakers? Yes, offence, that's right. We get offended with each other. Why do we get offended? – Because, we don't love. And why don't we love? – Because, our hearts are not pure. Why are hearts not pure? Yes, because of sin. What's the remedy of the sin? – Yes, repentance.

Saints, we take offence because we don't love, we don't show mercy, and we don't show grace. We don't realize that we too, are offenders. I want to share with you something I've spoken much about previously. It's the parable of the unforgiving servant in Matthew 18. Now, if I'm preaching to the choir forgive me, I'm just providing you scriptures to give to others. I know, oftentimes you come to Church and something's being preached and you think, "I wonder if he's preaching to me?" Well Saints, very often it's not for you though it might be. But mostly it's just to teach you so that you can teach others. Right, so I'm not having a go at anybody, and my heart is just very heavy for the Church.

Matthew 18 verse 21 and 22, *"Then Peter came to Him and said, "Lord, how often shall my brother sin against me, and I forgive him? Up to seven times?" Jesus said to him, "I do not say to you, up to seven times, but up to seventy times seven."* Really! Peter was asking how often I should forgive my brother. That was the question, how often should I put up with my brother's sin? Peter throws out a number, the number seven. But Christ takes it and he multiplies it by seventy, - that is, you are to forgive your brother 490 times. Let me ask you a question do you know any Christian who has sinned against you 490 times? Let's be honest, do you know of any Christian who has been sinned against 490 times? – Anyone? Now, let me ask you another question, have you ever sinned against another Christian 490 times? I haven't, trust me, I doubt I've even preached 490 sermons so I can't be accused of offending anybody 490 times. Why are people upset with you? Why are Christians upset with you, and why are you upset with Christians? If nobody has sinned against you more than 490 times, then there should be no reason in the Christian Church that anybody should be offended. Normally after about the fifth or sixth time you resolve the differences. Really, there should be no offence in the Church so where does the offence come from?

Verse 23 *"Therefore the kingdom of heaven is like..."* Every time we hear the words, *"the Kingdom of heaven is like,"* know that Jesus is about to share a principle of the Church, a principle of God's Kingdom –this is how the Kingdom of God works. Remember the 'Royal' parable, the parable of the sower; only those who hear the word, understand it, grasp it, adopted it and make it part of their life will produce fruit. If you don't understand that the parables are here for you to understand, embrace and live out, they will profit you nothing. We're about to look at a parable, which means you need to prepare your heart to receive. If you don't receive it, if you don't understand it, it's going to profit you nothing. You'll be futile. How many of us want to be barren? Praise the Lord; I'm at the right Church then.

Back to verse 23 and through to verse 26 *"Therefore the kingdom of heaven is like a certain king who wanted to settle accounts with his servants. And when he had begun to settle accounts, one was brought to him who owed him ten thousand talents. But as he was not able to pay, his master commanded that he be sold, with his wife and children and all that he had, and that payment be made."* (The servant then does the most ridiculous thing,) verse 26 *"The servant therefore fell down before him, saying, 'Master, have patience with me, and I will pay you all."* Now for many of you, you have no idea what ten thousand talents represents. Do you have any idea how much ten thousand talents represent in US dollars? Is it thirty, fifty or eighty million dollars? As of June 2018, ten thousand talents is "fourteen billion, one million, one hundred and sixty-five thousand seven hundred dollars". Let's just call it fourteen billion. This man comes to the king and his debt is fourteen billion dollars so he falls down and says, "Be patient until I pay you all." Yes, how many lifetimes do you need?

Verse 27 *"Then the master of that servant was moved with compassion, released him, and forgave him the debt."* The king in this parable represents God; the servant represents any one of us. It could be me it could be you; it's any one of us. Jesus, when He taught a parable, carefully worded the parable so that every word had significance. He uses a phenomenal sum of money; I mean it is unbelievably big. King Solomon's income at the height of his reign was only 666 talents of gold. He was the richest King that ever lived and at the height of his reign, he was 9334 talents short of what Jesus uses as an example to represent us before God. What Christ is trying to reveal, trying to say is that our sin before God is "un-payable". We could never ever, ever, ever, ever pay, for our sins to be redeemed. But God, who is gracious and merciful, forgives us. All He wants us to do is to fall down and repent. That's the only requirement God has, acknowledge your sin, acknowledge your debt, acknowledge that you can never make good. That there is no way you can enter Heaven, that there's no way you can earn God's favour, it's just impossible. If we had to update the Bible and Jesus came to United States and Bill Gates and a few of the other people were there, Christ would turn around and say; "There was once a man and he owed 1 million talents of gold. So that even Bill Gates couldn't pay it off.

What God is wanting to share with us is that our sin before God can never be paid by us. It is only God, in His abundant mercy that forgives us. This is what we need to understand, we're saved by the most amazing grace. We're saved by a Father who looks at our state and has mercy. That's the love of the Father; He looks at us and says you are so wretched, so broken, so destitute. The only way that you can ever be in relationship with me again is if I pour out in abundance my love. That is why the Cross of Christ is part of the love of God. God in His love sent Jesus. A price that had to be paid so that mercy could be given. Do you understand that, Saints? A price had to be paid so that mercy could be given.

Now we got back to our story in verse 28 Jesus continues and He says, *"But that servant."* That servant, that had been forgiven 'fourteen billion, one million, one hundred and sixty-five thousand, seven hundred dollars', that very same man. *"But that servant went out and found one of his fellow servants who owed him a hundred denarii; and he laid hands on him and took him by the throat, saying, 'Pay me what you owe!' So his fellow servant fell down at his feet and begged him, saying, 'Have patience with me, and I will pay you all.' And he would not, but went and threw him into prison till he should pay the debt. So when his fellow servants saw what had been done, they were very grieved, and came and told their master all that had been done."* Verse 32 *"Then his master, after he had called him, said to him, 'You wicked servant! I forgave you all that debt because you begged me. Should you not also have had compassion on your fellow servant, just as I had pity on you?"*

It's interesting that Jesus uses a figure of a hundred denarii. A Denarii, the Bible tells us, was a day's wage. Obviously, today all of us earn different salaries but let's just say a day's wage for an unskilled labourer is $150 dollars. So $150 times 100 is $15,000 dollars. It's one advantage of having a Jewish Pastor, when it comes to money we can work out sums really quickly. It's a genetic gift from the Father. Now, $15,000 for somebody who earns $150 a day is a lot of money. Let's take it to a professional who's earning a thousand dollars a day. 100 denarii amounts to $100,000. What Jesus is illustrating here is that one hundred denarii, has value. It's not something to be just scoffed at, it has value. What He's teaching is that when people sin against you it's not irrelevant. It's not something to just get over. Christ, the Lord Jesus, understands that when people sin against you there is hurt, there's value to it, it has substance, and it's not insignificant. Many preachers will tell you "Oh, just get over it." The fact is, when you're hurt you are hurt, isn't that right?

Your level of spiritual maturity will determine how you are able to deal with being hurt. If you're spiritually mature, then things do wash off your back, but even then there is still personal pain. If you're a young Christian it tends to hurt a lot more. The fact is when people hurt you, they hurt you. It doesn't matter how spiritual you are, it doesn't matter how much you love God. What Christ is saying here is when you're hurt you are hurt. God is a realist. Christianity is not some fairy tale; it's not some cult, "Yeah just deal with it." What God is saying is, "I acknowledge that when people hurt you, it does have substance to it." That's from the Lord's Prayer, which says, *"Father, forgive us our trespasses, as we forgive others their trespasses against us."* Other translations it says, *"And forgive us our debts, As we forgive our debtors."*

The fact of the matter is when people hurt us there is substance to it and what God is saying is He acknowledges that when you're sinned against it does affect you. However, He wants us to see that our sin has been forgiven – that is monumental. He wants us to see that when people sin against us, in light of how God has forgiven us, we need to forgive them. It's always a hundred denarii against ten thousand talents. What He's saying is, "There is no justification to harbour unforgiveness." Yes, you have been hurt, God acknowledges it. Yes, you have been robbed, God acknowledges it. Yes, it affects you, God acknowledges it. But do not lose sight of what you have been forgiven of as an individual. Nobody has ever sinned against you the way you, or I, have sinned against God. We can never compare the sin that we have been afflicted with, compared to the sin that we have committed against God. For us to even try is ludicrous and insane. Never try to justify your sin. Never try to excuse the way you treat somebody who has sinned against you.

That's what Jesus is saying. It's all about perspective, it's all about our sin in the light of those have sinned against us and nobody has sinned against us the way you or I have sinned against God. In light of that, in light of the mercy that God has shown us, and the abundance of His grace, that we are to forgive others with the same mercy and grace that God has given us. If we don't – let's go back to the beatitude – "*Blessed are the peacemakers, For they shall be called sons of God.*" If I hold an offence against anybody, if I am not prepared to walk in forgiveness and love with anybody, anybody – that is anybody which excludes no one. All the bodies are included, in anybody. If I am not willing to forgive 'anybody' then God will not forgive me. If I try to justify why I am vengeful against the person, why I have hatred against the person then God will not forgive me, because I'm not a peacemaker. Only the peacemakers are the sons of God. Those who walk around with an offence, those who walk around with unforgiveness, those who walk around with bitterness and those who harbour resentments are not sons or daughters of God.

Jesus continues in the parable speaking to the servant who refused to forgive although he had been forgiven much. He says in verse 33 and 34 of Matthew 18 "*Should you not also have had compassion on your fellow servant, just as I had pity on you?' And his master was angry, and delivered him to the torturers until he should pay all that was due to him.*" How do you pay God back? That is called eternity Saints. That is why Hell is for eternity because you cannot pay God back. If you want to reject the grace of God, if you want to reject the forgiveness of God then, God says, "Fine, but you need to be separated from me for eternity until you pay at all." That's why Hell is for eternity because you cannot ever pay God back. Then Jesus says these incredibly powerful words. Everything thus, so far has been a parable and now Jesus comes and He summarizes the parable. He says in verse 35, *"So My Heavenly Father also will do to you if each of you, from his heart, does not forgive his brother his trespasses."*

Jesus was speaking to those who were following Him. He says if you do not forgive your brother, My Father will do to you exactly what was done in this parable. You'll be delivered to the torturers until you are able to pay back. That means you're separate from God. There are many times in Scripture, many times, where Jesus says if we do not forgive then neither will God forgive us. I'll give you a few scriptures Mark 11:25-26, Matthew 6:14-15, 1 John 3:10-15, 1 John 4:22-21. Is that enough? If we don't forgive, God won't forgive us.

Let's take a look at the Lord's Prayer which is in Matthew Chapter 6. Verses 9 through 13 details the Lord's Prayer and then we come to verse 14. We all know the part of the Lord's Prayer where it says, *"And forgive us our debts, As we forgive our debtors."* – Verse 12. Now you understand why there are debts – because of Matthew 18. Then in verse 14 Jesus says *"For if you forgive men their trespasses, your heavenly Father will also forgive you. But if you do not forgive men their trespasses, neither will your Father forgive your trespasses."* Let me ask the question; "If I'm not forgiven by the Father then what is my spiritual state? That's right, I'm lost. There is no way I can enter eternity, there is absolutely no way I can enter into eternity and be in the presence of the Father if I'm unforgiven. Put it another way, to have unforgiveness in your heart is to sign your own spiritual death warrant. That is why we should not be vengeful, we should walk in peace, and we should understand how God has been so gracious to me, as an individual. Then I will not hold anything against any person, though I'm hurt, though I'm wounded by what is being said or being done to me, yet I will choose forgiveness, I will choose grace and I will choose mercy because I don't want to be separated from God. But more importantly if my heart is right before God, if I'm full of God's love, in God's grace and God's mercy I will not readily walk in unforgiveness.

Some years ago I was ministering to a family and we were praying for the baptism of the Holy Spirit. A friend of mine was with me, I was praying for this married couple and he was praying for the wife's mother-in-law. After I finished praying for these folk I heard this dreadful scream behind me. Those of you that have ever seen a demon manifest know, well they make an awful racket; they really are quite a nuisance. But here was this very sweet woman, probably in the mid 60's at the time, rolling on the floor, frothing at the mouth with this most horrendous growling and noises coming out of her – Not human at all. It didn't take a rocket scientist to realize that this woman was really demon-possessed so I started ministering to her. When you are ministering in these circumstances you are really sensitive to the Holy Spirit's leading. I asked the Lord, "What is going on here?" God answered me and said, "She has unforgiveness." The Lord went on to reveal to me that she had been molested as a young girl, by her own father. Isn't that terrible? Here's this woman, demon-possessed, carrying bitterness, unforgiveness and resentment because as an innocent young child she was molested. What did she do to deserve that? What did she do to deserve her father acting in such a wicked, despicable way? Nothing; she was a completely innocent child. And yet because of resentment there was a legal right for Satan to inhabit her body. Does that sound fair? No, but that's how things work in the spirit realm. Unfortunately, she was being possessed. After listening for a bit I just told the demon to be quiet. We have authority. Satan just makes a big noise and he's got to be silenced.

I then said to this woman, "You need to forgive your father. If you don't forgive your father this torment is going to continue." By God's grace and because the desire of her own heart she made a decision to repent. Right there and then, as soon as she repented that spirit departed from her. I knew it had left because you could see the peace in her heart. Her son, who was standing behind me, said surprisingly, "The spirit is gone." I said, "yeah, I know that it's gone." He says, "No, no you don't understand, I saw this black mess leave my mother and fly out the house."

Saints, you can come to Church, you can sing praises but if there's bitterness in your heart you're separated from God. If you don't repent and you don't surrender, you are opening up yourself to the enemy and he has legal rights. As Jesus said, *"His master was angry, and delivered him to the torturers"* You will be handed over to the tormentors. The tormentors are evil spirits and you will be tormented. Whether you're spiritually oppressed or possessed it is because of unforgiveness.

I preached this message of unforgiveness once at a friend's Church and afterwards this giant Texan came up to me. He must have been at least six foot six tall and his late 60s. He was weeping. He was a missionary and had been in Africa for about 25 years. He just fell on my shoulder, crying and he said, "I've carried unforgiveness in my heart for many, many years against somebody and tonight I've been released!" Saints, it affects all of us, whether we are in the full-time ministry or just in the laity. Satan wants you to get into unforgiveness. He wants you to get into bitterness because if he can get you there then he has legal right over your life. But we are the sons and the daughters of the Most High God who are peacemakers. *"Blessed are the peacemakers,"* those who forgive, those who are gracious, those who love their enemies and who do good to those who spitefully use them. We are the sons of God, we are the daughters of God therefore we do not have to fear the enemy. Christ calls us to clean our heart.

"God does not believe in atheists

Therefore, atheists don't exist"

Chapter 7

Beatitudes of Kingdom Living Part 4

W e need to continue examining the blessed attitudes of the citizens of the Kingdom which are found in the book of Matthew Chapter 5. We've explored verse 8, *"Blessed are the pure in heart, For they shall see God."* You'll also recall verse 9, *"Blessed are the peacemakers, For they shall be called sons of God."* A thought struck me as I recalled that song, "You are a chosen generation, a royal priesthood, a holy nation...." The Kingdom of heaven is made up of immigrants. It is impossible, absolutely impossible, to be born into the Kingdom at birth. No person at birth is born into the Kingdom of God. The only person ever, who was born into the Kingdom, is the King of the Kingdom – Jesus. Every other person is an immigrant. One chooses to forsake ones' homeland to enter the Kingdom. One chooses to surrender ones' citizenship to take on the citizenship of heaven. Now, I'm not preaching the Jehovah's Witness gospel. In my Church the majority are South African citizens but our true citizenship is in heaven and until you are willing to immigrate, you cannot be a citizen. I thought I'd just throw that in for free.

We need to continue exploring what are the characteristics of the citizens of heaven. What are the characteristics of the citizens of the Kingdom of God. In the United States of America, to become a citizen, once you're accepted you have to pledge your allegiance to the flag. You go through a whole ceremony, a legal ceremony where you pledge your loyalty. The same is true of the Kingdom of God. You don't just enter the Kingdom of God of your own free will. You don't enter the Kingdom of God on your terms and conditions. You enter the Kingdom of God in submission to the terms and conditions of the King of that Kingdom. The Beatitudes are the attributes and the characteristics that the citizens of heaven need to adopt whilst on earth. You're not a Christian by naming it. *"It is he who **does** the will of my Father,"* says Jesus. He is the one who is accepted. It's not joining a Church or saying the Lord's Prayer before you go to bed at night. It's only by adopting Christ as your King, as your Lord. We then strive, by His grace, by the mercy of God and by His Holy Spirit to allow God to transform our nature and our character so that we begin to live out the attitudes of the Kingdom.

Matthew Chapter 5, verse 10, *"Blessed are those who are persecuted for righteousness' sake, For theirs is the kingdom of heaven."* I guess I'd better recap so we can get the context right. Jesus starts the Beatitudes with *"Blessed are the poor in spirit, For theirs is the kingdom of heaven."* Blessed are those who know their spiritual state, who know their need for salvation. If you think you're okay then you are not blessed because you're deceived. If you think that you're a relatively good person and that God, because of your goodness, is going to receive you into his Kingdom, you are very mistaken - all have sinned and all have fallen short of the glory of God and all are bound for Hell. But because of God's love, God's goodness and God's desire for you to join Him in eternity, He sent His Son Jesus to die on a cross for you so that a way could be made for you to come into the Kingdom. It's imperative we recognize our spiritual bankruptcy. *"Blessed are the poor in spirit,"* blessed are those who know their spiritual state before God, that they need a Saviour.

Jesus continues in verse 4 *"Blessed are those who mourn, For they shall be comforted."* Blessed are those who not only know their state but mourn their state. Those who see that not only are they sinners but they understand what it is to have sinned against the Most High God. It demonstrates repentance. Some people when they get caught out doing wrong say, "Okay I'm sorry about that." That's not repentance. Repentance is mourning as you see your true state and to cry to God for mercy. Of course God is a loving, merciful, gracious and good God who quickly and willingly forgives us.

Verse 5, Jesus says, *"Blessed are the meek, For they shall inherit the earth."* The humble are those that will humble themselves unto the Lordship of Christ, those who will surrender themselves, who do not think highly of themselves. You can't be truly saved if you're not truly humble. Salvation requires humbling oneself, surrendering oneself to the Lordship of Jesus, to make yourself of no reputation, so that He can be Lord.

Verse 6, *"Blessed are those who hunger and thirst for righteousness, For they shall be filled."* – to see the righteousness of God is established. Verse 7, *"Blessed are the merciful, For they shall obtain mercy."* Can you can see how this progresses? From seeing ones spiritual state, to coming to salvation, to becoming co-heirs with Christ – *"The meek, For they shall inherit the earth."* Then Jesus says those who thirst for righteousness. It's not only that you are going to inherit the earth one day but that you want to see God's righteousness established and that produces character.

All the beatitudes so far lead us to salvation. Jesus continues with the Beatitudes and starts talking about things after we're saved, after we're part of the Kingdom. What are the attributes that we need to begin to display? Jesus says, *"Blessed are the merciful, For they shall obtain mercy."* When you look at the Church, generally speaking, it's a place where you do not find mercy. Christians tend to be hypercritical, intolerant, unloving and uncaring. Everything that Christ wants us not to be, we are. In fact, most times, if you want compassion, you want mercy go to the world. The Church seems to be the only army that shoots it's wounded. Christ wants us to be merciful.

Verse 8, *"Blessed are the pure in heart, For they shall see God."* In the previous Chapter we looked at Jeremiah and saw that our hearts, outside of Christ, are incredibly deceitful and that only God can cleanse our heart through the blood of Jesus. We also looked at verse 9, *"Blessed are the peacemakers, For they shall be called sons of God."* The Church is not here to destroy one another. The Church is not here to create enemies; the Church is here to reconcile men to God, to hold fast the bonds of unity in love, and in Christ.

That is the review. The context is that once you are a child of the Kingdom, once you begin to live according to the tributes of the Kingdom, then the good news is; *"Blessed are those who are persecuted for righteousness' sake!"* – Isn't that wonderful? You realize you need for God, you realize your spiritual bankruptcy so you come and you humble yourself, 'blessed are the meek.' You begin to thirst for God's righteousness and you begin to adopt the ways of the Kingdom. You begin to follow the ways of Christ, being merciful, being loving, being gracious, caring and compassionate. When you begin to do these things, well, 'blessed are you,' because you're going to be persecuted, you're going to be hated, – isn't it wonderful? Isn't being a Christian glorious? Absolutely.

It's because you joined a Kingdom that is not of this world. You're literally giving up your original citizenship, to obtain the citizenship of another Kingdom. Just to be clear, that doesn't mean you stop paying your taxes, or you stop obeying the laws of the land. One of the attributes of the Kingdom of God is that wherever a citizen of the Kingdom of God finds himself or herself, that citizen will then adhere to the laws of that land in which they live. Do you get that? Unlike the Jehovah's Witnesses who say, "Well we're part of the Kingdom of Jehovah therefore we do not recognize any other authority." That's not what the Bible says. The Bible says that we ought to recognize all authority, even the authority that is outside the Kingdom of God because all authority is given by God. Therefore you ought to submit to the laws of the land in which we find ourselves in. A child of God can never say that they are not bound by the laws of the land that they living in.

The truth of the matter Saints, is that if you want to serve God with all your heart, and you want to become Christ-like, then the more you desire to serve God, or the more you desire to be Christ-like, the more you're going to be persecuted. And the more you're persecuted, the more blessed you are. If you don't want to be persecuted that's fine, you will be least in the Kingdom – if you make it! If you're not persecuted, it means that you're not reflecting Christ, and therefore when Christ is not truly Lord you're in a very dangerous place. But those who desire to live upright in Christ will suffer persecution, the Bible says.

Back to verse 10, *"Blessed are those who are persecuted for righteousness' sake, For theirs is the kingdom of heaven."* There's something we need to learn. We often sing a song which says that 'we are a royal priesthood, that we are a chosen generation.' When you are born-again you enter into a different Kingdom. This is so important. Let's go beyond a new creation, you're entering into a new Kingdom. You've got to become a new creation to get into the Kingdom. Our problem is we think like Church people and not like Christians. There's a huge difference between the mentality of the Church and the mentality of the Kingdom of God. We are new creations; thank God we are new creations. We have to be new creations to become a citizen of the Kingdom of heaven. All our

Christian jargon, literally all of it, is just speaking about the necessary things that must take place in our lives for us to **enter** the Kingdom, so that we can become **citizens** of the Kingdom. However, we don't understand what it is to be a citizen.

A citizen has responsibilities. There is a certain conduct that is required of a citizen. All of us are bound by requirements of this land in which we live. In South Africa we all have to get an ID document at the age of 16 and we're all expected to obey the laws of this land. All of us are expected to pay taxes, so that the government of this land has finances to govern this nation. You and I cannot behave as we will in South African; do you agree? We do not have freedom to express ourselves in any way we want to. You can't go in and start cursing people, you'll get arrested. Even as South Africans we are restricted in our behaviour, so it is true in the Kingdom of heaven that God expects us to act like sons and daughters of His Kingdom. The Church has placed very little emphasis on that. We don't place, as Christians, and I'm talking about the Church in general, much emphasis on Christian conduct or Christian character.

Generally speaking, Christians are not nice people. I have to be honest with you. I've been a Christian and a part of this Kingdom now for twenty-five years and I must say it's a nasty Kingdom, made up of really nasty people. So much so that if somebody says to me, "I'm a Christian," my instinct is to run a mile. Am I the only one? It's an indictment against the Christian Church. The Church only speaks about membership. The Church only speaks about being loyal to the local Church. If you leave your local Church and go join another Church you are no longer their brother or sister, they treat you as an enemy, they treat you as a leper or as an outcast. That is why, Saints, it's so important that we grasp and understand the Kingdom of God. We must get our minds outside of 'Churchianity' and get our hearts into Christianity. Where Christ is King and Christ is Lord and Christ has rule.

That was a little bit of a tangent or a detour, but I'm trying to shock us into understanding the true state of the Church. If I've said anything that's untrue, I should be cautioned . Remember we're talking about, *"Blessed are those who are persecuted for righteousness' sake"*. This is very important *"Blessed are those who are persecuted for righteousness' sake, For theirs is the kingdom of heaven."* Notice, Jesus did not say "Blessed are those who are persecuted." Please, understand it's very important to grasp that truth. There are many people who are being persecuted today. There are many people groups and there are many folk who adhere to certain religions or cults, who are suffering persecution. But they are not necessarily going to be heirs of the Kingdom. It's only those who are persecuted for righteousness sake. That is, the righteousness that comes through faith in Jesus Christ, - those who have surrendered their lives to the Lordship of Jesus, those who are pursuing His Kingdom and His Lordship. Only those who are persecuted for righteousness sake will inherit the Kingdom. It's important Saints. Some Christians are persecuted for stupidity's sake. Some Christians are persecuted because of their behaviour, which deserves persecution, and then they claim that they're being persecuted for righteousness. No, they've being persecuted for their own stupidity, or their own sinfulness. There's a big difference. I've heard so many Christians say, "You know, they hate me at work." I reply, "Listen, if you worked for me, I'd probably dislike you as well, you're dislikeable.

Whether you're Christian, Hindu or atheists; it's got nothing to do with your religion, it's to do with your character. Some Christians deserve to be persecuted, just for their character's sake. There's no blessing to be persecuted when you act like the devil. Let's be honest Saints, there are a lot of Christians that, if I was allowed to and I had relapsed into a backslidden state, I'd likely minister the fivefold ministry in the shape of a fist! But Saints we can't do that. We've got to be persecuted for righteousness sake. If you're persecuted for righteousness sake it means that you're a son or daughter of the Kingdom.

1 Peter Chapter 4, verse 12, *"Beloved, do not think it strange concerning the fiery trial which is to try you, as though some strange thing happened to you;"* When fiery trials, persecutions and hardships come against you, you must not think it's strange because in the Christian life you will always experience persecution when you desire to follow the Lord. It has to happen and I am going to explain to you why in a moment. Peter encourages the Church and he says, *"But rejoice to the extent that you partake of Christ's sufferings, that when His glory is revealed, you may also be glad with exceeding joy. If you are reproached for the name of Christ, blessed are you, for the Spirit of glory and of God rests upon you."* If you're persecuted for

righteousness sake it is because the Holy Spirit is working in and through your life, changing you so that your life reflects the Kingdom of God, as you reflect Christ who is your Lord. That is why you're persecuted.

There are two Kingdoms that are in operation on earth today. There are two Kingdoms who are hostile to each other. We are in a war zone. There is no chance of there ever being a ceasefire or a truce or any peace between these two Kingdoms. One Kingdom must be totally destroyed and the other Kingdom must have total domination. That's the reality of the situation that the world finds itself in, whether knowingly or unknowingly. Jesus tried to explain this to the Pharisees in Matthew Chapter 12. It's very important that we see this - why are we blessed when we are persecuted for righteousness sake.

In Matthew 12, Jesus was ministering and He casts out a demon spirit from a man who was blind and mute. The people were deliberating whether this could be the Messiah. The Jews were pondering if this was the Messiah that the prophets had spoken about. The Pharisees, the religious leaders show up in all their religiosity and in verse 24 it says. *"Now when the Pharisees heard it they said, "This fellow does not cast out demons except by Beelzebub, the ruler of the demons."* Here the Jews and the common people of the Jews were wondering whether Jesus could be the Messiah. The Pharisees, the religious leaders, who cared more about their status, more about the traditions then they did about the Word of God, said "Take no notice of Him, He casts out demons by Beelzebub, the ruler of demons." To which Jesus responds in verse 25, *"But Jesus knew their thoughts, and said to them: "Every kingdom divided against itself is brought to desolation, and every city or house divided against itself will not stand. If Satan casts out Satan, he is divided against himself. How then will his kingdom stand?"* What He's saying is very important to understand.

There is a Kingdom, which is ruled by Satan. Please do not think that the rule of this earth is in the hands of God, you'll be most mistaken. In the Gospel of Luke Chapter 4, verse 6 when Satan comes to tempt Jesus he says to Him, *"All this authority I will give You, and their glory; for this has been delivered to me, and I give it to whomever I wish. Therefore, if You will worship before me, all will be Yours."* Jesus did not call Satan a liar. He didn't say to Satan, "You have no right to offer me the Kingdoms of the earth," because Jesus knew full well that Adam had relinquished all authority over the Kingdoms of this earth to Satan. Satan is the ruler of this earth's kingdom and will be until the Lord's return. Satan doesn't cast out Satan. Satan does not extend the Kingdom of God. This is what the Pharisees were saying. Satan never does anything, in any way, to help extend God's Kingdom.

This is what Jesus was in effect saying, "If I am casting out devils by the power of Satan then Satan's Kingdom is divided and that Kingdom will not stand." The reason that Satan's Kingdom still stands is because Satan doesn't destroy what is his. Jesus continues and He says in verse 28, *"But if I cast out demons by the Spirit of God, surely the kingdom of God has come upon you."* As I said at the start of this book Jesus was ministering to prepare the people to receive the Kingdom of God. The Kingdom of God had not yet come; it could only come at the resurrection of Jesus. That's when people began to enter the Kingdom. You couldn't enter the Kingdom until Christ died, paid for our sins and rose again. Only then by faith could we enter the Kingdom. Jesus was saying here that, when you see the power of God being ministered, know that the Kingdom of God has come.

All of us, who are born-again, were once citizens of the Kingdom of darkness – all of us without exception. There's never been a person, conceived by a human father, who was not part of the Kingdom of darkness. Every single one of us, whether willingly or unwillingly, whether knowingly or unknowingly, was once a citizen of the Kingdom of darkness. That's what Paul writes in the book of Colossians Chapter 1. Paul is sharing this truth and he speaks about the redemptive work of Jesus and he says in verse 13, *"He has delivered us from the power of darkness and conveyed us into the kingdom of the Son of His love,"* – all of us, who have surrendered our lives to the Lordship of Jesus. We have discussed true biblical repentance, which is something that happens in your heart, not something that happens in a counselling session. All those that have truly repented and surrendered their lives to the Lordship of Jesus are translated, or taken, from one Kingdom, by God, and placed into His Kingdom. *"Into the kingdom of the Son of His love, in whom we have redemption through His blood, the forgiveness of sins."*

Saints, we are part of a different Kingdom. We have relinquished our citizenship of the world, of Satan's Kingdom. And because we are part of another Kingdom, the Kingdom that we left, the Kingdom of darkness seeks to destroy us. We basically have changed sides and entered into a war. Whilst you're in the Kingdom of Satan, God is not fighting against you. God is a God of love. God is pouring out His love to bring you into His Kingdom. God's weapon is love, God's weapon is mercy, God's weapon is grace, God's weapon is goodness and God's weapon is forgiveness. God uses His love, His goodness and His grace, which are epitomized through the sacrifice of Jesus, to bring us into His Kingdom.

Satan is a dirty rotten scoundrel. He's a wicked, perverse creature. When you go from his Kingdom to the Kingdom of Light, into the Kingdom of God then the weapons of Satan are; destruction, death, murder, theft or whatever he can use to destroy your life. For this reason when you come into the Kingdom of righteousness you're going to be persecuted by your former king.

1 John Chapter 5, verse 19, tells us that, *"the whole world lies under the sway of the wicked one."* Therefore, if you're not in the Kingdom of God, you are in the Kingdom of darkness. Whether you have sworn allegiance to the Kingdom of darkness or not, is irrelevant. You don't have to be a Satanist to be a part of the Kingdom of darkness. To be part of the Kingdom of darkness all you have to be is unsaved. There is this war, between the sons and the daughters of righteousness and the ruler of the Kingdom of darkness.

The Kingdom of darkness will use its subjects to persecute the sons of righteousness. Satan will use people in his Kingdom to persecute the righteous in the Kingdom of God. Satan has never physically murdered anybody. A demon cannot murder a Christian; do you know that? A demon has no power, zero, nothing, over a child of the Living God. One of the biggest lies of the devil resulted after he obtained some pulpit time and preached that demons can get Christians. That is a whole lot of garbage. Jesus says, in Luke Chapter 10, verse 19, *"Behold, I give you the authority to trample on serpents and scorpions, and over **all the power of the enemy**, and nothing shall by any means hurt you."* [Emphasis added] If you have authority over all the power of the enemy, what power does Satan have against you? That's right, nothing, because you've got 'all'. Therefore Satan and his demons cannot, in any way, afflict a Christian. I don't care what minister preaches otherwise, they are lying sons of light living in darkness. The Word of God is true and let every man be a liar. If Jesus says He has given His saints power over Satan and all his demons and nothing shall by any means hurt them, then no demon spirit, not Satan himself, can hurt the Christian. That is a fact Saints.

I've never been attacked by a demon spirit. I've casted out many demons and have never been attacked by one of them. Why? – Because of Jesus. Not because of me but because Jesus said so. How then does persecution come? It can't come by Satan, it can't come by demons, how then are the righteous persecuted? It comes via the *citizens* of the Kingdom of darkness. Satan can't cause harm to you but he can influence people to persecute you, and if God should permit, to even take your life. Peter writes in 1 Peter 4, verse 14, *"If you are reproached for the name of Christ, blessed are you, for the Spirit of glory and of God rests upon you. On their part He is blasphemed, but on your part He is glorified."* If you're persecuted for righteousness sake it means that the Holy Spirit of the living God is upon your life. That you are reflecting the Kingdom, that your life is showing the fruit of the Kingdom of God and blessed are you.

Do you know Saints, that there is what's called, in the Kingdom of heaven, the crown of the martyrs? A crown reserved for those who are afflicted for the name of Jesus (Revelation 2:10) As we learnt previously, the whole point of our life, after coming to Christ, is that we might labour for God, that we might find ourselves faithful, so that in the Kingdom of heaven, we will have authority. All of us are going to have different authority in heaven. That authority is not based on how dynamic your ministry was on earth. This is so important and I'm compelled to say this a thousand times a day, until people get it. The authority you will enjoy in heaven has got nothing to do with how dynamic your ministry on earth was. Whether you led twenty five million people to Jesus, or you faithfully served in the Church kitchen, what you did is irrelevant. What is relevant though, is your faithfulness and your attitude. God wants us to be faithful to what He has called us to do as individuals and not to compare ourselves with each other. We're training for a reigning, and as I said before, it's our faithfulness to what God has called us to do that's going to determine the authority we'll have in His Kingdom. We're not just going to go to heaven. Heaven is the capital city of the Kingdom of God but there's going to be a whole lot of stuff that's going to be going on in eternity.

Now after such a long detour let's get back to Matthew Chapter 5. Matthew Chapter 5 verse 10, *"Blessed are those who are persecuted for righteousness' sake, For theirs is the kingdom of heaven."* Then verse 11, *"Blessed are you when they revile and persecute you, and say all kinds of evil against you falsely..."* It says that those who are persecuted for righteousness sake get into the Kingdom. It is those who are reviled against falsely, persecuted unjustly, those are the blessed. *"Blessed are you when they revile and persecute you, and say all kinds of evil against you falsely for My sake. Rejoice and be exceedingly glad, for great is your reward in heaven, for so they persecuted the prophets who were before you."* The reality is that we're in a war zone.

There is no such thing as easy Christianity. Whoever told you that was deceived. The more you want to serve Jesus the more you're going to get on the enemy's case, the more he's going to try and break you down to destroy you. That's the hardship and the reality. However, the joy is that the closer you become to God the more joy He puts in your heart. The more hope you have the more He gives you – a 'forehead of flint' so that things don't bother you, to quote from the Old Testament (Ezekiel 3:9). This persecution doesn't break you but in fact, strengthens you and gives you joy. That is the reality Saints.

So, how do we then live in this place? The closer I draw near to the Lord, the more I thirst and hunger for His righteousness, the more I'm going to be persecuted but the more blessed I am – how do I live here. How do I live in that space? You know, the next thing Jesus says in Matthew 5 is *"You are the salt of the earth; - You are the light of the world."* When we join the Kingdom of heaven we join the quest of the Kingdom. The quest of the Kingdom is the quest of the King, who desires that all should come to repentance and that all should come to salvation. We serve a good God, we serve a loving God. We serve a God who wants to see souls saved and who wants to see souls coming into His Kingdom – we serve a very loving, caring, good God. You and I are the salt of the earth, we are the light to the world and we are the reflection of God to this world. If people are going to seek Jesus they need to see Jesus in you and in me. We then become ambassadors of this Kingdom.

I want to finish with a scripture in 2 Corinthians which is more often than not misquoted and misused. In 2 Corinthians Chapter 5, verse 20, Paul is writing to the Church at Corinth. He's writing to a Church that is doctrinally very unsound, they are full of strife, division, bitterness and sin. You might say he's speaking to the

Church of this century as well. The Apostle Paul writes on behalf of himself and his ministry team to the Church of Corinth and he says these words; *"Now then, **we are ambassadors for Christ**, as though God were pleading through us: we implore you on Christ's behalf, be reconciled to God."* [Emphasis added] Note that Paul did not call the Church of Corinth, ambassadors for Christ. So many times you hear people saying we are Christ's ambassadors. No, you're only an ambassador for Christ when you're living in obedience to Christ. You're not an ambassador for Jesus when there is strife, when there's contention, when there is sin, when there's unforgiveness and when there is pride in your heart. If those things are present then you're not a minister of reconciliation, you are no longer an ambassador, you have disqualified yourself from being an ambassador. You are just like the Corinthians. Therefore you need true ambassadors to plead with you to be reconciled with God.

I think that in our time, God is raising up Christians within the Church to become ambassadors to the Church. To plead with the Church to be once more reconciled to God and begin to act like citizens of the Kingdom and not like citizens of the world because that's what we are witnessing. We're witnessing Christians who have the same morals, the same standards and the same conduct as the world. They're citizens of the Kingdom but they behave like citizens of the world. God wants us to become ambassadors – each one of us. Everyone who is washed in the blood of Jesus, He wants to become ambassadors of righteousness.

It's there that Christ ends the Beatitudes. It's only when we surrender ourselves to the teachings of Jesus, by making Him Lord and allowing the Spirit of God to change us from the inside that we will become ambassadors. You will be persecuted but then you will be highly blessed and favoured in the Kingdom. God shows no partiality, He loves us all equally and desires us all to fully experience everything that He's done for us and everything that heaven is. However, when it comes to your eternal authority it is in your hands somewhat. The more obedient, the more submitted, the more willing, the more authority God will give you. Authority always means closeness to the King. Authority is given to those who are close to the King. We've covered that previously.

If you want to know the Lord, if you want His closeness in your heart, in your life, if you want the sweet fellowship of His Spirit now, then become obedient. If you're willing and obedient you will reap of the good of the Kingdom.

God allowed Job to be tested. That wasn't a persecution, that was a test or a trial. Job wasn't persecuted by any person. God allowed Job to be tried and tested by Satan because God wanted Job to grow. As we study Job we see that Job started off knowing of God and by the end of his trials and tribulations he knew God. He went from knowing about Him to knowing Him personally. That's why God allows trials in our life so we can get to *know* Him, not *about* Him. Most Christians know about Jesus. Most Christians know about God, but God doesn't want Christians to know about him, God wants all His sons and daughters, all He's drawn to know Him, just like your parents wanted you to know them.

Persecution should always come from outside the Church. If it's inside the Church then it's exactly what Jesus told the Pharisees; *"If Satan's Kingdom is divided against itself that Kingdom cannot stand."* The same truth must then be true of God's Kingdom. If God's Kingdom is divided against itself it cannot stand. That is why the Church is generally powerless and pathetic because Christians spend more time trying to destroy each other than to unite and come against the world's system. Think about it. How many Christians rejoice when another Church begins to prosper in the things of God? How many Christians are broken-hearted when they see another Christian falling? Many Christians rejoice and say they were rotten anyway. We behave atrociously. I've been in the ministry for many years and I've met many ministers and been to many Churches and I tell you Christians act atrociously. We persecute each other and we destroy each other when we don't show grace, or love, or mercy and goodness. We don't show any reflection of Jesus to one another.

Persecution should in theory always come from outside the Church, because the Church should be united as one body, one Spirit, one baptism and one Lord, - that's the Church. Obviously if somebody's serving the Lord with integrity and sincerity they will not persecute anyone. Think about when you got saved; think about when you came to the Lord. Did you immediately hate anybody? Didn't you find all of a sudden you just loved everybody? Even the people that you previously hated you now had this incredible love for them! What changed? Why do some go from having this incredible love for people, to again begin to hate, divide and create strife? Because they moved their position. When you get saved you humble yourself before God. You're just falling all over the Lord, you're crying out for mercy please. You so filled with His love and you're filled with His nearness. Therefore His character rubs off onto you. After you've been in the way for some time you become a mature Christian but you may have drifted from nearness to God and exchanged relationship for knowledge. And now there's strife, there's division and there's contention, – you're not mature, you're backslidden. That's what happens in the Church, you get people who think they mature because they can, you know, recite the book of Job, but that's not maturity. Maturity is when you act like Christ, that's true maturity.

Let us strive for the unity of the faith, let us be peacemakers, let us be merciful and let us be vessels in extension of the Kingdom of righteousness. That's what Church is about, that's what Christianity is about. You are part of the Kingdom of God. All of us are immigrants; none of us were born into the Kingdom. We are born-again into the Kingdom, it's a rebirth. Let us make the King proud by making Him Lord.

Let's Pray.Lord, Father, my God, in Your incredible love, in Your wonderful mercy, in Your unspeakable compassion, You sent Jesus to pay for our Redemption. We've gone through these Beatitudes and Lord we ask of You that by Your Spirit You would engrave these teachings, these words of our Lord on to our heart. My God, help us to draw close to You. Please forgive us for being agents of strife and division, Lord, of bringing the Kingdom of darkness into Your Kingdom, through attitudes, through things we have done and through things we have said. Merciful Father, forgive us and give us grace to be truly salt of the earth. Give us grace by Your Spirit, my God, to be the light that will reflect Your mercy so that souls will be saved and that the Kingdom of God would be extended. In these times have mercy on Your Church. We ask in Jesus' name.

*"If you don't love God
Go to Hell"*

Chapter 8

Kingdom Authority

W hile on leave recently I found myself standing on the beach staring towards Australia. The sunlight was warm and the birds frolicked as the waves crashed at the shore. As I stood there in my tee-shirt and shorts, with the sun beating down, the Lord kept stirring my spirit, saying to me that unless we come under authority we will have no authority. I meditated continuously for two weeks on that, on what God had put in my spirit. Looking at us, as a Church and the body of Jesus as a whole, we see that in this area we are doing incredibly poorly. We generally are not under Authority. Authority is a principle of the Kingdom that is so important. What I'm going to share in this Chapter is so incredibly important. I'm not sharing it to strike a point. Please hear me, I'm not sharing something to make a point or to try and validate things that have happened in the past as a Church. What I'm sharing is something that God has put in my heart. This is so crucial to understanding the Kingdom.

In the past few Chapters we examined the Beatitudes spending four Chapters on them. The Beatitudes, or put differently, the blessed attitudes of the citizens of the Kingdom. The attitudes a citizen of the Kingdom needs to adopt. But now Saints, we need to go a bit further. If we want to experience, if we want the authority of God in our lives, if we want to see God move in our Churches, if we want to see souls saved, if we want to see healings and miracles, if we want to see the power of God amongst us then there is something we need to learn. There is a vital principle of the Kingdom that needs to be established and rooted in our hearts which is that we need to understand that authority is only given to those who are themselves under authority. You cannot have any authority in the Kingdom of God unless you are first under authority.

This is such a broad subject. It's not just speaking about Authority in one aspect but it's speaking about Authority in its fullest context. Authority to the Word of God, authority to God and authority to one another, it's so incredibly diverse. As the Spirit leads I want to see how God directs where we go with this. Please, I'm not trying to score a point. There's so many times people think, yeah the pastor is just saying that because he's trying to justify something, just trying to convey a hidden message. By now you should know I don't speak in hidden tones. I do not disguise what I want to say. If you've got spinach between your teeth, I'll tell you that you've got spinach between your teeth. If your breath smells, I'll tell you that maybe you should buy a new toothbrush or perhaps get some "tic-tacs". The Bible says speak the truth in love. What I'm sharing today is from the heart of God.

Turn with me in your Bible, to the book of Matthew and the eighth Chapter. Again this ties into the subject we're speaking about, which is the Kingdom of God. We're going to take up from verse five and go through to the end of verse 12. *"Now when Jesus had entered Capernaum, a centurion came to Him, pleading with Him, saying, "Lord, my servant is lying at home paralyzed, dreadfully tormented." And Jesus said to him, "I will come and heal him." The centurion answered and said, "Lord, I am not worthy that You should come under my roof. But only speak a word, and my servant will be healed. For I also am a man under authority, having soldiers under me. And I say to this one, 'Go,' and he goes; and to another, 'Come,' and he comes; and to my servant, 'Do this,' and he does it." When Jesus heard it, He marvelled, and said to those who followed, "Assuredly, I say to you, I have not found such great faith, not even in Israel! And I say to you that many will come from east and west, and sit down with Abraham, Isaac, and Jacob in the kingdom of heaven. But the sons of the kingdom will be cast out into outer darkness. There will be weeping and gnashing of teeth."*

There are only two accounts in the Gospels where Jesus commends people for having great faith. Are you aware of that? In the three-and-a-half years of His ministry only on two occasions does Jesus marvel at the incredible faith of individuals? It happens only twice and there are two individuals both of which are Gentiles. They are not Jews; they are not the people of God. Remember that at this time Jesus was called to the Nation of Israel. It was the Nation of

Israel that God worked through to establish His presence on earth. No Jew ever exhibited faith as God would have them have faith, except two Gentiles. These verses in Matthew 8 are one such account and we're going to look at this in a bit more detail.

What's very interesting is what Jesus says in verse 11 and 12, *"And I say to you that many will come from east and west, and sit down with Abraham, Isaac, and Jacob in the kingdom of heaven. But the sons of the kingdom"* – that is the Nation of Israel, that nation that God appointed to be His chosen people. Many in Israel will not enter the Kingdom of heaven! They were once the chosen of God; they were once the only nation that God would minister to and minister through. But God said that many of *"the sons of the kingdom will be cast out into outer darkness."* Why? Why would Jesus, after speaking about the centurion having such great faith, make the claim that many will come from the East and the West –speaking about those outside of the nation of Israel. That they'll come and enter into the Kingdom but the sons of the kingdom, those to whom the Kingdom was first offered, will not receive it.

Why is Jesus warning Israel in light of the Centurions few words that he had spoken? Let's look at this same account in Luke's Gospel. In Luke 7 we have a little insight into the Centurion. It says that he had built synagogues for the Jews and he had shown much kindness to the Jewish people. But he comes and pleads with Jesus for one of his servants. He's not asking anything for himself, he pleads that Jesus would heal his servant. Jesus responds to him and says, "I'll come to your house." This man is a professional soldier, he's a Centurion. That word Centurion comes from the Latin meaning one hundred. Therefore, he was a commander over a hundred and so an officer within the Roman occupation force in Israel. He turns around to Jesus and says it is not necessary that you come physically to my house. He says all you need to do is to speak a word. He says because *"I also am a man under authority."* He understood that Jesus had authority and that Christ was under authority.

What authority was Jesus under when He came, when He walked on earth? Yes, the Father's authority. Remembered the Bible is very clear that Jesus laid aside the power of His deity. When Jesus came to earth He did not come as God, although He was God, although He pre-existed, although He was the one who created the heavens and the earth. He did not come to earth in the form of God. He did not come in His deity, He came as a man. That is why at the age of thirty He had to be baptized in the Holy Spirit. It was the Spirit of the living God in Him and upon Him, which enabled Him to do the miracles that He did. Just like you and I need to be baptized in the Holy Spirit for God to do miracles and signs and wonders through our lives. Jesus was a perfect man. Jesus had to be as a man under authority to the Father. We need to understand this, Saints. We need to see Jesus as our highest example of how we are to conduct ourselves as believers and as sons and daughters in the Kingdom of God. To this end, we need to see that Jesus was a man, who placed himself under the authority of the Father.

When the Roman centurion, this officer, sees Jesus he recognizes Jesus' authority. He recognized that Jesus himself had authority but that Jesus was also under authority. How do we know this? Because he says so! He says I am also under authority. He says, "*I also am a man under authority, having soldiers under me. And I say to this one, 'Go,' and he goes; and to another, 'Come,' and he comes;*" That's exactly how authority works, especially in a military environment. For those of you who were involved in the military, through your national service or voluntarily, you understood that in the military you do not question an order. If somebody of a senior rank gives you an order, you obey – it's not a negotiation. That's how the Kingdom of God works. It works like the Roman army worked.

The Kingdom of God, Saints, works exactly like an army. There is one Commander-in-Chief. In fact, the word 'The Lord of Hosts' in the Hebrew is not actually a name but a title. You know that Jesus was called the Lord of Hosts. That word host in the Hebrew is 'tsaba'. 'Tsaba' is actually a rank, not a name, it's a rank. Its means commander-in-chief, it is the highest military rank in an army. We find ourselves then in an army, we're in a family but the family itself is an army. Does that make sense? If you were a Spartan, you'd understand that. We are in an army, saints. We are born-again into the family of God, we become adopted as sons and daughters of God but this family we find ourselves in is also an army, We need to understand this. There are various ranks in the army although we're all equal. None of us are greater, in the sight of God, than the other. This is so important - there are no favourites in the family of God, we're all equally loved.

God is impartial. He loves you and me equally but the truth is we all have different levels of authority in the Kingdom. Some have been given greater authority for the purpose of serving. Authority in the Kingdom is not given to rule and lord. Remember what Jesus said when the disciples were haggling over position because Mrs Zebedee had the hutzpah, (sorry that's a good Yiddish word for 'the cheek'), to ask Jesus that, may be, if it's all right, one son sits on His right and the other son sits on His left. The disciples got bent out of shape and started haggling over who'd be the greatest in the Kingdom. Jesus turns round and says to them, "You don't understand. The Gentiles lord over one another... But whoever desires to become great among you shall be your servant. And whoever of you desires to be first shall be slave of all." When we speak about authority in the Kingdom of God Saints, were not talking authority to rule and dominate, we're talking about rule and authority to serve.

The rulers in the Kingdom are there to serve, they are there to lift up, and they are there to build up the Saints. How different it is from the gospel of the Church where the rulers of the Church dominate, control, manipulate and seek to be served. It's not so in the Kingdom. it's very important that I share this with you because if we're going to be speaking about authority and submitting to authority we need to understand what authority is. Authority is God-given. Now I need a good English word – a synonym for authority. It's a God-given responsibility but you can't have responsibility without authority. Permission, yes possibly, instruction, command, accountability, no, no sorry not accountability. Empowered! Yes, thank you, we are empowered by God to serve.

Let's go back to our Roman Centurion; he's getting a bit cold out there so let's go back to him. When Jesus offered to come to his house this Centurion understood authority and he says, "You don't need to do anything Lord. You have the authority; all You need to do is give a command, because I know that. As a Centurion, all I need to do is issue a command for somebody to carry out a particular task. All I need to do is write a letter or tell one of my troops that I've given instruction to a third party and that command will be exercised and carried out. Why? Because I have authority." Just like the Romans soldiers had to obey their Centurion so all things are subject to Jesus Christ and must obey Him, - all things.

Jesus, after His resurrection comes to the disciples, as we read in the book of Matthew Chapter 28, verse 18, and says these words: "*All authority in heaven and on earth has been given to me.*" That means Christ has *all* authority. Therefore, if Christ has all authority how much authority does Satan have? Yes, he has nothing. The authority that Satan has is the authority that's been given him by God which he usurped from Adam. You and I are under authority. When Jesus heard what the Centurion said He stood in awe. Because here was a Gentile, a person who did not grow up with the ways of God, with the scriptures of God and the experience of God, had caught what Israel never comprehended. The Kingdom of God works on authority. Unless we are under authority God will never entrust us with authority. This is really what I want to share today.

There's authority in many areas. As I said, as I watched the waves crashing, the seagull gulling and the breeze breezing, I realized that we in the Church are not under any authority. How can I say that? Many will respond and say, "Yeah Jesus is the Lord of my life." To which of course I'm going to say, "Really." I'm speaking to myself too, of course. I really was challenged by God during my time away and I believe I've come back very different from the way I left. God is wanting total submission. He wants us to be totally and utterly submitted to Him. The time of playing Church and having an inkling of Christianity is for babies. God is looking for all or nothing Christians. You are either in or you're out. You're either 100% committed or you're 100% out of it. This is what I believe God is speaking into our hearts.

Saints, think about our own lives. Are we in absolute submission to authority? Is Jesus Christ really the Lord of our lives? This message is going to be very encouraging at some point. I don't know where to start as there is so much to share on the subject and I'm probably going to have to continue it for a couple of additional Chapters. Let's look at the various areas of submission. Can we just start with the most painful and get it over with? I really don't like talking about this, but let's talk about submission to Godly authority. I want to talk about submission to God's Word and a few other things but I want to do the toughest one first. It's the toughest for me because I don't like talking about authority because people think yeah he's just trying to establish his own authority. For those of you who know me understand I don't have a problem with identity. I don't really care what you believe about me or not. But I want to share this not for my sake but for your sake.

God has placed authority in the body of Christ – Godly authority. God has placed people in authority. One of the greatest lessons I learned from the army that I still apply today – there were many lessons I learned, some I had to give up when I became a Christian – but the greatest lesson I learned in the army was about submission to authority. I'll tell you a story because I can and I've got the floor. When I did my national service way back in 1985 they only taught us how to salute in about the middle of basic training. They think that a civilian doesn't know how to salute which is quite true because as civilians we didn't understand authority. Our instructor began the salute training with these words, "You do not salute the person you salute the rank." I want to say that again because in the military there were professional soldiers. In fact, and he's passed away so I can speak about him, when I was in Army Headquarters there was this one sergeant major. He served as a rear gunner on a Lancaster bomber in the Second World War which was probably the most dangerous place to be in an aircraft. Poor man was absolutely shell-shocked. The guy was really just a lunatic and when I came into the office of a morning he would start singing any old song that popped into his head – he was plain crazy. If I had not learned to honour his rank above the person I could never have submitted to him.

The army taught me one thing which is that you give honour to the rank, not the person. That is how Authority works and it's the same when God says submit to governments. You might not like the government or you might not like what the government is doing but that is irrelevant. God says submit to every ordinance of man (1 Peter 2:13). It's not whether you like it or not, it's got nothing to do with your opinion or my opinion. t is the way of the Kingdom. God can't expect His children to have authority if they will not submit to His authority. There are authorities in the Church that are ordained by God and there are authorities in the world which also are ordained by God because the Bible says all authority is from God. That's another thing we're going to get into later. Christians need to start submitting to the authority of the land. Not because you like the politician but because you honour the One who has given him that authority. We need to start to honour the authority; you honour the rank not the person. It's very helpful Saints.

There's an incredible lesson in Scripture which we're going to look at today. In the Church, Saints, there is God given authority. I'm only going to share two very brief examples of this. In 1 Corinthians Chapter 12 the Apostle Paul begins to teach the Church of Corinth about spiritual gifts, - the gifts of the Holy Spirit. He outlines the nine gifts to the Spirit and then he begins to equate the Church, the body of Jesus Christ, with our physical bodies. He says that just like the physical body is made up of many parts and all the various parts are needed so that the body can function in like manner, in the very same manner, the Church is made up of so many diverse individuals. Yet every person is vital for the health, the well-being and the functioning of the Church. However, I would say that 80% of you don't believe that – that you are a vital part of the body of Christ. Most Christians don't get involved much because they don't think they're important. But that's my message just now.

Paul goes on to say that we're all equal and we're all important. And that's right, all of us are important. Every member of the Church is vital, Saints. Many of you don't believe me. Many of you think that you're not that important to the body of Christ and the functioning of the body. You can't be in any deeper error! Every one of you is vital to the Church. What we are doing right now, is not Church, it is but one very small expression of Church. I'd like to say it's almost one of the least important expressions of Church. Your place is not in the Sunday service necessarily, but the expression of the body is so diverse that it touches every sphere of life. It's very probable that your gifting is not for Church at all but to be used out there among the unsaved. But whatever your gifts, you are vital in the Church.

Paul goes on to say in verse 27 of 1 Corinthians 12, still speaking about the body, but he moves on and introduces the subject of authority. Although we're all equal we are absolutely co-dependent. All of us are co-dependent on each other. We have such need of each other. That's another revelation we need to get to, another thing we need to begin to submit to – our mutual need one for another. This is where the Church is not submitting and it's an area that we need to get into. Paul writes in verse 27 *"Now you are the body of Christ, and members individually."* Did you get that? All of us make up the body of Christ just like all your cells make up your human body.

Paul goes to say in verse 28, *"And God has appointed these in the Church: first"* – the Greek word for first here is próton, meaning first in order of importance or rank. *"First apostles, second prophets, third teachers, after that miracles, then gifts of healings, helps, administrations, varieties of tongues. Are all apostles?"* Paul was a very methodical teacher of the word of God. The subject that he is addressing is spiritual gifts and as Paul lists the gifts so he warns the Church because he knew that we're all going to be crazies in the last days. He warns the Church by saying you need to understand something; we're all part of the body, we all need each other, but there is authority in the body. The first authority and the highest authority the body is the apostle followed by the prophet and thirdly the teacher. After that, after those three, he lists everything else in descending order; the evangelists with their spectacular signs, wonders and miracles that all the Church flocked to. When the evangelist says, "The Lord showed me that on the 27th of September at 11:37pm He will return." Many of the saints says, "Well he's got to be right because he's the guy that's raised the dead, he's the guy that healed the sick, he's the guy that we see all the spectacular stuff from therefore the Church listens to that doctrine and make absolute fools of themselves. Why, what have they done? They have usurped God's authority. Because when it comes to doctrine the word says; *"first apostles, second prophets, third teachers, after that"* is the stuff we love. After all the good stuff, you know, mass rallies, people getting saved, the gifts of the Spirit functioning, which are lovely, we all love them, we all desire to see that. But Saints, it must have its place under the authority or, I should say, in the authority of God.

In the Church, God places a higher authority on certain gifts than others. I've shared with you many times, what is it that unites the apostle, prophet and teacher? What is the common denominator of those three offices - apostle, prophet and teacher? Yes, it is doctrine. Doctrine, that's what the apostle prophet and teacher all have in common – sound, solid, Biblical doctrine. The Church today generally has lousy Godless weak incorrect doctrine. Why? Where are the true apostles, where are the true prophets and where are the true teachers? They have been discarded for signs, wonders and miracles. It seems that unless you've led a hundred thousand people to the Lord, raised the dead, healed the sick, cleansed the lepers or poured gold dust on somebody's head, nobody listens to you.

Saints, in the body there is authority – God-given authority. Not for destruction, not to lord over but to nurture. Sound doctrine brings life. You can't live on emotion. It is great to be amongst evangelists and it really is awesome to see God move, but you cannot be sustained by their ministry. That ministry won't sustain you. It's vital that we appreciate that, that we embrace it and want to see more of it, but it will not sustain you.

Paul talks to the Church at Corinth in 2 Corinthians Chapter 10 and verse 8. For those of you who have attended the Bible studies will know that Paul stayed in the city of Corinth for a year and a half. He planted the Church there, he raised up elders and then he departed. However, soon after his departure, false brethren came in and brought the Church back under bondage, back under law and told the people that Paul was a false apostle and that they shouldn't listen to him. So, Paul writes to the Church at Corinth and he says in verse 8, *"For even if I should boast somewhat more about our authority, which the Lord gave us for edification and not for your destruction, I shall not be ashamed."* Paul tells them that authority is given for edification. Authority in the body of Christ is to build you up, it is to equip you. Being built up, does not mean to be mollycoddled. Sometimes to be built up can hurt. Building up does not mean to be left in your sin; it's to build you up into a son or a daughter of the Most High God.

Paul says this in verse 9 and 10, *"Lest I seem to terrify you by letters. "For his letters," they say, "are weighty and powerful, but his bodily presence is weak, and his speech contemptible." Let such a person consider this, that what we are in word by letters when we are absent, such we will also be in deed when we are present."* Paul says, "Listen, I've got authority to build you up. You guys say that when he's with us he's so weak and gentle. But when I come again I'll come with the same authority that I write to you in." You see there's an authority given by God which is seen through the ministers of God. This is something we need to understand, it's a lesson that the Lord taught me as a young man.

I had an incredible salvation experience. I had the most amazing salvation experience, you may have heard by testimony but it was absolutely out of the ordinary. At a very young Christian age God began to use me. It was amazing; people were being healed, demons being cast out and folk were being saved – it was incredible. It was all God; it wasn't me it was all God. But I became a bit puffed up. Actually puffed-up would be an understatement, I became extremely proud and arrogant. I thought I was God's man for the hour, full of power. I became so puffed up and so arrogant that I used to look at other ministers and think, yeah, such Dodos! I couldn't submit to authority because I thought was better than everyone else. I thought I was more anointed. And the fact was that at that time I was. There was a great anointing on my life as there was on most of the Pastors in the Church I was at. But I never understood authority and authority wasn't correctly taught well, so I stumbled, because of pride, because I thought I was somebody and didn't understand authority. I didn't understand that God puts people in the body as He chooses and He gives them authority irrespective of what we might think of them. This is very important because we look at people and think that because God uses me more than He uses them therefore I'm greater. No, none of us have anything that we contribute to the Kingdom. Everything we have is a gift from God. The anointing on your life is not your anointing, it comes from God. It is a grace from God. You and I have nothing save what God gives us. So I had to learn submission.

I've it said before and I'll say it again. Prior to starting my current Church, I had sworn by an oath that I will not come into the ministry again, ever! However, no matter how much I tried to duck the ministry God kept putting me into ministry. The last Church we were at before we started the Church here, the man that God called us to submit to, his doctrine was really poor, very poor. In fact, there was very little common ground that we had, yet I could willingly submit to him and it was not a problem. I would submit to him even though his doctrine was wrong. I'd finally learn submission. I'd finally learned not to look at the man but to honour the position. Are you hearing me Saints? we honour authority.

The greatest example that I'm aware of outside of the Lord Jesus Christ, when it comes to the subject of understanding of authority, is King David. I think he understood authority as much as the Roman Centurion understood authority. Turn with me, as we begin to close and don't get optimistic or excited it's going to be a long close, to 1 Samuel. First a bit of background; the nation of Israel came out of Egypt under the leadership of Moses, Joshua then took them to the promised land where they go through a period of judge's ruling over them. By and large Israel was a theocracy. God had purposed that Israel, the nation of Israel, would be a theocracy. The nation of Israel was a theocracy ruled under God. It was never supposed to be a monarchy, rule by a king. It was never supposed to be a democracy ruled by elected leaders and it was never meant to be a dictatorship. The Kingdom of God is, and always will be, a theocracy. Israel was an example of how the Kingdom was supposed to function with God in control. God appointed leaders but God was the ultimate ruler.

Israel looks at the nations around them, then turns to God, or I should say, to Samuel who was the Prophet at that time and says, "We want a king like the nations around us. We don't want God to be our Lord, we don't want God to be our King, we want a man." God very reluctantly gives them Saul. Saul starts out incredibly well. The Bible says of Saul that he was a head and shoulders above any other man in Israel. He was a giant. I mean some of us Jews get to quite big sizes. Saul was at least seven and a half feet tall. The Bible says he was good-looking plus he came from a wealthy family. What more could a Jewish girl want? He's a looker, he's rich and he's King! Saul starts off humble, such a humble man. He's appointed King and as you know the story, things go to his head and he becomes proud, he becomes puffed up, he becomes arrogant until he finally rebelled against God.

The Lord then raises up another King. God appoints a teenager. He gets Samuel, the Prophet, to go and anoint the youngest son of Jesse as King of Israel. It would be another thirteen years before David actually takes the throne. Round about the age of seventeen David is anointed as king over Israel by the Prophet sent from God. Although he was anointed or you might say, there's the calling on his life if we bring this into a New Testament understanding. Remember the Old Testament is written for our instructions so let's try and understand it with a New Testament mind set. Here's a guy born-again and God just bestows on him the most incredible calling, the most incredible gifting but he's not walking in it yet, not in the fullness of it.

We see that David goes out to bring some cheese and bread to his brothers and there sees Goliath and he slays Goliath. We see David's faith in God and that God's hand is upon his life. When he kills the Giant he's promoted to be a general in Saul's armies and he goes and slays all the enemies of Israel. We're starting to see the fruits of the anointing but he isn't in his calling yet. Are you seeing this? Okay I'm getting excited because it's actually really good what I'm saying, this is of God, and so that's why I get excited. When I don't get excited then it's just me. I'm not excited about me at all but I'm excited about God. David starts to see the fruit of his calling but he's not in the fullness of his calling. Saul, now backslidden from God, because of his arrogance, because of his pride, because of his rebellion, begins to resent David. He begins to persecute David who remains incredibly faithful not only to King Saul but to the nation of Israel. David's probably one of the greatest Patriots that has ever lived. Saul however is eventually so consumed by hatred and jealousy of David that he seeks David's life, he seeks to kill David.

David had legitimately been anointed by the prophet of God to be the next King. He carries a legitimate anointing over his life and there is evidence of the fruit of this calling but he finds himself fleeing from Saul who is still the King. I want to read just two accounts in the scripture where David is fleeing from Saul. Over a period of several years, on two occasions, God literally brings Saul into a much compromised position, where David is able to kill him. I want you to catch the heart of a man who understands submission because this is a heart that you and I need to have if we are going to carry authority in the Kingdom. We need to have a heart that understands authority.

I want make a quick tangent at this point. The demons know those who have authority in the Kingdom. Do you know that? I shared this many times from the book of Acts Chapter 19. Satan knows those who carry Godly authority. I'm not talking about a ministry position I'm talking about authority. You don't need to be a five-fold minister to have authority. In fact, remember the fivefold ministry is there to train and equip the saints to function in the authority that God's given you. As a layperson you have as much authority as any other minister of the Kingdom. You have the authority, you just need to understand that and you need to walk under authority, for their authority to have effect. But Satan knows those who carry authority.

Let's go back to David. 1 Samuel Chapter 24 and reading from verse 1. *"Now it happened, when Saul had returned from following the Philistines, that it was told him, saying, 'Take note! David is in the Wilderness of En Gedi.'"* Then Saul took three thousand chosen men from all Israel, and went to seek David and his men on the Rocks of the Wild* Goats. *So he came to the sheepfolds by the road, where there was a cave; and Saul went in to attend to his needs."* In other words; he went to the toilet in a cave and guess who was at the back of the cave? *"David and his men were staying in the recesses of the*

121

cave." Saul is in a very compromised position, going to the loo, while very quietly in the back of the cave are David and some of these mighty men. Verse 4, "*Then the men of David said to him, "This is the day of which the Lord said to you, 'Behold, I will deliver your enemy into your hand, that you may do to him as it seems good to you.'" And David arose and secretly cut off a corner of Saul's robe.*" The men who followed David said, "Go and Kill him. This is a fulfilment of prophecy. God has said, "I'll give you your enemies.""

David's mighty men were a real ragtag bunch of people. The Bible says that the disgruntled, those in debt and those that were just generally fed-up, came to David. They weren't exactly outstanding citizens. These were not the finest men in Israel. They said to David, "God has said, I'll give you your enemies." But that's not what God said to David at all. God said, "I'll give you your enemies." That is the Philistines, the Amorites and the Amalekites. I'll give your 'enemies' into your hand. He wasn't talking about Saul.

So, David creeps up and cuts off a part of Saul's garment. Continuing with verse 5, "*Now it happened afterward that David's heart troubled him because he had cut Saul's robe.*" David came into conviction, - he realized he had sinned. All David wanted to do was to shock Saul and say, "Listen I could have taken your life." But even the act of damaging a garment of God's anointed was sin in the sight of God. David's spirit troubled him because he had sinned against God by simply cutting off a piece of Saul's garment to make a statement to him. We read in verse 6, *And he said to his men, "The Lord forbid that I should do this thing to my master, the Lord's anointed, to stretch out my hand against him, seeing he is the anointed of the Lord." So David restrained his servants with these words, and did not allow them to rise against Saul.*" Isn't this incredible; a man is seeking to kill David. David has been told, not only by the Prophet but he knows in his own heart that he's the anointed king. He is the next King of Israel and he knows that the current King is so backslidden, yet he doesn't lift up his hand against him. This is an incredible demonstration of truly understanding authority.

I want to read this whole portion from verse 8, "*David also arose afterward, went out of the cave, and called out to Saul, saying, "My lord the king!*" He doesn't say, "You dog." Listen to the language, "My lord the king." He respects and honours the authority. It's like saluting in the army, 'lieutenant,' 'captain,' it is giving honour to the rank, not the person. David comes out and gives honour to the King. He might not like the king. You might not like me; that's okay, my dog doesn't like me either. I'm not here for you to like me; I'm here to serve you. David might not have liked King Saul. He wasn't very likable. I mean who wants to go and listen to music with a guy who throws spears at you. Every time David took up his harp to play Saul threw a spear at him. How's that for a social visit! I'm sure David didn't like Saul but he honoured the rank and therefore he honoured the man. Do you get that? Because he honoured the rank he honoured the man that carried the rank.

It goes on to say in verse 9, "*And David said to Saul: "Why do you listen to the words of men who say, 'Indeed David seeks your harm'? Look, this day your eyes have seen that the Lord delivered you today into my hand in the cave, and someone urged me to kill you. But my eye spared you, and I said, 'I will not stretch out my hand against my lord, for he is the Lord's anointed.' Moreover, my father, see!*" – again showing respect - "*Yes, see the corner of your robe in my hand! For in that I cut off the corner of your robe, and did not kill you, know and see that there is neither evil nor rebellion in my hand, and I have not sinned against you. Yet you hunt my life to take it.*"

There is also something else there that we need to look at. David didn't seek to undermine Saul. He didn't seek to lead a civil war against Saul. Think about what we do in the Church; we don't like a Church, we don't like a ministry or we don't like a denomination, what do we do? We get an army together to destroy it. How many times have Churches split? More than we should. Why, because we don't honour God-given authority. David did though, he said so. He said, "My king, my father, I have not tried to rebel against you. I've not trying to usurp your rule. Don't listen to the men who are saying he's trying to take over your Kingdom." David says, "Don't listen my father. Don't listen to those who are telling you that I'm trying to take away your Kingdom. I'm not, I'm honouring you. I could've taken your life just now but I will not touch you. You are the Lord's anointed. You are my father. You are my master. You are my king."

You see Saints, what really I want to share with you is that to understand authority is to understand the heart of God, because everything in the Kingdom works by authority. David honours Saul. He honours Saul because he honours God. Because of David's love for God and his desire to serve God and obey God then he honours all the authority that God puts in place. David knew that God was in control. He knew that when God wanted him to be king he would make a way. He says that in the second account but you can read it for yourselves because I think you've got the point here. I don't need to belabour it. Read 1 Samuel Chapter 26, which is the account of the second time, that David spared Saul's life. You'll hear that it says; "Listen, when God wants to make me king, he'll take Saul out. It's not for me to take him out. It's not for me to bring myself into the place that God has ordained for me."

That's another mistake I made as a young Christian. As a young Christian I had these prophecies that came from the strangest places. They were the same thing. God put something in my heart and burned it into my spirit. Then for a period of a year or two, people I never knew, people that I met once would just come up to me and begin to prophesy, or phone me, just the craziest things. They all confirmed this same prophecy which hasn't yet come to pass. So I thought well, okay God. I mean, I've got all these prophecies, I'm so proud and arrogant, I'm highly anointed, let's make a place for myself in the Sun. Except that the Sun wasn't ready for me to make a place in it and doors shut tight. Nothing ever works out because I didn't know authority and therefore God couldn't entrust me with authority until I had learned authority.

David knew that God had anointed him King. He knew that one day, when God deems that the time was right he would be king. Stop trying to make a place for yourself. Be faithful; be faithful to God given authority because when serving under authority you'll be given authority. However, if you rebel against authority everything that you set out to do, will fail and those who come alongside you will in turn rebel against you. The spirit that you start with will form the spirit of your work. God has placed and given authority. You're not called to like the authority but we are call to submit to it. Very often – okay this Church is an exception because you haven't the most amazing minister to submit to. His wife certainly thinks so! Saints, all I really want to say is; when we submit to authority, we're called to submit to authority so that that authority can build us up. So that authority can cause us to mature in Christ. If that authority which God has placed in your life doesn't impart to you doctrine, nor example, nor understanding, then that authority has been appointed to teach you, patience, love, endurance and suffering. There's always a purpose for authority in your life. Don't look at authority and think I'm not learning anything therefore I cannot submit. Oftentimes the greatest lessons that you and I need to learn are not doctrinal they're character.

"You have one new friend request

Jesus

Confirm Ignore"

Chapter 9

Unity of the Body of Christ

I don't want to summarize what I've written about already but we see that there are two Gospels being preached today, - the gospel of the Church and the gospel of the Kingdom. We saw that the gospel of the Church is not what Jesus came to preach. He preached the gospel of the Kingdom. He died for the Kingdom of God so that people would be saved, redeemed and adopted as sons and daughters, as children of God and then they in turn would extend the Kingdom. This is done by going to the highways, the byways, the prisons, to the poor and preaching the good news so that sons and daughters can be adopted through the blood of Christ and the Kingdom of God can advance.

We've examined what the Kingdom of God is and compared the gospel of the Kingdom to the gospel of the Church. We've investigated the beautiful attitudes to the citizens of heaven which the Church really needs to start adopting. Then we observed a particular Kingdom principle – 'submission'. You cannot have authority until you're under authority. In this Chapter I want to look at the subject of unity, - unity in the Kingdom of God. Generally, in the Church there is no unity. We will find within local congregations there are divisions. Paul had that problem in Corinth. He says some say I'm of Paul, some say I'm of Apollos and some say I'm of Peter and of course the super spiritual who say I am of Christ.

Within any local community you're going to have division. Between communities – between local Churches – there is division. Then we have divisions of denominations so the Church really is a horrible place. I'm not really fond of the current state of the Church because it's full of strife, bitterness, one-upmanship, and suspicion and all the things that we hear about that goes on in prisons. That is the result of what happens when you preach the gospel of the Church. "Come to our Church, we are the best Church. Don't go to them down the road they don't know anything. Don't you know their Pastor, you know, well, he's got a waffle problem - he waffles." That's why the Kingdom of God is not advancing because while the Church is devouring itself, Christ cannot build it.

My message in this Chapter is really simple but vitally important. As with any spiritual truth about the New Testament we need to go to the Old Testament so turn with me if you would in your Bibles to 1 Samuel Chapter 31. I'm not going to be preaching for hundreds of pages as really I don't have much to say. I could actually say it all in one line but you have paid good money for this print therefore you should get full service. As I start reading from the Word of God you might have asked the question, "What on earth has this got to do with the Church and more specifically what on earth has this got to do with the unity in the Church?" Because what we're going to be looking at is the very tragic death of King Saul. As I expect you know, King Saul was the first king of Israel, a man who started off humbly before God but ended up full of pride and full of rebellion. In fact, he was about to go into battle against the Philistines and he goes to visit the Witch of En Dor. There they have a séance and call up a familiar spirit, whom he thinks is Samuel, who tells him he's going to die in battle. We know from the previous Chapter that Saul hunted David down for years and years seeking to take his life. Yet David, although anointed king, spared Saul's life on two occasions and never lifted up his hand against Saul even when Saul was seeking his life. David joined himself with the enemies of Israel under the pretence of fighting against Israel but every time they went to battle he would flip sides and fight with his people, Israel.

Enough of the background, let's get to the Word of God. 1 Samuel Chapter 31 starting from verse 1, "*Now the Philistines fought against Israel; and the men of Israel fled from before the Philistines, and fell slain on Mount Gilboa. Then the Philistines followed hard after Saul and his sons. And the Philistines killed Jonathan, Abinadab, and Malchishua, Saul's sons. The battle became fierce against Saul. The archers hit him, and he was severely wounded by the archers. Then Saul said to his armorbearer, "Draw your sword, and thrust me through with it, lest these uncircumcised men come and thrust me through and abuse me.*" Basically Saul doesn't want the Philistines to torture him. "*But his Armor-bearer would not, for he was greatly afraid. Therefore, Saul took a sword and fell on it. And when his Armor-bearer saw that Saul was dead, he also fell on his sword, and died with him.*" – "Praise God!"

So, I hope you all got the idea of unity from that? Well, the story continues, that's why there's a second book of Samuel. 2 Samuel Chapter 1, verse1 "*Now it came to pass after the death of Saul, when David had returned from the slaughter of the Amalekites, and David had stayed two days in Ziklag, on the third day, behold, it happened that a man came from Saul's camp with his clothes torn and dust on his head. So it was, when he came to David, that he fell to the ground and prostrated himself. And David said to him, "Where have you come from?" So he said to him, "I have escaped from the camp of Israel." Then David said to him, "How did the matter go? Please tell me." And he answered, "The people have fled from the battle, many of the people are fallen and dead, and Saul and Jonathan his son are dead also." So David said to the young man who told him, "How do you know that Saul and Jonathan his son are dead?" Then the young man who told him said, "As I happened by chance to be on Mount Gilboa, there was Saul, leaning on his spear; and indeed the chariots and horsemen followed hard after him. Now when he looked behind him, he saw me and called to me. And I answered, 'Here I am.' And he said to me, 'Who are you?' So I answered him, 'I am an Amalekite.'*" He forgot to add, "I'm also a flipping liar." You see this man was never on Mount Gilboa and this man did not speak to Saul, he's lying. Did you pick up on that?

Verse 9, "*He said to me again, "Please stand over me and kill me, for anguish* (or agony) *has come upon me, but my life still remains in me." So I stood over him and killed him, because I was sure that he could not live after he had fallen. And I took the crown that was on his head and the bracelet that was on his arm, and have brought them here to my lord.*" Well to cut a long story short David mourns. He mourns the death of Saul, they weep and they fast for this loss to Israel. Then in verse 13 the Bible says, "*Then David said to the young man who told him, "Where are you from?" And he answered, "I am the son of an alien, an Amalekite." So David said to him, "How was it you were not afraid to put forth your hand to destroy the Lord's anointed?*" David thinks about this whole affair and says "Sorry where did you say you're from; the First Church of the Half Dead? Well, how come you weren't afraid to kill your pastor? How come you weren't afraid to kill the Lord's anointed? Verse 15 continues the account. *"Then David called one of the young men and said, "Go near, and execute him!" And he struck him so that he died. So David said to him, "Your blood is on your own head, for your own mouth has testified against you, saying, 'I have killed the Lord's anointed.'"*

What does all that have to do with unity in the Church? This is something that God has been dealing with my heart about and God just bought this portion of scripture to my heart. David, when he hears about the death of Saul and the death of Jonathan and his brothers, the natural heir to the throne, he is heartbroken. He's heartbroken because of the loss to Israel. The nation of Israel had been defeated, the king and the princes of Israel lie dead and David's heart is broken. Why, because David understood Kingdom. The Kingdom of Israel had suffered loss.

Now, in the New Testament the Apostle Paul writes in the first book of Corinthians Chapter 12 and he speaks about the Church being like the human body. He says that if one part of the body aches the rest of the body hurts with it. David understood this. There was no celebration that Saul was dead. There was no rejoicing that the princes of Israel had died with their father. There was great morning and this Amalekite thought, "Hey you know what. I'm going to bring good news. I'm going to tell David that the king is dead so now he can just march on and take the Kingdom." That's so much like the Church. There are Christians that take great delight when they see another ministry suffering. Or another if a pastor falls then all of a sudden they think that's great. But we don't ache, we don't mourn and we don't all weep and we don't hurt with those who hurt because our mentality is not for the Kingdom, our mentality is for our little Church. And even within our little Church we have a little holy huddle. Saints, these things ought not to be. They are an abomination in the sight of Almighty God.

I believe that now is the time that God is wanting to bring unity in His body. I mean unity between those who are washed in the blood of Jesus Christ. I'm not talking about all people uniting because, hey you know, there's more than one way to God. That's baloney! Jesus said I am the way, the truth and the life and no man, comes to the Father, but by me. All who have faith in Jesus; all who have made Jesus the

Lord of their lives are our brothers and our sisters. It doesn't matter what denomination – denomination is an abomination. I have it on absolute brilliant authority that Jesus the Son of God, from the tribe of Judah, of the seed of Abraham, was born a Jew, circumcised on the eighth day. At the age of thirty, the age of the Levitical priesthood when they could go and minister, He began His earthly ministry. He fulfilled every single requirement of the Law. As a Jew He was crucified, as a Jew He died, as a Jew He rose again and it was as a Jew that the Church was formed. Right, so denomination is not part of the scriptures – one body.

Remember the cry of Jesus in the Garden of Gethsemane just before His arrest and subsequent crucifixion. Let's look at what Jesus cries out in praise to the Father in the Gospel of John Chapter 17. That Chapter contains the prayer of Jesus but I only want to look at a specific portion of that prayer found in verse 20 of John 17. Jesus is praying to the Father and he says, *"I do not pray for these alone,"* - He's not praying for His disciples. In the earlier part of this prayer He prayed that the Father would keep the disciples in the world but to keep them from the world. But then Jesus begins to extend His prayer, the influence of His prayer. He says, praying the Father, *"I do not pray for these alone, but also for those who will believe in Me through their word;"* That's you and I Saints. That's every Christian who is alive today because of the fruit of the Apostles. This prayer, therefore, is a prayer for the Church today. This prayer is as relevant today as it was nearly 2000 years ago when Jesus cried it out to the Father. This is the heart of our Saviour; this is the heart of God for His own Kingdom.

Verse 20 says, *"I do not pray for these alone, but also for those who will believe in Me through their word; that they all may be one."* That they may be 'one'; in ancient Greek this word 'one' is heis. It means the numeral, number one. To be one, in oneness, not in twoness or threeness or fourness! The prayer of Jesus was that those who would believe on His word and the words of the Apostles would be one. – One Church, one body, one family, because there's only one Kingdom with one King who desires one Church and one body. *"That they all may be one, as You, Father, are in Me, and I in You;"* Notice what Jesus says. He doesn't say, "Lord I want the Church to be one," He says," I want them to be one like you and I are one." This is not some superficial unity, some form of cooperation or brotherhood.

Jesus is saying "I want them to be one, as you and I are one." It needs to be an absolute bond of unity, same heart, same spirit, same purpose and same goals. Jesus said in John Chapter 5, verse 19, *"the Son can do nothing of Himself, but what He sees the Father do;"* Jesus says in John Chapter 14 verse 9, *"He who has seen Me has seen the Father;"* That's the 'one' which he is talking about. That's what God wants through his body that we are united. United under what, what is the common denominator? What's the common denominator what unifies us as Christians? It's the Lordship of Jesus. Is He the Lord of your life? Yes or no. Well, if He's the Lord of your life, and you're a son or daughter of God, then you are one with any other son or daughter of God who has made Jesus Christ the Lord of their life.

I'm not talking about Churches now. There are people sitting in Churches that aren't Christians, because sitting in Church doesn't make you Christians just like sitting in the garage doesn't make you an automobile. Being a Christian is something that happens on the inside when you surrender your life to His Lordship and when you taste of His amazing grace and forgiveness. All who have experienced that, no matter where they find themselves, are one body in Christ. God's heart and God's cry is that we would be one with each other just as the Father and Son are one. Saints, this is not the great suggestion, this is a command of God, that the Church be one.

He then goes on to say in John Chapter 17, verse 21 *"that they also may be one in Us, that the world may believe that You sent Me."* I'd better read that again from verse 20 because it's so important. His prayer is; *"I do not pray for these alone, but also for those who will believe in Me through their word; that they all may be one, as You, Father, are in Me, and I in You; that they also may be one in Us, that the world may believe that You sent Me."* Saints I need to reiterate this as this is the greatest testament the Church has, that it does not use, because it cannot use it legitimately. The greatest testament the Church has is that we are one body, one family and that we love each other, care for each other and stand together. That is a testimony that God has given the Church but the Church cannot legitimately use it because it's not true. His prayer, the cry of Christ, is that the Church would be united, that the Church would be one, so that the world would know. That the world would know that we are Christ's disciples.

Saints, where do we start with this? There has to be unity in the body. Now, that doesn't mean that I'm going to have to start telling all the Christians, "Hey you better start getting your act together." It starts here in my heart. It starts with the revelation that I am part of a huge family. I'm not the oldest brother, I'm not the smartest brother, I'm not the richest brother or the most popular brother. I'm just one brother who is as much loved as every other brother and sister. That there is one Father and one God, who loves us all equally, but whose heart is broken, whose Spirit is grieved when there is conflicts in His Church. God's hands are tied, Saints, while the heart of His Church is set on destruction. It is so sad that that is the current state of the Church right now. You can read the rest of John 17 as I'm trying to keep this short and not waffle too much, – actually I don't want to waffle at all.

In the book of Ephesians, the Apostle Paul encourages the Church at Ephesus. The background to Ephesus is that Paul encourages the Church of Gentile believers reminding them that they're not second-class citizens. And that they are as much loved by God as the Jews. The early Church was all Jewish, all the apostles were Jewish and all the leaders were Jewish. If you wanted to know anything you just spoke to a Jew. Paul by the Spirit of God was encouraging the Ephesians by assuring them that they were equally loved by God and that there are no favourites in the Kingdom. He reminded the Galatians in Chapter 3 verse 28, *"There is neither Jew nor Greek, there is neither slave nor free, there is neither male nor female; for you are all one in Christ Jesus."*

In Ephesians Chapter 4 starting from verse 1, we read; *"I, therefore, the prisoner of the Lord, beseech you"* Strong words "I'm begging you," *"to walk worthy of the calling with which you were called."* Saints, we have an amazing calling. You are a son of God or a daughter of God, that's a high calling, that's an incredible privilege. Paul writing by the Spirit of God says; let your conduct match the calling. Let your conduct confirm your high and regal call – sons and daughters of God. Act like a son or a daughter, I beg you, says Paul. *"With all lowliness and gentleness, with longsuffering, bearing with one another in love,"* I've been speaking about this for a while in the Church, we are to love each other patiently and graciously but also we are to bear with each other. Verse 3 *"endeavouring"* – striving, working towards – *"to keep the unity of the Spirit in the bond of peace.*" There should be an active pursuit in the Church to unite believers. Notice that. I'm making a huge distinction with this; it's 'believers' uniting. Believers are those who believe in Christ, those who have been redeemed through faith in the sacrifice of Jesus. We are to endeavour or strive to unite the Church. Not a specific church but I'm talking about the Church of Jesus.

We start with my Church, the Church of Benoni and then we've got the Church of Benoni United then we'll unite the Church of the East Rand and we've got that united, we'll unite the Church of Gauteng, then the Church of South Africa, the Church of Africa and finally the Church of Jesus Christ. We need to endeavour, there is a working out, a striving, for unity. Because as verse 4 continues, *"There is one body and one Spirit, just as you were called in one hope of your calling; one Lord, one faith, one baptism; one God and Father of all, who is above all, and through all, and in you all."* This whole Christian deal revolves around one person; His name is Jesus Christ, the Son of the Living God. He's coming back for one Church; that is all who believe on Him, who have made Him the Lord of their lives. You don't get baptized into Buddha; you don't get baptized into Allah; you get baptized into the Lordship of Jesus Christ – the Father, Son and the Holy Spirit. The Church needs to pull together.

Psalm 133; now I shared on this at the home Church on Wednesday night but it's been burning in my heart since. 'Hin·nêh mah- tō·wḇ ū·mah- nā·'îm; še·ḇet 'a·ḥîm gam- yā·ḥaḏ' *"Behold, how good and how blessed it is For brethren to dwell together."* This is a beautiful song from the messianic community. This song has been sung in every messianic group I've ever been to. They sing the Psalm 133 *"Behold, how good and how pleasant it is For, brethren to dwell together in unity!"* Not, 'how good and pleasant it is for the brethren to be together', but to dwell together and that togetherness with unity. - The unity of love, the unity the Spirit and the unity the Lord. The Psalmist provides a metaphor of the unity. He says, when the brethren dwell together, when the people are one, *"It is like the precious oil upon the head, running down on the beard, the beard of Aaron, Running down on the edge of his garments."* The first time I read this I thought, "What"? That makes no sense at all, how can oil running down beards and heads and garments onto floors be beautiful in the sight of God. Then just to confuse it even more, David by the Spirit writes in verse 3, *"It is like the dew of Hermon, descending upon the mountains of Zion; For there the Lord commanded the blessing-- Life forevermore."*

This is such a profound metaphor, such a deep picture. When the brethren dwell together Saints, it is like God's anointing oil upon the priesthood. Without the priesthood, there could be no presence of God in the nation of Israel. It was the priesthood that brought reconciliation between God and man through the sacrificial system. The day that Aaron was anointed by Moses, and that oil for the first time flowed down the head and the beard, it instituted reconciliation between man and God through the high priesthood. Another comparison is where David, by the Spirit of God writes, *"It is like the dew of Hermon."* Those of you who have been to Israel to Mount Hermon you'll know that it's the highest peak in Israel and it catches snow. Throughout the summer the snow slowly begins to melt and run down the mountain into the Jordan River. The Jordan River in turn feeds the entire Jordan valley which is incredibly fertile and lush. If you've been to Israel and Tiberius, you will recall that it's incredibly green. There are farmlands that grow strawberries the size of apples – it's such an amazing place.

Where there is unity there's life. It enables God to bring life and that's what the Psalmist is saying and he closes with the conclusion, *"For there the Lord commanded the blessing -- Life forevermore."* With this unity, God commands the blessing – life forevermore. God's life, the life of the Spirit, can come into the Church of Jesus when there is unity and when there is oneness. God can only be in a place of holiness, in a place of unity, in a place that is open to Him. God can only be where He's welcomed. If there's strife or division or contention and the fruit of the flesh is evident in a heart, in a community, in a denomination or in the Church grouping then God cannot be there. All that we've got left then is religion, theology and darkness.

Practically; how do we do this stuff? Saints, we need as an individual to determine in our hearts not to enter into strife with anyone. To have a revelation and understanding by God that whoever is, and I'm going to use the word born-again because it's the only word in scripture that describes it, whoever has come into new life through Christ Jesus, is family. Yes, we might be at different stages in our spiritual walk but which family murders their two-year old because the two year old doesn't have the understanding of the teenagers in the family. Do we not show grace with babies? Why don't we all learn to show grace in the family of God. We're all at different places in our spiritual walk, in our spiritual understandings. But as long as somebody is born-again and they desire to serve Jesus, then we do everything to maintain a love relationship with them, no matter what they do to us. I've learned a few things by being a parent. I've had my children throw tantrums at me because they think I've been unjust. I could have reacted by clobbering them back or I could just ignore them, send them to the room, and just love them later on. When babies in the Church act like babies, love them, if you think you are mature.

I believe our unity is something that's in the heart of God. We need to start making a conscious effort to love one another and take no delight when somebody falls. We are not to be jealous when God starts to use another brother or another Church. In fact, we rejoice with them. Above all else we learn that we are totally dependent on each other. The greatest lesson which we need to learn as Christians is that none of us can stand by ourselves. No matter how gifted you are, no matter how anointed you are, no matter the size of your ministry, God in His wisdom has purposed that we are totally dependent one on another. The spirit of independence needs to leave the Church because we are bound; we are intertwined with one another through the love of Christ. We are one body made up of many parts and God has placed each of us in the body as He pleases. Therefore, we need to begin to cooperate and realize our dependence on each other.

You know, it's not in my heart to go and minister in the prisons. It's just not my calling but does that mean it's unimportant? Absolutely not, it is a Biblical mandate. We've got to start broadening our perspective of Church. See yourself like this; as a little pipsqueak in a huge Kingdom. You're a pipsqueak in a massive Kingdom - you don't call the shots, you don't know what's going on so just be faithful where God has placed you. As soon as you think of yourself as anything you can't keep unity, because when you think you're important you believe you need to know everything and that God has to run everything past you. Like that you can't walk in unity.

I just want to encourage you and this is where we're going to get really charismatic, Pentecostal or whatever you like to call it. If you have been a voice of dissension in the Church either with your attitude or your words you need to make it right with God today. We each need to make a commitment and ask God to guard our tongue and to guard our heart. Ask God and say, "Lord make me a peacemaker." Remember we saw in the beatitudes where Jesus said, "B*lessed are the peacemakers,"* (the reconcilers*)" for these are the sons of God."* Saints, the Cross is wonderful but as I've taught a thousand times the Cross was the starting place of God's plan of redemption. We are not saved sinners; we were saved to be adopted. – Adopted to become sons and daughters, to reflect the character of Jesus, who was the ultimate peacemaker.

As a Pastor I don't want to hear anything about any person. I don't want to hear a negative word. Just to be clear, I'm not talking about sin. If there is sin, we'll deal with it in love. We'll always do that, we will never excuse sin but we'll deal with it in love. But I don't want to hear about somebody who might have left this Church and something bad has happened to them. I really don't want to hear that, I want to hear something good. I want to hear a positive report. I want to hear words of blessing spoken. Where there's sin we'll talk about it, where there's false doctrine we'll talk about it. But we'll not judge anybody, we'll not condemn anybody and we will not gloat when one member of the Church hurts. I want you to make that commitment because I'm going to hold you responsible. I want you to be responsible for the words that come out of your mouth from the attitudes of your heart. Let each of us affirm what Joshua declared, *"But as for me and my house, we will serve the Lord."* That we will love those who see us as enemies until they get the revelation that we are their best friends.

If you've been reading this and you know that your mouth has said things that you shouldn't have said or your heart has had an attitude that you shouldn't have had. I want you, right where you are, to just talk to God and ask the Lord to forgive you and to give you grace. – Grace to walk in His love and that His unity will be birthed within you.

Father, as I bow my head before you, my God, I ask that you would forgive me, as a believer, for every word of judgment, every word of criticism or anything that I might have said to hurt another brother or sister. Forgive me for not understanding that your love is for one body and that you desire the unity of every believer all over the face of this earth. My God I want more than just to be forgiven. Father, I want to be transformed by your Spirit. Lord, change my heart and put a greater measure of your love in me so that I would love each one, my God, with the love with which you have loved me. Dear Lord, please minister to me Father and change my heart. In Jesus name.

Chapter 10

Not in Word but in Power

———◆———

The Bible states in 1 Corinthians Chapter 4, verse 20, *"For the kingdom of God is not in word but in power."* Paul writes that to the Church at Corinth. The Kingdom of God, God's Kingdom, is not about doctrines and theologies. Although doctrine and theology is important it is not the foundation of the Kingdom. The Kingdom of God is about the dunamis of God, – dunamis, in the Greek. It's about the power of God. The Kingdom of God is advanced and is established through the power of Almighty God. Not in debates on doctrines and theologies. Where the Kingdom of God is, the power of God should be evident. However, if we're truthful we see that that is not so of the Church of Jesus Christ, in general. There is much word but very, very, very, very little power. These things ought not to be so my brethren.

Turn with me to the Book of Luke Chapter 9 as I want to show you a Biblical pattern that God has established in His Kingdom. It's a pattern that transcends the New Covenant. It's found in the Old Testament over and over again; where we see that our God is a God of power and a God of might. God begins His interaction with mankind in great power. He creates the universe; that takes some doing. He creates man. Every time God interacts with man He interacts in power. God, giving life to the womb of Sarah and to the body of Abraham. God, consuming the altar of Elijah with fire. God, pouring out the flood of Noah, splitting the earth so the waters under the earth would burst forth. God, pouring out his wrath upon Egypt with ten mighty plagues. Parting the Red Sea. Providing manna on a daily basis to the Israelites. Every morning, for forty years, there was a pillar of cloud over the camp and every evening that same pillar turned to fire. God, through Elijah, raising the dead then through

Elisha raising two more. God, cleansing Naaman the leper in the River Jordan. Elijah calling down fire from God which consumed a hundred men. God, God, God always showing power. And then comes Jesus.

In Luke Chapter 9 and reading from verse 1 the Bible says; *"Then He called His twelve disciples together and gave them power and authority over all demons, and to cure diseases. He sent them to preach the kingdom of God and to heal the sick."* Notice what Jesus did. This is what Jesus did, what Jesus does and what Jesus will do. Jesus called these disciples to Himself and the Bible says He 'gave' them. – He 'gave' them 'power.' He gave them dunamis – the very power that He had because He was baptized in the Holy Spirit. Remember when Jesus walked the earth as a man He had absolutely none of His deity, none of His power. That is why for the first 30 years of His life Jesus did nothing miraculous, because He couldn't. It was only when He was baptized by the Holy Spirit, after being water baptized by John, that Jesus began His ministry. The Bible is absolutely, abundantly crystal clear on that.

Jesus imparts authority to the disciples and He gives them power and authority over all demons – that means every single demonic host. He gave them authority to cure diseases. He sent them to preach the Kingdom of God and to heal the sick. Why was it necessary for Jesus to give the disciples authority of demonic spirits and power to heal the sick if His commission to them was to go and preach the Kingdom? Why was it necessary that they have authority over demons and the ability by God to cure diseases, if the mandate was to preach the Kingdom of God? Because the two go hand in hand. The Kingdom of God proclaims about a God who is almighty, a God who is omnipotent, a God of mercy, a God of grace and a loving God. But the Power of God confirms that proclamation. What good is proclaiming a gospel about a God who does not confirm that gospel?

The worst thing that happened was when the Jews lost control of the Church because then Gentiles came in, with no pedigree and no history of the ways of God. I'm talking about hundreds of years ago. I'm talking second and third generations of the Church. Gentiles came in not knowing about the miraculous exodus from Egypt – things that Jews grew up with. Young Jewish children knew the power and the might of God. A different mind-set started coming into the Church. People that were divorced from the God of the Hebrews, bringing

139

new theologies - oh the time of healings and miracles are over because they ended at the last apostle. That's just absurd because God's might and power was poured out upon humanity long before the apostles were ever born. Which apostle was around at the time of Moses? Which apostle was around when Joshua prayed to God and God caused the sun to stand still. Or when God confirmed to Hezekiah that he's healed and brings the sundial back fifteen degrees. To which apostle can we attribute that miracle? To say that God's power stopped with the last apostle means to say that it began with the first apostle. In a way, that is true because the first apostle is Jesus; He is the great apostle of our faith.

The Kingdom of God is a Kingdom of power because the King of that Kingdom is the Almighty. This is a pattern, Saints. When you look at the New Testament it is a clear pattern of God's dealing with humanity. God speaks, and then confirms His word with signs following. When the Apostles returned for the first time what's interesting in verse 10 is the play on words when it states that Jesus took His disciples aside to Himself. They are no longer called disciples; it says, "*And **the apostles**, when they had returned, told Him all that they had done. Then He took them and went aside privately into a deserted place belonging to the city called Bethsaida. But when the multitudes knew it, they followed Him; and He received them and spoke to them about the kingdom of God, and healed those who had need of healing.*" [Emphasis added]. There is so much in this verse, about five sermons worth. The 'Apostles' came back and proclaimed what had been done. The disciples are the ones who followed Jesus. The apostles are sent as messengers, doing the works of the Lord. They are telling Him that they'd cast out devils and had done amazing wonders. When the multitude heard that Jesus was in town, Jesus immediately began to preach the Kingdom and heal the sick. Preach the Kingdom heal the sick, preach the Kingdom heal the sick, it is a pattern throughout Scripture that God wants to confirm His word with signs following.

When we look at the Church today, and again I'm generalizing, we don't see the power of God and that is a great tragedy. But there's a greater tragedy which is the complacency of Christians – they don't mind not perceiving the power of God. I think one of the greatest sins that we all commit against God is a lackadaisical, disinterested attitude towards God's power. I'm not trying to scold anybody, I always feel like I'm doing that so I apologize in advance because that's not my intention. But my heart is grieving that we as a Church are complacent. That we're okay if God doesn't pitch up, that we're okay if God doesn't move, that we're okay to have intellectual arguments to bring people to salvation. I remember many times when I would share the gospel with folk and you know they'd say, 'look, it's a load of nonsense'. Then God would tell me to do some peculiar things. I remember one time this guy was a drug addict, horribly addicted to drugs and he was Jewish. I said to him, "If your Messiah will deliver you from drugs, will you bow your knee to him?" He says, "If anybody can deliver me from drugs I will bow my knee and serve them." I said, "You're on." I prayed for him and got in touch with him the next day. Actually, his wife phoned me and she said, "He's been sober for 24 hours, that's never happened before." And he never touched drugs again after he bowed his life to Jesus.

Another occasion I was sharing the gospel with a Jewish man and he was just arguing. God said to me to tell him to, 'stand up, shut up and bow his heart to my Lordship.' I don't know what came over me but I said to him suddenly, "Stand up, shut up and bow your knee to Jesus." It was like this guy was in a trance; he literally jumped up because he had encountered the power of God, the power of the Living God. This is what God wants. He wants to confirm His word with signs following. This is Mark's testimony as he finishes off his gospel account. Take a look at the last part of Mark Chapter 16 when Jesus tells his disciples in verse 17, "*And these signs will follow those who believe:*" Not these signs *might* follow but these signs *will* follow. Not these signs will follow until the last apostle dies. Not these signs will follow until we get all those denominations that don't believe that these signs will follow! These signs will follow those who believe. What is the condition for the signs to follow? – Belief and faith - "*If you believe.*"

"*And these signs will follow those who believe: In My name they will cast out demons;*" My goodness, mention demons in Church these days and everybody dashes for the door. The average Christian is petrified of Satan, petrified of demonic manifestations, – absolutely petrified. That is crazy. It's like watching those huge circus elephants, monstrous beasts, tied with a little chain fixed to small peg in the ground. How does that work? How does this huge powerful animal not venture beyond the reach of the chain? Because of its mind, it

141

remembers that when it was a baby elephant it was on the same chain and couldn't move it then. He doesn't realize that now it's grown to four tons it could rip out not only the peg but the entire circus with it. We're so like that elephant. We don't know who we are.

"These signs will follow those who believe." He goes on to say, *"They will speak with new tongues; they will take up serpents;"* – which of course we don't do, to test God, – *"and if they drink anything deadly, it will by no means hurt them; they will lay hands on the sick, and they will recover."* And this is what I want to get to, verse 19 and 20 says *"So then, after the Lord had spoken to them, He was received up into heaven, and sat down at the right hand of God."* Seated there, He is making intercession for you and me. He's done His work and He's seated at the right hand of God the Father. Don't pray for Him, He's too busy praying for you. Don't pray to Him, you'll be disturbing Him, He's praying for you. We now pray to the Father in His name.

Verse 20 says, *"And they* (that is the disciples who believed in His name) *went out and preached everywhere, the Lord working with them and confirming the word through the accompanying signs. Amen."* – Because they believed. They preached the word and God confirmed the word with signs following. God confirmed. They didn't try to do anything, God the Father confirmed. Saints, there are hundreds, no I exaggerate, but there certainly are many, many, many scriptures in the New Testament where the preaching of the Kingdom of God is accompanied with healings, signs and wonders and miracles. It comes as a complete package.

Remember in Luke Chapter 5, where Jesus was in Capernaum and as He was preaching in somebody's house and the scribes and the Pharisees were present, the Bible says in verse 17, *"the power of the Lord was present to heal them."* Four men brought a paralyzed friend and lowered him through the ceiling. Jesus wanting to make a point to teach the Pharisees and scribes a Biblical truth turned round to this man and says *"Man, your sins are forgiven you"* The religious leaders had an absolute demonic fit. Who is this man that says he can forgive sins, for God alone can forgive sins. Jesus reverts to them as the Messiah and begins to teach them the very things that their scriptures taught about the Messiah. He says, *"But that you may know that the Son of Man has power on earth to forgive sins"*--He said to the man who was paralyzed, *"I say to you, arise, take up your bed, and go to your house."* Jesus was just teaching Isaiah 53; *"Surely He has borne our griefs and carried our sorrows; yet we esteemed Him stricken, Smitten by God, and afflicted. But He was wounded for our transgressions, He was bruised for our iniquities; the chastisement for our peace was upon Him, and by His stripes we are healed.*" He was just preaching, as part of the redemption of man. The power of God made manifest is not only for salvation but that God may use His power for healing and miracles and signs and wonders. This is the pattern.

If you don't believe me, that's fine; I'm certainly unimportant in this equation. Let's see what the Bible teaches. Paul wrote in 1 Corinthians Chapter 4, verse 20 speaking to the Corinthians. The Greeks were very intellectual, they loved debates and Paul speaks to the Greek Church and he says, *"For the kingdom of God is not in word,"*- it's not in great debates. Paul appreciated that debating would not bring the Kingdom. He'd had a great debate in Athens with the Greek philosophers and the fruit of that debate was not much. He then goes to Corinth but he doesn't debate with the Corinthians. He doesn't debate the gospel; he doesn't show them some CD or DVD from some intellectual Christian confirming that the earth was indeed created by God. Now listen, I'm all for Kent Hovind. He's brilliant and the creation guys they're brilliant, they're excellent. But, you know, there comes a time when you stop arguing. I've found that most Christians are not super-intelligent. That's not an insult it's just a confirmation of what Paul says in 1 Corinthians Chapter 1, verse 26 *"For you see your calling, brethren, that not many wise according to the flesh, not many mighty, not many noble, are called."* We are simple folk who knew we needed salvation, we came to Christ. The intellectuals don't come to Jesus, they can reason out why they don't need Him. Don't enter into an intellectual debate with somebody that's smarter than you. That was one of the greatest things my father ever told me. He said "David, it's better to lose an argument to a clever person than try to win one with a fool." The Bible says in Proverbs Chapter 9, verse 10, *"The fear of the Lord is the beginning of wisdom, and the knowledge of the Holy One is understanding."* Therefore, any intellectual person who does not know God is a fool. So, don't debate them.

Paul wrote that very important lesson after failing in Athens. He failed miserably with the preaching of the gospel, he strayed from his mandate. You can read about it in the book of Acts. I won't tell you what scripture as you can find it yourself. It's called personal Bible study. Paul learned a valuable lesson. He failed in his ministry in Athens; he botched it completely because he entered into an intellectual debate with the Athenians. He goes to another Greek city and we read in 1 Corinthians Chapter 2 from verse 1 where Paul recounts to the Corinthians the events surrounding their salvation. He says, *"And I, brethren, when I came to you, did not come with excellence of speech or of wisdom declaring to you the testimony of God. For I determined not to know anything among you except Jesus Christ and Him crucified. I was with you in weakness, in fear, and in much trembling. And my speech and my preaching were not with persuasive words of human wisdom, but in demonstration of the Spirit and of power, that your faith should not be in the wisdom of men but in the power of God."*

Saints, one of the greatest mysteries is how God chooses His vessels to do certain things for Him. Peter was a fisherman, he knew about fish, he knew about boats and he knew about nets. Yes, he was a Jew – not a very well-studied one. But God said, "I want you should go to the Jews. I want you to preach to the Pharisees. I want you to preach to those who know the Law." Then he calls Paul, a Pharisee of the Pharisees, one who knew the Old Testament better than any Pharisee in the whole of Israel and had lived out the law. But God says, "I want you to go to the Gentiles, who know nothing about the law." Why did God do that? I can guarantee you if Paul and Peter were in the 'First Church of the Almighty Christians,' the council of elders in their great wisdom would say, "Well you know Peter, I know you have such a calling and a passionate heart for the Jews but really you're an ignoramus. Obviously, God has ordained that you should go to the Gentiles. But Paul you've got a master's in theology and a masters of a masters in the expounding of the Mosaic Law. You're a teacher of teachers; you are a natural choice for the Jews." That's what we do, don't we?

That's what we do. We look at somebody's natural strengths and say that's your ministry. In fact, we Christians are so brilliant that we even have these little how to discover your ministry gifts questionnaires. No silly, that's how you discover your carnal gifts, your natural gifts are of no use to the Kingdom of God. God does not want you to be strong. God wants you to be uncomfortable, out of your depth, broken, scared and petrified. How can I say that? Because Paul says I was with you in much fear and trembling. When Paul went to Corinth he was in fear and trembling, he was out of his depth and he was uncomfortable. I mean 'Paul' was out of his depth, he was uncomfortable and that's where God wanted him. When Paul was in Athens on the steps of Areopagus philosophizing, because he was so educated, he began to quote Greek literature to win over the Athenians but he failed. However, when he came to Corinth, he determined to know nothing except Jesus Christ him crucified. He said I will not fail my God again by trying to intellectualize. I will not again come in my own strength, in my own power or my own wisdom. I'm going to come broken. I'm going to come just as I am. I don't know what to do, I don't know what to say, I don't know how to do this thing. I'm going to come in the power of God. The end result was that Paul did amazing things by the Spirit of God in Corinth. There were healings, miracles, signs and wonders and the Corinthians came to Christ because they saw the power of God demonstrated. The gospel preached with the power of God confirming it.

I don't want to belabour this but I'm trying to establish pattern. Let's look in the book of Romans, Chapter 15. Paul writes to the Church of Rome and tells them something in verse 18 which he repeats in verse 19. He says *"For I will not dare to speak of any of those things which Christ has not accomplished through me, in word and deed, to make the Gentiles obedient-- in mighty signs and wonders, by the power of the Spirit of God, so that from Jerusalem and round about to Illyricum I have fully preached the gospel of Christ."* Paul says I preached the gospel in word and deed, in mighty signs and wonders, in the power of God. Then he says, *"so that."* I've done these things; I've preached the gospel in word with signs and wonders following, *"so that,"* he says, *"I have fully preached the gospel."* You see saints; we don't fully preach the gospel. The gospel is not just that God loves you and Jesus died for you. That's not the gospel of Jesus Christ that's not the gospel the Kingdom.

The Church has lost the understanding of the gospel of the Kingdom and it is time for restoration. The Cross of Jesus Christ speaks of our salvation. It is where Jesus bled to death and gave up His Spirit so that we could be saved, so that our sins could be cleansed. He was the fulfilment of every blood sacrifice to the Old Covenant. He is the Lamb of God who 'takes away the sins of the world.' All that is step one. Step two is our response, we either accept or reject. Either bow your knee to the Lordship of Jesus Christ or reject His Lordship. Step three is where we begin the journey as sons and daughters. It is where the Church, by and large, has not begun. We are hovering around the Cross of Jesus, "Dear God, forgive me. Dear God, forgive me. Am I forgiven? Forgive me my sins." We do not realize that we already are sons and daughters of the Most High God. That God is in us by His Holy Spirit, transforming us into the image of Jesus.

Romans 8, verse 29 *"For whom He foreknew, He also predestined to be conformed to the image of His Son, that He might be the firstborn among many brethren."* And 2 Corinthians Chapter 3, verse 18, *"But we all, with unveiled face, beholding as in a mirror the glory of the Lord, are being transformed into the same image from glory to glory, just as by the Spirit of the Lord."*

God wants us to be His Ambassadors to take the gospel to a lost and dying world. Not with arguments but in the power of the Spirit of the Living God. That is why Jesus had to be baptized in the Holy Spirit. Saints, at the age of 12, Jesus was confounding the Rabbi's in the temple – at the age of 12. Nobody was able to argue with the boy Jesus. He knew the Word of God. He knew who He was, that He was the Messiah. He turned around to His Mum who was anxiously looking for Him. Just like any normal Jewish mother, she must have been frantic but He says, "Do you not know I must be about my Father's business." At 12 He knew His identity. He knew His mission, He knew who He was. So, why were there 18 more years before Jesus did anything, before Jesus made himself known publicly? There are a number of reasons. Jesus had to fulfil the law. He had to be the high priest. Only at the age of 30 could a priest begin to function. That's why He waits until He was 30.

It's only when He's baptized in the Holy Spirit, only when the Spirit of the Living God comes upon Him does He begin His ministry. Does that mean Jesus didn't have the Spirit in Him before? Of course He did. He was in perfect relationship with God so of course the Holy Spirit was in Jesus. But the Holy Spirit wasn't upon Jesus. There's a huge difference Saints. There's a massive difference between the Spirit of God coming into our hearts at salvation and our baptism of the Holy Spirit. The Spirit of God coming upon us, it is colossal, it is gigantic. I teach on this extensively in my basic foundation's series.

I want us now to look at the Gospel of Luke because I want to share with you a mystery. How many of us are baptized in the Holy Spirit? You know when you're baptized in the Holy Spirit. You know that you know that you know that you know. The evidence is there because you're speaking in tongues. Has God done anything through your life recently? How many people have you prayed for who have been healed? Anyone cast out a demon recently? What's gone wrong Saints? What's gone wrong with the Church? You know there are so many Churches that offer courses on how to get full of the Holy Spirit. They even teach you how to pray in tongues. I say that with the heavy dose of sarcasm as you cannot 'learn' to speak in tongues. What then is wrong?

Acts Chapter 1, Jesus is about to ascend into heaven. He's got with Him a minimum of 12 men, at least, if not many more. They have all done three and a half years with the finest Bible College the world has ever seen. They'd had the most incredible discipleship, the most amazing privilege that any Christian might have ever had. They had all graduated and given a commission. They've been given their calling to go into all the world to make disciples of all nations, teaching them all things that Christ had taught them. Then the Dean of the Bible College turns around – and please I'm not having a go at Bible colleges, but I want you to understand that doctrine is important. Those of you who know me appreciate I'm a stickler for doctrine. Theology is important; I'm a stickler for theology. But neither doctrine nor theology make any sense without the Holy Spirit.

Acts Chapter 1, verse 4 says, *"And being assembled together with them, He commanded them."* – And I just need to say, Hebron College is a brilliant college. That was my advert. Alright! Now back to our verse, Jesus is about to ascend to Heaven, the disciples believe they have everything they need then Jesus says this. *"And being assembled together with them, He commanded them not to depart from Jerusalem, but to wait for the Promise of the Father, "which," He said, "you have heard from Me; for John truly baptized with water, but you shall be baptized with the Holy Spirit not many days from now."* Let me ask; were the disciples Christians? – Absolutely. Jesus had been with them for forty days after His resurrection. They were born-again. And you can't be born-again unless the Holy Spirit of the Living God dwells in your spirit. Got that; do you all believe that? Good. So was the Spirit of God in them? Yes. Were they born-again?

Yes. Were they ready for service? No, they weren't ready. Jesus says you wait, don't go anywhere. I am not releasing you until you receive the promise from the Father. *"For John truly baptized* (you) *with water,"* – speaking about John the Baptist – *"but you shall be baptized with the Holy Spirit not many days from now."* Verse 8 Jesus continues, *"But you shall receive power* (dunamis) *when the Holy Spirit has come upon you; and you shall be witnesses to Me in Jerusalem, and in all Judea and Samaria, and to the end of the earth."*

You cannot be a witness for Jesus unless you are baptized in the Holy Spirit. Come on Saints, how is it that you accept that statement? Why weren't you angry? I've just said you can't be a witness for Jesus unless you are baptized in the Holy Spirit. Think about my question and I want you to get angry with me. Any emotion will do me. Show me some life! Ok, so people do want to be angry but these days you can't actually. Okay, what about the Churches that don't believe in the baptism of the Holy Spirit? Aren't they witnesses for Jesus? Not really. They are witnesses for a part of Jesus but not the Kingdom of God. They do not represent the Kingdom of Heaven. Does that mean they're going to Hell? No. It just means that they're only preaching half of the truth. It means that they're ineffective; it means that it's fleshly and carnal. David, don't you know you're obviously making it an enemy of yourself. Actually, I do that all the time, I've realized this is my gifting, so I may as well jump in with hands and feet. I've tried to be nice but it doesn't work so now I just preach the truth in love. I mean, I love you but you need to hear this. You've got to hear but don't hate me, just hate God. Then try and figure that one out, fight with God, don't fight with me.

Saints, Jesus wants witnesses unto him. I love the Authorized Version, that's the old King James Bible which says *"and ye shall be witnesses unto me."* The first time I read that something just burst in my spirit. Christ wants us to replicate His ministry. Did you get that? Jesus wants us to replicate His ministry, that's why He says to the disciples at the supper. "Truly, or *"verily, verily,"* or surely, *"I say unto you, He that believeth on me, the works that I do shall he do also; and greater works than these shall he do;"* John Chapter 14 verse 12. Jesus wants us, that's you and I, whoever is a believer, whoever is born-again, washed in the blood of Jesus. He wants us to be baptized in the Holy Spirit so that we can be witnesses unto Him, so that our lives will replicate His ministry, so that we don't just preach the gospel of "Jesus loves you, this I know, because the Bible tells me so," etc. etc. That's insipid, Saints. That's not the God of the Bible. The God of the Bible sent His Son Jesus Christ to set at liberty the captive, to heal the sick, to cleanse the leper, to give sight to the blind, hearing to the deaf, to proclaim the acceptable time of the Lord and to bring the Kingdom of God and its' influence upon earth. That is the God we serve. That is the type of disciples that Christ is looking for.

Even this amazing band of men and woman, who had witnessed the most incredible things and had been taught a phenomenal doctrine were not equipped until they were baptized in the power of God. It is only by the power of God that the Kingdom of God will be established. It's only by the power of God that people's hearts will be changed, as people come under conviction of the Holy Spirit.

Now, I come back to my previous question which I asked about 5 pages ago. Why then, if you are, if we are born-again and even baptized in the Holy Spirit, why then are we not seeing the manifest presence and power of God through our lives? I ask this question of myself often, because I once witnessed the most incredible things on a weekly basis. We've seen demons being cast out, people healed, and people crying under conviction of the Holy Spirit. It wasn't like when we witnessed to people, they would say, "Ah, okay, okay I think I'll give my life to Jesus. Huh, what do you think doll, huh, good idea?" No, people wept. They said, "God forgive me." They came under the convicting power of the Holy Spirit and were radically changed. What has gone wrong?

I want to share with you something and I pray by the grace of Almighty God He will open your hearts to catch this. It's in the Gospel of Luke Chapter 3 and I'm going to read verse 21, and 22. The scripture says, *"When all the people were baptized, it came to pass that Jesus also was baptized; and while He prayed, the heaven was opened. And the Holy Spirit descended in bodily form like a dove upon Him,"* – have you got that? The next portion is the genealogy of Jesus and there are no great revelations there so let's go on to Chapter 4 verse 1. *"Then Jesus, being filled with the Holy Spirit, returned from the Jordan and was led by the Spirit into the wilderness, being tempted for forty days by the devil."* What is the first thing that happens after His baptism? He's full of the Holy Spirit and the Spirit of God takes Him into where and to do what? Yes, He was praying and fasting in the wilderness forty days, that's right.

We know that the devil tempted Him and He overcame all temptations but notice what verse 14 says. *"Then Jesus returned in the power of the Spirit to Galilee."* Did you notice the subtle change? Jesus is full of the Spirit and goes into the wilderness. There He's tempted, there He prays and there He fasts. But when He has finished fasting, when He has withstood all the temptations of the devil, the Bible says He comes out in the *power* of the Spirit. Saints there is a big difference between filled the Spirit and being filled with the power of the Spirit. This is what I wanted to share with you. Now I can start my message.

Because the Church does not preach the Kingdom we feel that once somebody is filled with the Spirit and speaks an unknown tongue, we then believe that's it. They have now experienced the fullness of everything God has. Once somebody can speak in tongues, we say, that is it. Saints, we not are baptized in the Holy Spirit so that we can speak in tongues. Tongues are only an evidence of the Spirit in us. The Holy Spirit is not about tongues. We are baptized in the Holy Spirit so that God's power can flow through our lives, to touch others with the power of God so that they can know who God is. I got born-again, not because of intellectual arguments. I was a lot smarter before I came to Jesus. I could argue so well. I wasn't as passive, loving and gentle as I am now. When Christians came with their argument it did nothing to me, it did nothing for me, it was silliness. But when one young man put his hand upon my shoulder and the dunamis of God – the power of God – flowed right over my being. Right then from the very depth of my heart, from a place I never actually knew existed, I began to sob with such remorse. I could hardly breathe because I was crying so deeply. I had such a sense of my wickedness before God and I broke down and surrendered my life to God. Why? – Because this guy told me about Jesus? No. He just said, "I want to pray for you," and the power of God simply flowed through this young man and overwhelmed me. Okay, before that I saw the presence of God, but that's just by the by. The fact of the matter is that I experienced God. Not a theology. I hadn't experienced the Christian doctrine; I experienced the Christ of Christianity.

That is what God wants to do. He wants to empower us with His Spirit so that those who we minister to may encounter the God that we're speaking of. God doesn't want us to be witnesses **about** Him; He wants us to be witnesses **to** Him. That they see Him, when they see us and that they are in the presence of God when they're in the presence of us. The only way to get to a place where God can use you is to go from being filled, to being in the power of the Spirit. For that transition to take place a few things need to happen. You need to go to a place and be broken. Where you are willing to give up your life rather than compromise the truth of God. Jesus could have starved to death out there. But hungry and parched He resisted the temptation of food; He resisted the temptation of power, of glory and of position because He was sold-out for God. Until we are broken and have come to a place where it is God, His Kingdom and nothing less, we will not know the power of God.

This lackadaisical, half-hearted, que sera, sera, Christianity is useless to everybody. God is warning us to capture His heart. He has given you and me so much. He has given us everything that pertains to life and Godliness so that we should come short in no gift. He has given us His Spirit. Paul prays for the Church at Ephesus and says in Chapter 1 verse 18 and 19, *"That you may know what is the hope of His calling, what are the riches of the glory of His inheritance in the saints, and what is the **exceeding greatness of His power** toward us who believe."* [Emphasis added] We need to start getting hungry, passionate and sold out so that power of God can begin to flow through our lives. God is looking for vessels that are yielded, that are contrite, that are humbled, and that are full of compassion and full of his love.

The question is; are you and I willing to be those vessels? – Or are we just okay with this normal-dry powerless Christianity. There's a word in Afrikaans that means 'a hole being filled' and that's how I am with the Christian Church. I'm tired of looking at this Ferrari with a lawnmower engine. Who's going to join me and get serious for God?

We have spoken through these pages about the Kingdom of God. We've spoken about the attitude to the Kingdom, attitudes that we see are not prevalent in the Christian Church. We need to adopt those attitudes. We need to see the Kingdom of God as it really is. I really encourage you to reread the teachings in the preceding pages. Understand this completely because it's not about the gospel of the Church. We have seen the effects of the gospel of the Church with its division, strife, backbiting, rumours and jealousies. It's time for the Kingdom of God.

Will you sell-out for Christ?

Do you really want the power of God? Answer that question seriously. Do you really want the power of God on your lives?

Are you willing to pay the price?

This is only between you and God. I can't pray a magical prayer over you. I can't do anything, believe me I've tried. This is between you and God, what we need to offer God is a willing heart.

Before I close this chapter, I want to talk briefly about communion. We need to learn to take communion biblically, not traditionally. We need to understand that communion is a covenant meal where we reflect on our obedience to the covenant. Traditionally, and historically, Christ took communion when He had finished laying out the conditions of the New Covenant. In doing so He would have said in Hebrew "sav'raw ma'ra'nat v'rabotah" which means what is your opinion or what is your response to the Covenant, to what I've just spoken. The Jewish response would be "le'chaim" which means to life, to your life, to your way, to your truth. We hear what you're saying Lord and we give ourselves that we might have life. The Rabbi Paul with this Hebraic understanding speaks to the Church at Corinth and he says, and I paraphrase, "How is to that when you come together to take communion one is drunk and one of you has consumed all the communion wine and others have eaten all the food." But then he goes on to say, "*For he who eats and drinks in an unworthy manner eats and drinks judgment to himself, not discerning the Lord's body.*" (1 Corinthians 11:29.)

Saints, we don't take communion to ask God to forgive us for our sins, that is so unscriptural and yet so traditional. Sin is dealt with in your quiet time it is dealt with between you and God. When you come to take communion, what you're doing is, you're examining yourself to see whether you are in covenant. Jesus, are you my everything? Are you truly Lord of all my life? Do I truly desire to abide in you? Notice my words; I'm saying none of us are perfect, but **do we desire** to obey Him? Are there areas in our lives that are not submitted to our Lord? Because if so Paul says don't eat and drink judgment upon yourself. Don't take the cup and bread and say I'm in perfect relationship with God, I am obeying him, my will is to obey Him, but your heart isn't. The problem is that when you hold these seemingly innocent objects in your hand you are declaring covenant with God. A God, who is faithful to always uphold His part of the Covenant, but who is also a God that will judge us if we lie. We tend to say, "Lord I'm one hundred per cent in relationship with you, everything's perfect, hunky-dory." Don't do that. Take communion the traditional way with this new understanding. This examining yourself, of course, should have all been done before coming to Church. I want you to take a deep look at yourself and your commitment to Christ. Ask the Lord to show you where there is compromise, where there is disobedience in your life. I'm telling you Saints, God will not pour out His Spirit upon us where there is sin or disobedience. It doesn't matter how anointed you are. It doesn't matter how gifted you are. You will never function in them if there are areas in your life where there is disobedience or rebellion.

"If you've been praying for snow:

Please stop?"

Chapter 11

The Parable of the Ten Virgins

ometimes when we're confronted with very new concepts it shakes us even though we might see it clearly in the Bible. Paul said, "It's imperative that you study these things for yourselves." What we've done in the previous pages by the Spirit of God is to open up your mind to consider things that you possibly haven't thought of before. The Kingdom; yes, we're all awaiting the Kingdom. The Kingdom of God is at hand was the message Jesus and His disciples preached. This Kingdom came about on the day of His resurrection and it is advancing. However, it does not advance as we generally perceive and envisage it. The Kingdom of heaven advances in the Spirit, it doesn't advance in the earth through our understanding. The Church does not become stronger and stronger and eventually take over this earth. This world is fallen, it is judged and the god of this age has been judged. The Lord is not going to come and share His throne with man. He's coming to rule supreme.

I want to continue with this theme of the Kingdom and look at one of the parables of the Kingdom –the parable of the ten virgins is found in Matthew Chapter 25. You and I need to be alert because we are living in the end times and the Lord's return is imminent. If you believe in the pre-trib rapture it's more imminent than those who believe in an intra-seal, rapture. Regardless of what you believe the fact of the matter is, the rapture of the Church is imminent. There's only about four or five years difference between the different views on when the rapture occurs. Therefore, if you believe in pre-trib you go earlier. If you believe in intra-seals, well you wait another five years. If you believe in the pre-trib and you see the Jews building the third temple and the start of the daily sacrifices, then your belief was wrong and you simply just wait. If you believe in the intra-seal rapture and you love the Lord you'll be taken before the persecution, which is a bonus. Okay, I'm not here to talk about the timing of the rapture which is my favourite subject but today I really feel that the Lord would have us look at, Matthew 25.

Matthew Chapter 25 starting at verse 1, "*Then the kingdom of heaven*" – oh, there it is again. "*Then the kingdom of heaven shall be likened to ten virgins who took their lamps and went out to meet the bridegroom.*" Let's just pause there for a minute. Whenever, in the Bible, we read 'the Kingdom of heaven is like' then Jesus is about to illustrate a Spiritual truth. A parable is not a sweet story; it's not there to share some moral. A parable is a graphic illustration of a Spiritual principle. Did you know that the Church is going to be divided when the Lord comes back for the inhabitants of the Kingdom? It's going to be divided up into two groups as we'll see as we take a look at these ten virgins. Virgins, as we know speak of the Church. These virgins take their lamps and go out to meet the bridegroom. The bridegroom is Jesus. The lamps; this is interesting, what are their lamps? Well you might say this is just a story. It's a lamp; a lamp is just a lamp that one carries to guide one. But the lamp is interesting because in the Bible the lamp doesn't mean a lamp. In the parables it means something else.

Keep your place in Matthew 25 and let's go to Matthew Chapter 6 to understand what the lamp is. The Virgin's took their lamps. Now, as I lay the foundation before we delve into this parable of the ten virgins it might seem as if I'm jumping all over the place, but I will bring everything together eventually. Matthew Chapter 6 verse 22 and 23, "*The lamp of the body is the eye. If therefore your eye is good, your whole body will be full of light. But if your eye is bad, your whole body will be full of darkness. If therefore the light that is in you is darkness, how great is that darkness!*" 'The lamp of the body is the eye.' What does it mean, 'the lamp of the body is the eye'? The eye reflects what's inside. If the eye is light, then there's light in the soul. If the eye is dark how great that darkness is; that means the soul is void of understanding, void of the Spirit of God and void of anything of God. Your lamp is your person, your soul and your spirit.

So, these virgins go out to meet the bridegroom, - it doesn't sound right does it? The lamp is the soul, the spirit but they are going out with their soul and spirit! Clearly then these virgins together with their soul and spirit are all one. What God is doing in this parable is that He's segmenting man. Man is a spirit being; has a spirit, lives in a

155

body and has a soul. Man is a triune being, we know that. The spirit of man is born-again. You can't be born-again in your soul. Your soul cannot be born-again but your soul can be renewed. Your soul can come into line with your born-again spirit so that your 'lamp' can be all light. When the spirit influences the soul and the soul wills to submit to the Word of God and the Lordship of Christ then the lamp is perfectly lit. When a spirit is born-again but the soul refuses to submit then the light will go out. Is that clear? So, they take their lamps; it's who they are – their soul and spirit. Is there unity or is it disunity? This will become clearer as we move on.

Back to Matthew Chapter 25 and in verse 2 we read, *"Now five of them were wise, and five were foolish. Those who were foolish took their lamps and took no oil with them, but the wise took oil in their vessels with their lamps."* Remember, the lamp of the body is the eye. The soul of man; is there light in the soul, is there light in the heart? Five were wise, and five were foolish. Let's start dissecting this. Five were wise; the Greek word for wise is phronimos. Phronimos means sagacity, discerning and perceptive. It doesn't mean intelligent necessarily, it is being able to discern events and circumstance. These five virgins, this part of the Church, this segment of the Church, were discerning they understood the times. They had a keen perception, they were alert and they were aware. They knew that the bridegroom's return was imminent and they'd made preparation by bringing extra oil, which speaks of the Holy Spirit. Oil is always synonymous with the Holy Spirit. Remember the parable of the Good Samaritan; he takes oil and wine – speaking of the Holy Spirit and the blood of Christ. The oil in scripture and certainly in the parables always refers to the Holy Spirit. The wise virgins are those who are perceptive, who understand that the hour is at hand and that it is clearly the season of the Lord's return. Therefore, they make sure they have sufficient oil, that they are sufficiently full of the Holy Spirit. Because they have discernment, they are alert.

The Bible says, however, that the five foolish virgins had no oil. That word foolish is an interesting Greek word. In the original Greek the word translated foolish here is móros. Maybe you're smiling because yes, it sounds a whole lot like the English word moron. Now of course, you know, the translators of the King James couldn't imagine them using the phrase "the five moronic virgins." "That just would not do when translating scripture," you could hear them say.

But the reality is that it's exactly what the Greek word implies. The word moron or móros doesn't actually mean 'somebody that is stupid.' Móros means wilful or intentional ignorance. That's a profound difference, isn't it? Someone that's stupid could be excused for their behaviour. They're naive or a simpleton. One has mercy and grace for such. But that's not the word that the Bible uses. It's not the word that Jesus Himself is using. He's using the word móros, these virgins are wilfully ignorant. It's the same word that Paul used in Romans Chapter one where he speaks of those who can clearly see, in creation, the hand of God. That God is not concealed because the very creation speaks of a creator.

Paul in Romans Chapter 1, verse 22 says *"Professing to be wise, they became fools,"* Those professing to be wise; professing to be phronimos they became móros. He uses the same word, móros. He's really talking about the equivalent of today's scientists and professors who despite the evidence against evolution insist on believing in evolution. It is absolutely clear that there is no evidence for evolution. Every one of their theories has been thoroughly debunked. There is not one theory of evolution that has not been debunked and yet they wilfully hold on to it. They're not stupid men but in fact men and women of great intellect. However, claiming to be wise, claiming to have knowledge they make themselves fools. They wilfully deny the obvious. It's like the Church, "We're living in the end times." "No, no, no we're taking dominion, brother – we're influencing the world." Really! Have you read the news lately? Have you compared today's news from last years and last years from the year before? Can you not see that the earthquakes are increasing exponentially, that there are more natural disasters, that there are many more wars now and that men are more bloodthirsty and wicked and that homosexuality has gone from the closet to the classroom? And we're advancing? Are you a moron? Are you móros, brother?

We have segments in the Church that are purposefully wilfully ignorant. Five wise – discerning and five wilfully – undiscerning. The five, who are unwilling to be realists, want to appease their sin nature. Incredibly there is an extraordinarily large segment of our Church that is catering for the base nature of man. You want to be wealthy? – Join our Church. You want to get that promotion? – We've got the answer. You don't even want to be sick again? – The Jesus we preach heals you every time. Sadly, they are drawing in the masses. Laying down your life? – Never, God is too gracious. He understands that you're a sinner; just ask Him to forgive you morning and night then live like the devil – it's all okay! Willy blinded.

So, these ten virgins go out to meet the bridegroom. One group has oil in their lamps; they are full of the Spirit of God. The other group has not taken any extra oil. Matthew 25, from verse 5 says, *"But while the bridegroom was delayed, they all slumbered and slept. And at midnight a cry was heard: 'Behold, the bridegroom is coming; go out to meet him!' Then all those virgins arose and trimmed their lamps. And the foolish said to the wise, 'Give us some of your oil, for our lamps are going out.' But the wise answered, saying, 'No, lest there should not be enough for us and you; but go rather to those who sell, and buy for yourselves.' And while they went to buy, the bridegroom came, and those who were ready went in with him to the wedding; and the door was shut. Afterward the other virgins came also, saying, 'Lord, Lord, open to us!' But he answered and said, 'Assuredly, I say to you, I do not know you.' Watch therefore, for you know neither the day nor the hour in which the Son of Man is coming."* At midnight, at the darkest hour in human history the Lord comes. What are all the virgins doing? They're sleeping. Is that sinful? No.

There's coming a time upon the earth when you will not be able to labour for the Lord. Jesus says in John Chapter 9, verse 4, *"I must work the works of Him who sent Me while it is day; the night is coming when no one can work."* The night is coming when no man can work or labour. Now, I have to warn you again but I am intruding into some people's eschatology and their view of the rapture, so mind your feet for a bit as they're going to get trodden on. We somehow think that we're going to be witnessing, witnessing, making disciples and preaching the gospel then all of a sudden the Lord's going to come. That's not what the Bible teaches. The Bible teaches that there is going to come a time where nobody will hear anymore, where the world will be divided into the believers and the non-believers. The believers themselves will be divided. Even the Benny Hinn's and the Joel Osteen's, if they're your heroes I'm sorry, but no, I'm not sorry! I mean, their TV programs will be off the air and nobody will be joining their Churches. The same will be true of those meeting in sound fellowships and home Churches. Nobody else will be joining, nobody else will be responding to the gospel. That is midnight. It's going to come a time when there is such darkness on the earth that nobody will be interested. You're either in the Church or you're not in the Church. But the Church itself will be divided; there will be the wise and the unwise.

As a bridegroom comes, speaking of the rapture now; remember this is a parable. You're not going to have time to quickly get your heart right with the Lord when the rapture takes place. The Bible says in 1 Corinthians Chapter 15, verse 52, speaking about the rapture, "*in a moment, in the twinkling of an eye, at the last trumpet.*" It will be as lightning that flashes from the East unto the West. It's going to be instant. But this is a parable to illustrate the state of heart and their attitude. So the Bible tells us that in verse 7 that they trim their lamps. They get ready to trim their lamps and get them going but there's no oil. The foolish have no oil. What did they say? They said to the wise, "Give us some of yours." How do we give the Holy Spirit to somebody? We can't give the Holy Spirit to anybody. Then they say, "Go to those who sell." Well who's the one that gives the Holy Spirit? Yes, Jesus himself. How on earth do you receive the Holy Spirit from the giver of the Holy Spirit when the giver of the Holy Spirit has closed shop? He's not giving the Holy Spirit anymore. He's coming back for those who have the Spirit. The Bible tells us in Ephesians Chapter 1 verse 13 that, "*You were sealed with the Holy Spirit of promise, who is the guarantee of our inheritance until the redemption of the purchased possession.*" If you do not have the Spirit, if you are not filled of the Spirit of God, Jesus is not coming back for you. You can't in that moment ask the Lord to fill you with His Spirit, because He's not coming to fill, He's coming to receive to Himself His bride.

The Bible tells us that those who were ready, those who were full with the Spirit of God, went in. I'm not talking about being baptized in the Holy Spirit. I wish you would all be baptized in the Holy Spirit, I wish you would all be filled with the Holy Spirit, in the sense of the baptism. Actually, we do have a prophecy and a promise in Joel that says that is going to happen. Thank God, and then we'll all be charismatics in the proper way. – Proper charismatics; not the mad, insane craziness that we see today. Good old-fashioned Charismatic or Pentecostals. Anyway, that's something that will happen in the future. Praise the living God for that.

In the meantime, we need to be full of the Spirit in our hearts. Will you be full of the joy the Lord and have a passionate desire for

God? You and I do not know when we are going to meet the Lord. We're all focusing on the rapture but the way some of you guys drive you might not even make it home today, I thought South Africa was bad. My lord, I thought we were bad. I don't know how you guys survive in London. I've never prayed so much in a car and been so conscious of the briefness of my life until driving with some of you folks on these English roads. It's horrible, if I was scared of death I think I'd have taken a train back to Heathrow and flown out of this country already! None of us know when we are going to die. It could be at any moment. We need to be ready now, today, to meet with the Lord. Are we filled with the Spirit? Because when the Lord returns for His Church there is no more time. Time is over.

The Bible continues and says in verse 10, "*And while they went to buy,*" – now obviously you can't buy the Holy Spirit. You know that? Where did they go to seek the Spirit? Well, you can't seek the Spirit when the giver is no longer giving. The Bible says of Israel in Ezekiel Chapter 35 that during the Millennium God will put His Spirit in them and He'll make them to obey His commandments, His law. But that's a very different work of the Spirit which we as believers experience. The Bible says that I will take out your heart of stone and I'll give you a heart of flesh. I'll put my Spirit within you and I will cause you, or make you, to keep my Commandments. That's not being born-again because they've got to keep the law. God will cause Israel to keep the Mosaic Law. Read the rest of Ezekiel and you'll see it's all based around observance to the resurrected Mosaic Law. This dispensation of grace, this short two-thousand years is a special dispensation. Before Jesus came it was Law and when He returns it'll be Law. Read your scriptures, the Bible is very clear about this. One cannot receive the Spirit unto salvation once the Lord returns.

These virgins, they're not going to receive favour in the Millennium. These are those who purposefully rejected Jesus. These are móros. They knew what the word said, they read the word and they wilfully disobeyed it. When they do try to get into the wedding hall they find the doors are shut as we read from verse 11 – 13. "*Afterward the other virgins came also, saying, 'Lord, Lord, open to us!' But he answered and said, 'Assuredly, I say to you, I do not know you.' Watch therefore, for you know neither the day nor the hour in which the Son of Man is coming.*" There's an intense urgency in the Spirit. To be born-again is to enter into a relationship with Jesus, would you agree? God is seeking relationship; God's heart's desire is to be a Father to those who will receive Him as Father. But how do I know if I'm in relationship with the Lord? What evidence is there? Well, Jesus says to the five foolish virgins, "I never knew you." There was no relationship. The word "to know somebody" in the Old Testament, is used to describe the consummation of a marriage; "he went into her or he knew her." It's talking about a very deep intimacy. The Lord wants to have a deep intimate relationship with us. He wants us to know Him.

When we go to Matthew Chapter 7 we see this Biblical theme, the spiritual truth, that not everybody who professes to be a Christian is a Christian. There are a lot of people in evangelical Churches who are singing the same choruses as you, attending the same teachings, going to the same prayer meeting but they are not born-again! Therefore, they are not believers. It's a very disconcerting truth, isn't it? Nevertheless, it is true because, unfortunately, we have watered-down the gospel message. We're more concerned about numbers on our pews then people's eternal souls. We place a higher priority on meeting the budget, meeting the expenses and keeping the lights on than making sure people are born-again. We have become so obsessed with these 'Church' monuments that we're neglecting the living stones.

If you are in the ministry or you believe you are called to the ministry you have a responsibility. We know the old fashion picture of the country Pastor on his bicycle being very sweet to Mrs Jones and…. No, no, no, that's just religion. We need to speak the truth in love but the truth nonetheless. In Matthew Chapter 7 Jesus speaking about the end of the age says in verse 21, "*Not everyone who says to Me, 'Lord, Lord,' shall enter the kingdom of heaven, but he who does the will of My Father in heaven.*" Not everyone who says to Me, "Lord, Lord" will enter the Kingdom of heaven, only he who does the **will** of My Father in heaven. What distinguishes a true saint from a foolish saint? It's the doing. Are we saved by our works? No, but works are an evidence that we are saved. Do you see the difference? There is nothing that you and I can do to earn God's favour. In fact, if we try to earn God's favour through works, we displease Him greatly. The more we try to work for our salvation the more His wrath is incurred. However, once we receive His incredible mercy and grace something happens inside of us. The person who is truly born-again is compelled by the life of the Holy Spirit to labour for the Lord. It's not that you try to earn favour. It's simply that you can't help yourself.

I tell you, in my natural self, I want to go and live in a small village with a very good confectionary store nearby and mostly just be left alone. I'm a serious recluse by nature but I am compelled, every moment of my life to think about the Church. The plight of the Church compels me and I'm driven. It's against my human nature; it's against who I am outside of Jesus. Isn't that true of you? The more you love the Lord, the more you draw close to Him, then the more you want to live for Him, the more you just want to speak of His Kingdom and do those things that He puts upon your heart to do. You see, that is a proof of our salvation. The true evidence is when I'm compelled to speak of my Lord, I'm compelled to labour as He leads in directs. I find I cannot sit still. I find I cannot withdraw myself from the activities of His Kingdom.

Depart from me, I never knew you! "*Not everyone who says to Me,*" verse 21 again, "*'Lord, Lord,' shall enter the kingdom of heaven.*" Notice it's the Kingdom of Heaven. It's the Kingdom, 'Heaven' being the capital city. "*But he who does the will of My Father in heaven.*" verse 22, "*Many will say to Me in that day, 'Lord, Lord, have we not prophesied in Your name, cast out demons in Your name, and done many wonders in Your name?'*" These are impressive works, aren't they? Jesus then, "*will declare to them, 'I never knew you;*'" That's the Greek word 'ginōskō', - I never had intimacy with you. There was no intimacy. "*'I never knew you; depart from Me, you who practice* (Greek word anomia) *lawlessness!'*" – You who wilfully disobey My word.

I wasn't around in the 30s, 40s, 50s, or the early part of the 60s but I do know from older folk who I've had the pleasure of speaking with that the preachers from that era didn't mince their words. Sin was sin, right was right, there was no confusion. Today we don't talk about forgiveness, we don't talk about bowing the knee, we do not talk about submission, we don't talk about repentance of sin and we don't talk about confessing our sins one to another. Today in the Church – and again I am generalizing, I am aware of that – we've watered down the gospel. The problem, however, with watering down the gospel is you have a generation of Christians who, by and large, don't know the Lord. They don't know His ways. When it comes time to stand before Him Jesus will say, "I don't know you because you practice lawlessness, you are wilfully disobedient. You have access to My word but you refused to heed it. You are móros. You're not stupid you are wilfully ignorant, wilfully rebellious.

Saints, are we ready? Are we ready right now? If we were to die at this very moment, do you know, that you know, that you know that your heart is right with the Lord? Is He your everything?" Do you love Him with all your heart? Do you wake up in the morning to passionately seek Him? Do you think of Him through the day? Does He occupy your thoughts even through the hustle and bustle of our lives? Does He knock on your heart and say, "Draw aside for a moment, let's just chat a little?" – Do you love Him? You see, that is what separated the wise and the foolish virgins. The wise had oil, they were in relationship.

How do I know this, how do I know that oil speaks of relationship? Well because the scripture teaches me. Turn with me to Ephesians Chapter 5. This is such a well-known portion of Scripture so we'll read from verse 15. I want to encourage you. God loves you, God will never let go of you. You have to let go of God to fall outside His love. Do you understand the difference? God's grace, God's mercy, God's goodness, God's love, – He create the universe for you. That's how He loves you. He sent His son to win you back to Him. There is no greater love than that. I'm a father but I couldn't do what Abram did in presenting his son Isaac as a sacrifice. I'm sorry I'm an inferior person compared to Abraham. God stopped him but our Father went all the way. I am a father who loves my son very much and I realize when I look at the sacrifice of Jesus just how much God loves me and how much He loves you to give His Son like that.

In Ephesians Chapter 5 Paul encourages the Church and says in verse 15, "*See then that you walk circumspectly, not as fools but as wise,*" – "See that you walk carefully, not as fools but as wise, not as móros but as phronimos," – "*redeeming the time, because the days are evil. Therefore, do not be unwise,*" (do not be móros) "*but understand what the will of the Lord is.*" What is the will of the Lord? The Lord's will is for you to be with Him. The Lord's will is for you to give yourself to Him. The Lord's will is that you find your life in Him so that He can give you His Kingdom. That is His will.

Verse 18, "*And do not be drunk with wine, in which is dissipation; but be filled with the Spirit.*" Be continually filled. That is perfect present tense in the Greek. Be, being filled with the Spirit, or being continually in the process of being filled. Being filled with the Spirit here is not a once-off occasion. It doesn't just happen at your salvation. It doesn't just happen when you got baptized in the Holy Spirit. It's not a once-off, it's a continual filling. "Are you continually being filled?" "No." "Why?" "I don't know how to." Praise God because you've come to the right place today. I'm going to show you from the scripture. The truth is, though you actually do know how to if just keep reading. Verse 18, *"And do not be drunk with wine, in which is dissipation;* (excess, or sin) *but be filled with the Spirit, speaking to one another in psalms and hymns and spiritual songs, singing and making melody in your heart to the Lord."* Do you wake up with a song? I appreciate you live a busy life but was there a song of worship as you're washing, bathing, showering, shaving or preparing breakfast this morning? Was there a praise song to the Lord in your heart?

Verse 20 *"Giving thanks always for all things to God the Father in the name of our Lord Jesus Christ."* How am I in a position of continually being full? Because I love Him, I speak of Him, I speak to Him, I worship Him and He occupies my thoughts so that even when I'm busy and distracted I find time in the day just to refocus on Him. We might be standing in the checkout at the supermarket while everybody's complaining about the weather or the slowness of the cashier or something about a political decision – do we stay in the EU or do we leave the EU. You know, while everyone's grumbling and moaning around you as is the nature of mankind, do you just within yourself, in your heart, worship God? Are you a lover of Jesus? The lovers of Jesus are continually filled. They spend their time in worship and blessing and speak to each other about the things of God.

When you meet with a fellow Christian do you talk about the things of God? Do you edify each other? This is how we are continually filled, by being Christ centred? Are we truly Christ centred or do we just go to Church on a Sunday for a top-up? It may be that we're really, really, really fanatical and we go to a midweek meeting. Perhaps you're way over-the-top and add a prayer meeting to that as well! But we don't go beyond that because it's just excessive, isn't it? Are you insane? We separate our lives and say, "Well this is my Christian box." I come to Church and I put on my Christian face and speak my Christianese. That's a whole dialect, you know; "bless you brother and how are you sister." That dialect, you know it. Then we go out into the world and it's "hello mate." Three faces, my work face, my social face or my Church face. No, to be filled with the Spirit is to be Christ centred at all times. Do you love Him? Because that's what it means to be born-again. It's to respond to a God whose love is beyond my comprehension, to speak of Him and to worship Him. It is then that I'm filled with the Spirit, but it continues.

If you want to be continually filled with the Spirit, it doesn't mean just singing songs. The next verse, verse 21 then seems out of place, *"Submitting to one another in the fear of God."* Submitting to one another in the fear of God! Paul is not introducing a new subject he's still talking about being continually filled with the Spirit. So, you're singing songs and melodies in your heart, giving thanks, submitting to one another, then – wives submit to your husbands, husbands love your wives! He goes on to say children submit to your parents, parents don't grieve your children, masters treat your servants well and servants respect your masters. The rest of the Chapter and continuing into Chapter 6 is all about dealing with submission until verse 10 of Chapter 6 when Paul says, "Finally brethren." It appears that he's now changing subject but from verse 21 of Chapter 5 to verse 10 of Chapter 6 Paul is establishing that submission is an expression of our love for God which therefore enables God to fill us with his Spirit. God is not going to fill us with His Spirit if we are groaning, complaining, backbiting, causing strife and division, husbands not loving their wives as Christ loved the Church. I had to learn this myself, had to learn to love my wife, oh yes. My wife is dainty, delicate, soft and gentle but I'm a bull in the china shop by nature. And I've had to learn to love my wife as Christ loved the Church which means that since God forgives me twenty-five thousand times a day so I forgive my wife. Husbands are we loving them, are we reflecting Jesus to them? Wives are you honouring your husband or are you nagging him? Children are you obeying your parents?

Do you see this? To know Him is to obey Him. In obedience the Spirit is released to work in our hearts. Saints, if we are wise virgins then let's have oil, let's be filled with the Spirit. Being filled with the Spirit is desiring the Lord, a desire to be obedient, enjoying the blessing and assurance of salvation, – the joy of the Lord, the peace of God. Do you have joy, do you have His peace and do you walk with a confidence? There's nothing worse than being in doubt as to your relationship with God. There's nothing worse than not being able to come boldly to His throne room because you're so ashamed of your lifestyle. That's not the life that God wants you to live. Let's put Him first, let's love Him, let's walk as sons of light, let's walk with a confidence, acquired confidence and where need be, a noisy confidence in Jesus that comes from being filled of the Spirit, the assurance of salvation and of His coming. There is only one question that we must now each ask ourselves, "Do I know him?" Saints, He loves you. Every one of you can have an intimate relationship God.

As I bring this to a close, I want to correct a fallacy in the Church. Those of you who have been Pastors in Churches or leaders in Churches, you know that people come up to you and say, "Please brother would you pray for me?" Somehow Christians believe that certain individuals have a greater prayer connection with God. Somehow Christians have been led to believe that God is less likely to answer their own prayers then He would answer that of a Pastor. I want to assure you, I'm not trying to encourage you, whether you're encouraged or not I really couldn't care. I'm hoping you'll be encouraged but my motivation is not to speak soft cosy words to you. I want to speak to you about a reality which is that you have just as much access to the throne room of God as any man or woman that has ever walked this earth. God is waiting passionately for you to come to Him, do you know that? We must separate anointing and gifting from relationship. I am gifted to teach. How do I know this? God has given me an ability that does not come naturally to me. I am NOT a natural teacher; I cannot teach anybody the simplest concepts. You want me to teach you to make us an egg omelette, I'll say, "Sit down I'll make it for you." I just don't have the capacity, the ability, the patience or the wherewithal to teach in the natural. However, when it comes to the Word of God I can teach and talk for hours. I'll answer your questions and discuss the Word for hours and hours and hours. That is called gifting and all of us have gifting of some sort but it's got nothing to do with your relationship. That is rooted in God's grace. That's a gift, undeserved, unmerited – just given. Relationship is equal footing. You can have a relationship with the Lord that's as intimate as any other human being that has ever walked this earth. You can hear His voice as clearly as any other human being that has ever walked this earth. You don't have to be a Pastor to walk closely with God. On the contrary, I've met folk who are not Pastors, they just get on with the simple thing of being a Christian and they have a great intimacy with God. God loves you passionately. He wants you, not the Church, not the Pastor, not your denomination He wants you to enter into relationship with Him. In doing that your vessel becomes filled with oil. Let's pursue Him.

Father God. Lord I ask that you would set aside any words they had not come from your Spirit or from your Word but my God that that which is true, would find a fertile and good soil within our hearts. Dear Father I pray that you give each precious soul reading this today, the Spirit of Revelation in the knowledge of You. That they would know by your Spirit and through the power of your word how precious, how valuable and how loved they are by you. My God we ask that you would provoke each one to come into your throne room boldly. Lord, to be set free from the tradition that binds their minds, in fact every spirit of tradition, every lying spirit that would seek to keep my brothers and sisters in bondage I rebuke, in the name of Jesus. My God help us so that there would come a liberty in our thinking where we take your word at face value and believe it. Father, I pray that you would fill your children with your Spirit that they will be able to stand in these dark days. In the name of Jesus Christ. Amen.

"This Church is on Fire

Come burn with us"

Chapter 12

The Work of the Kingdom in this Age

In the previous pages we've considered the various aspects of the Kingdom and what are the characteristics of a person in subjection to the King of this Kingdom. We looked at the power of the Kingdom and the fact that on this earth we are training for reigning. Since that is true it's a good idea if we understood then what is the work of the Kingdom. Our role in the everlasting Kingdom is determined by the King Himself. The Apostle Paul tells us in 2 Corinthians 5, verse 10, *"For we must all appear before the judgment seat of Christ, that each one may receive the things done in the body, according to what he has done, whether good or bad."* Paul wrote this to the Church of Corinth, believers in Christ. The Church will be judged, Saints. This however, is not a judgement regarding our sinful state. Our sinful nature was totally done away with when we became redeemed through the blood of Jesus. This judgement is the fulfilment of the parable of the ten minas, which we looked at earlier. We will be judged with regard to the mina, the gifts or the tasks that the King has given us here in this lifetime. The reward of this judgement, we saw, is cities, reigning with Christ. This judgement will determine our eternal work and position in the Kingdom. It is imperative therefore for us to understand what we as Christians should be focused on during our lives here on this earth, if our works are to be judged and awards given based on those works. What then is the work of the Kingdom that a born-again believer should apply effort to, day by day, while still on this earth?

Now we have to be clear on one point here. If you are truly born-again you will see the Kingdom. We see that in John 3 verse 3 when Jesus was conversing with Nicodemus, a ruler of the Jews. *"Jesus answered and said to him, "Most assuredly, I say to you, unless one is born-again, he cannot see the kingdom of God."* In plain speak; if you are born-again you will see the Kingdom. We do not earn our salvation through our works on this earth. The redemption we have through the blood of Jesus is a gift from God. Our best efforts before God, without Jesus, the Bible tells us, are as filthy rags. However, if we truly comprehend our redemption, we will become passionate and work to advance the Kingdom.

We looked in the first Chapter of this book at the meaning of what Jesus says in Mathew 11 verse 12, "*And from the days of John the Baptist until now the kingdom of heaven suffers violence, and the violent take it by force.*" We saw that the Kingdom of heaven is entered when one understands the value of the Kingdom, together with one's absolute need and desire to obtain it. Many of Jesus' parables speak about the value of the Kingdom and what an individual is prepared to sacrifice to obtain it. Jesus on one occasion says the Kingdom of heaven is like a treasure in a field which, when a man 'finds', he sells everything he has to purchase the field that he may obtain the treasure. The Kingdom of heaven is so valuable that I will give up everything, absolutely everything, so that I may obtain it. That's its value to me. It is more precious to have than anything and I will gladly, willingly, sell everything so that I may obtain the Kingdom.

Saints, do you have passion? Are you so overwhelmed by a desire to enter into all that the Kingdom is to the extent that everything else, including your very life and everything in it, has no value? In this life we are to walk, live and exist with our sole focus on the Kingdom of God. Now, that may sound extremely pious and surely Jesus wouldn't require that of me? Well let's look at what Jesus says about the subject in His own words. In John Chapter 12 Jesus is talking to Andrew and Philip when they came and told Him that some Greeks wanted to meet Him. As a part of that answer He says in verse 25, "*He who loves his life will lose it, and he who hates his life in this world will keep it for eternal life.*" I would suggest that if you regarded your life in this way it would have little value to you. Now, before you track off into suicidal considerations believing you're totally worthless let's be clear on what this means. Hating your life indicates your own personal regard for the things of this life, not life itself. We go through life with a different viewpoint, not caring for the things of this life but with a mind-set focused on the things that are above. Colossians 3, verses 1 to 3 explains this best, "*If then you were raised with Christ, seek those things which are above, where Christ is, sitting at the right hand of God. Set your mind on things above, not on things on the earth. For you died, and your life is hidden with Christ in God."*

When we come to Christ, when we are born-again, we die from our old life, our old self. Our former self exists no more and in Christ Jesus we are a new creation. Everything we did and knew previously from that old life is dead and utterly finished. Our new life therefore, is not a reformat of our old life; it's completely different, completely new. Many Christians come to Jesus, rejoice in the gospel of the forgiveness of sins and fail to comprehend what it means to live a life in Christ. That's the gospel of the Church. They fail to live out a life on this earth of being a new creation in Christ. If we are a new creation, what then does that life look like and what does a born-again Christian do, on a day to day basis, while living our allotted time on earth?

Fortunately, Jesus provides us the key to that in John Chapter 12 verse 26 *"If anyone serves Me, let him follow Me; and where I am, there My servant will be also. If anyone serves Me, him My Father will honour."* If we want to be honoured by the Father, if we want to receive cities at the judgement seat of Christ, we must learn to serve now, in this life to be a servant. To be a faithful servant involves obedience – complete and total obedience.

There's and interesting portion of scripture in the book of Hebrews Chapter 5 where in verses 8 and 9 the writer, speaking about Jesus, says, *"Though He was a Son, yet He learned obedience by the things which He suffered. And having been perfected, He became the author of eternal salvation to all who obey Him."* What does this mean, that Jesus learned obedience and if Jesus had to learn obedience, where does that leave us? Remember we discussed previously that while Jesus was and is fully God, when He came in flesh, He chose to put the power of His deity aside and live His days on earth as man. Jesus learned obedience not in the sense that He was prone to disobedience and had to bring rebelliousness under control, but in the sense that He fully entered the human experience. As a child, He obeyed His parents (Luke 2:51); as an adult, He obeyed the Law (Matthew 5:17) and fulfilled all righteousness (Matthew 3:15). All His life, Jesus completely fulfilled the Father's will (John 8:29; 15:10). Obedience is not a gift, it is learnt and experienced. Jesus learnt obedience on earth by experiencing it in every situation, no matter how difficult. As a Son, He was obedient to His Father even to death on the cross.

During our days on this earth in this life we live in a body that even though the spirit might be born-again the soul, while being renewed, is still capable of sinning. Jesus lived in this same fallen world as we do and he learnt obedience and never failed once. He is our standard and example when it comes to obedience. Fortunately, He has provided the born-again believer with the Holy Spirit of God who dwells in us and empowers us to be obedient. It is only through that means that we have any hope of doing what we're told because the prominent character of the sin nature that once controlled us is always disobedience and rebellion.

So, with Christ as our model and the power of the Holy Spirit within us, the born-again believer is fully equipped to do what he or she is told and walk in obedience. As we progress through our Christian walk we learn how to fully submit to the working of the Holy Spirit within us, who in turn gives us the capacity to be obedient. This is what Paul meant when he wrote in Philippians Chapter 2 verse 12 *"Therefore, my beloved, as you have always obeyed, not as in my presence only, but now much more in my absence, work out your own salvation with fear and trembling;"* We do this by actively pursuing obedience in the process of sanctification.

If we are to be obedient, what then are we to be obedient to and why? Firstly, it's necessary to dispel some myths which are based on humanistic values and, unfortunately, have become widespread in the Church. A few decades ago a man wrote a book that went on to sell millions of copies around the world. Whole Churches have made the book required reading and studied it in their services and in small groups. I'm talking about Rick Warren's book 'The Purpose Driven Life.'

On face value the aspirations of the book are indeed very real. The question of why we're here is certainly a question that many believers and unbelievers struggle with. However, the inference given is that God has this amazing plan for your life, here on this earth and somehow if you can follow the 40-day plan which the writer expounds upon then you'll discover this plan. Doing so, he claims, will reduce your stress, focus your energy, simplify your decisions and give meaning to your life. Sounds amazing except is it Biblical? The writer uses a large number of scripture to support his theories. However, many are out of context or are plucked from any number of translations that best suits the narrative. Scripture speaks for itself and the doctrine of God's plan for our lives is in no way obscure. *"Take up your cross and follow Me,"* (Luke 9:23), *"hate your life,"* (John 12:25), *"crucified with Christ,"* (Galatians 2:20), *'in the world you will have tribulation,"* (John 16:33), just to name a few.

The book seeks to demonstrate how the Christian life will bring great benefit to you on this earth now. It suggests that by following certain rituals or studies over a period of 40 days you'll discover your identity and will give meaning to your life. The Bible however is very clear on what my identity is, if I am born-again – I am a son or daughter of God, seated in heavenly places and a joint heir with Christ. I am what I am because of the work of Jesus on the cross. I don't become a better person because of my own efforts or increased understanding. God allows things to happen in our lives that helps build character, to help us understand Him better as in proving our knowledge of Him through experience. Life experiences are never used to build identity. Immediately we're born-again our identity is fixed. We come into the full effect of the redeeming power of the blood of Jesus immediately. However, it's clear that the Lord uses tribulations in our lives to help us experience the meaning of identity as we read in Romans Chapter 5 verses 3 and 4, *"And not only that, but we also glory in tribulations, knowing that tribulation produces perseverance; and perseverance, character; and character, hope."*

I don't want to belabour the point regarding this book but its' unfortunate consequence is that it has spawned a whole generation that has grown up believing their purpose on this earth is to seek-out the Lord's purpose and individual plan for their life while on this earth. And that somehow if they can tap into that plan then their life on this earth will be fulfilled, enriched and enjoyable. While it is true that many Christians do experience an enjoyable life on this earth that cannot be taken as conclusive proof they have lived out God's plan for their lives.

Jeremiah Chapter 29 verse 11 has become the catch phrase for these disciples. *"For I know the thoughts that I think toward you, says the Lord, thoughts of peace and not of evil, to give you a future and a hope."* That verse however has nothing to do with Christianity except perhaps a reference to our eternal state. That statement was made to the Jews specifically in a letter that the prophet Jeremiah sent to the captives in Babylon. Verse 4 of Chapter 29 makes that very clear; *"Thus says the Lord of hosts, the God of Israel, to all who were carried away captive, whom I have caused to be carried away from Jerusalem to Babylon:"* Nowhere in scripture are we told that during our Christian walk here on earth everything will be a bed of roses.

Just consider our situation for a moment. We live on this earth which the Bible tells us is ruled by Satan, the very same evil fallen angel who 2000 years inspired wicked men to gruesomely murder our Lord and Saviour on a cross. Do you really believe that this ruler, who is still in control on this earth until Jesus returns, is going to allow you to have an enjoyable life within his realm? Especially while you're out making *"disciples of all the nations, baptizing them in the name of the Father and of the Son and of the Holy Spirit, teaching them to observe all things that I have commanded you*?

Saints, we were not saved to have a good life here on this earth. Yes, if we trust in the Lord, He will take care of us and provide everything we need to carry out His will on this earth. However, we are never guaranteed a good life now; in fact, Jesus states the opposite very clearly. In John Chapter 16 verse 33 *"in the world you will have tribulation."* Not might, not possibly, but, you 'will' have persecution. It is to be expected. The apostle Paul tells us in 2 Corinthians 4, verse 7 *"But we have this treasure in earthen vessels, that the excellence of the power may be of God and not of us."* We live our earthly lives on this earth as we learn to know the Father better while we carry out the work of the Kingdom.

So what is this work that the King of the Kingdom requires us to do that determines our reigning position in His eternal Kingdom? Jesus is our model and answer to this question. In John Chapter 6 verse 38 the words of Jesus are recorded. *"For I have come down from heaven, not to do My own will, but the will of Him who sent Me."* Jesus, living on this earth as a man, lived in complete subjection to the will of the Father. If we are born-again and have submitted to the Lordship of Jesus, then our only desire will be to do whatever He wills. We will not be anxious for the things of this life as He takes care of everything for us. We're told this in Matthew Chapter 6 verses 31 to 33 *"Therefore do not worry, saying, 'What shall we eat?' or 'What shall we drink?' or 'What shall we wear?' For after all these things the Gentiles seek. For your heavenly Father knows that you need all these things. But seek first the kingdom of God and His righteousness, and all these things shall be added to you.*" When our focus is on the Kingdom, the things of our Lord, then it brings a tremendous peace. The Father knows what we need.

How then do we know the will of the Lord in our daily living? I've met many Christian who are continually seeking the Lord's will for their lives. As if the Father has some special hidden task for them to carry out. Of course it is true the Lord does call some for specific responsibilities which He equips and prepares them for. He places gifts in certain individuals to carry out a variety of functions in His Church. We read this in Ephesians Chapter 4 verses 11 and 12. "*And He Himself gave some to be apostles, some prophets, some evangelists, and some pastors and teachers, for the equipping of the saints for the work of ministry, for the edifying of the body of Christ.*" The operative word in those verses is 'some'. If Jesus is calling you for a specific ministry you don't need to seek it. He'll clearly let you know.

The vast majority of born-again Christians are not called to ministry, although we are all called to be witnesses and spread the gospel of the Kingdom. But is simply being a witness really what it means to do the will of the King of the Kingdom? What is the talent that the King has given you that you are to trade with that will gain you cities at the judgement seat of Christ? If we love Jesus and are desirous to do His will then we must know what He's doing, what He's accomplishing on a day to day basis. The only way to know that is to spend time with Him. That's what His disciples did. They were always there and when you read through the gospels you see that on many occasions Jesus had things done by those around Him. Trading with our talents does not usually involve great exploits.

It's the myriad of little things that make up the work of the Kingdom. Some are glamorous, some are definitely not so, but everyone is of great importance in advancing the Kingdom. Matthew Chapter 10 verses 41 and 42 make this clear. "*He who receives a prophet in the name of a prophet shall receive a prophet's reward. And he who receives a righteous man in the name of a righteous man shall receive a righteous man's reward. And whoever gives one of these little ones only a cup of cold water in the name of a disciple, assuredly, I say to you, he shall by no means lose his reward.*" Having a prophet or another saint (a righteous man) to stay or giving a little one a cup of cold water are not big tasks yet Jesus tells us that all of these are rewarded.

Turn with me to the gospel of Matthew Chapter 14 from verse 14. *And when Jesus went out He saw a great multitude; and He was moved with compassion for them, and healed their sick. When it was evening, His disciples came to Him, saying, "This is a deserted place, and the hour is already late. Send the multitudes away, that they may go into the villages and buy themselves food."* Interesting isn't it? The disciples took-in their surroundings, looked at their watches, discussed it together then jointly set off to advise Jesus. Thankfully we're not like that in the Church today. We know Jesus is in control, that He's building His Church so we support Him unquestionably and let Him get on with it! Or perhaps not much has changed.

Jesus' answer is interesting. It says in verse 16, *"But Jesus said to them, "They do not need to go away. You give them something to eat."* Notice He didn't say, "Don't worry, I've got this sorted." No, he turned it back to them and said "You feed them." It's not recorded as a suggestion but as a command. We don't need to surmise what their reaction was because the Bible records it. The record of the same event in John 6 describes the account a little differently so we'll pick up the rest of the report from there.

John chapter 6, verses 8 and 9 *"One of His disciples, Andrew, Simon Peter's brother, said to Him, "There is a lad here who has five barley loaves and two small fish, but what are they among so many?"* Andrew is mentioned specifically. He certainly didn't have much faith, judging by his comment. But you see Jesus was only looking for a response, something for Him to work with. He wasn't about to create a meal out of fresh air, although with God anything is possible. He asked His disciples to feed the multitude and Andrew stepped up saying "Lord, this is all I've got!" Andrew had very little faith but he made himself available. Without that it's possible this miracle may have never happened.

Verse 10 continues, *"Then Jesus said, "Make the people sit down."* Jesus could have easily instructed the people directly to sit down. There are several instances where Jesus spoke directly to large crowds. But Jesus gives an order, a command *"Make the people sit down."* Jesus knew what He was doing. He already knew the location was perfect for a picnic as the verse goes on to record, *"Now there was much grass in the place."* By this time the disciples perhaps began to realise Jesus was about to do something special. They didn't question any longer and set to their task with gusto. They got everyone seated and nicely, *"So the men sat down, in number about five thousand."*

Verse 11, *"And Jesus took the loaves, and when He had given thanks He distributed them to the disciples."* This is where the story gets interesting. Jesus took what Andrew had made available, five barley loaves and two small fish, and gave thanks. We read this account fully aware of how it ends up. The five thousand got fed and the disciples had leftovers for weeks to come. However, just put yourself in the actual event as it was unfolding. None of the disciples knew how it would end up. It's not recorded when the actual multiplying of the food took place but it's unlikely to have occurred when Jesus gave thanks. If the five loaves had suddenly multiplied into enough, sufficient to feed the crowds, think about it, Jesus would have been enveloped in a vast mountain of bread and fish. Let's get practical, that didn't happen. Instead it says Jesus gave to the disciples *"and the disciples to those sitting down; and likewise of the fish."*

It's likely it was only the twelve disciples doing the distributing, there may have been more but the only named ones mentioned were of the twelve. So, five loaves and two small fish by simple arithmetic means each disciple received less than half a loaf of bread and a sixth of a small fish. Jesus, after thanking the Father for the food, hands the small portions to each disciple and says, "Off you go, feed the multitude with that." Visualise the disciples as they walked from Jesus holding the tiny portion in their baskets as they looked at the vast crowd who hadn't eaten all day. What was going through their minds as they looked as the first burly guy at the front of the group? But the fact is they went and they did give it to the crowd. They were obedient to Jesus and that's when the miracle occurred. The account concludes saying they gave the crowds, *"as much as they wanted. So when they were filled, He said to His disciples, "Gather up the fragments that remain, so that nothing is lost." Therefore, they gathered them up, and filled twelve baskets with the fragments of the five barley loaves which were left over by those who had eaten."*

Jesus of course had compassion for the crowd but He didn't do the miracle for their benefit. He was teaching His disciples obedience. He was teaching them to trust and obey what He asked them to do. This truly was a great miracle but its' purpose was to teach the disciples a great principle of the Kingdom. The Kingdom is advanced by doing the will of the King. None of the disciples were asked to do anything great, they were just asked to serve, to wait tables. But when they did that the King of our Kingdom was honoured and the power of the Kingdom was on display for all to see.

We get so hung up on doing the great. We believe the great evangelist, the great pastors, the mighty men of God are the gold standard when it comes to our work in the Kingdom. Unless we've won hundreds of souls to Christ then we've achieved or succeeded in nothing. Your work might be to win souls too, but it also may be to just give cups of water to disciples. The point is that whatever we are asked to by our King we do it with great passion knowing that we're building up our reward in heaven. Men and women around us might not notice or even know what we're doing but that matters not. If we're doing what the Lord wills, then He notices and records it.

There's another example in scripture I'd like to refer to quickly. It's the report of the resurrection of Lazarus found in John Chapter 11. The account starts with a description of Lazarus and his two sisters Mary and Martha, and that Jesus loved them. The sisters send a message to Jesus saying "your favourite disciple, the one that you love, is sick". For two days He stayed where He was then declared to His disciples that He was going back to Judea, the very area when the religious leaders of the day were desperate to get hold of Him and kill Him. Naturally the disciples weren't too excited about that and tried to talk Him out of it but He told them He was going anyway because His friend Lazarus had passed away.

We pick up the account from verse 14, *"Then Jesus said to them plainly, "Lazarus is dead. And I am glad for your sakes that I was not there, that you may believe. Nevertheless, let us go to him."* Jesus was talking to His disciples and He says He was glad that Lazarus had died so *"that you may believe"*. Did that mean that Jesus had decided that if His disciples just witness one last big miracle, like raising the dead, then they would believe? Let's continue with the account as it unfolds.

The disciples eventually decide to follow Jesus and they arrive at Bethany where Martha begins to scold Jesus for not being there earlier and healing her brother before he died. Jesus replied to her in Verse 23. *"Jesus said to her, "Your brother will rise again." Martha said to Him, "I know that he will rise again in the resurrection at the last day." Jesus said to her, "I am the resurrection and the life. He who believes in Me, though he may die, he shall live. And whoever lives and believes in Me shall never die. Do you believe this?"* Jesus was teaching who He was, not what He was doing or about to do. Sometimes we get so carried away with the work or works that we forget who Jesus is. Martha had a little problem with that as you'll recall in Luke 10: 42 when she demanded Jesus tell her sister Mary to help with the serving instead of sitting at the feet of Jesus. Martha was focused too much on the service and not on who she was serving. That's an important lesson to learn in servant-hood. We serve the King because He is King. We don't serve for the sake of serving just to obtain accolades. We serve out of love and desire to do the will of the King.

The account goes on as Mary meets Jesus and also scolds Him for showing up late. Jesus asked where they have put him and told Jesus to come and take a look. Verse 38, *"Then Jesus, again groaning in Himself, came to the tomb. It was a cave, and a stone lay against it. Jesus said, "Take away the stone."* Jesus was about to raise a man dead for four days but He paused to ask someone to roll the stone away. Why? He already told His disciples that He wanted them to believe. Jesus didn't ask anyone specifically to roll the stone away. He simply asks that it be done with the intent of observing who came forward. If we are near Jesus our King, we'll always be ready to do whatever He needs to be done. It's so easy to get distracted with other stuff and be very busy doing life when actually our King needs us for a small task. That's called training for reigning. We're always available when needed.

Martha protested at the order, complaining about the smell but Jesus reminded her she needed to believe, or trust Him. Verse 41, *"Then they took away the stone from the place where the dead man was lying. And Jesus lifted up His eyes and said, "Father, I thank You that You have heard Me. And I know that You always hear Me, but because of the people who are standing by I said this, that they may believe that You sent Me."* Jesus wanted the people who were witnessing this pending miracle to fully understand that He was who

He said He was and that He was sent of the Father – *"that you may believe."*

Verse 43 *"Now when He had said these things, He cried with a loud voice, "Lazarus, come forth!" And he who had died came out bound hand and foot with grave clothes, and his face was wrapped with a cloth. Jesus said to them, "Loose him, and let him go."* Again Jesus uses others for a small task. Jesus could easily have spoken and the grave clothes could have fallen off. Wouldn't seem a very big thing after just raising a man from the dead, would it? But no, Jesus involved others because that's how the Kingdom operates and He needed His disciples to learn that. There's stuff to be done in service of the King.

The result of this incredible miracle is provided in verse 45, *"Then many of the Jews who had come to Mary, and had seen the things Jesus did, believed in Him."* The result was that the Kingdom was advanced. Souls were saved. Yes, Jesus did the heavy lifting but it was achieved with the help of others. None of these helpers are mentioned by name, they didn't do it for the glory. They did it to help the King advance the Kingdom.

We are to learn from these examples in scripture. If we're surrendered to Jesus and He really is Lord of our lives, we'll know what has to be done. If we're spending time with Jesus, in prayer, in reading His word in a state of surrender, then the Holy Spirit will prompt us. He'll drop names of people into our hearts to pray for that person or to drop by and have a coffee with them. If you see something that needs doing no matter how small, do it with all your heart. If the church steps need sweeping then be the very best steps sweeper known to man. Our King is looking for faithful servants. Let's conclude with Luke chapter 12, verses 43 and 44, *"Blessed is that servant whom his master will find so doing when he comes. Truly, I say to you that he will make him ruler over all that he has."*

Let us learn to be obedient servants doing the daily work advancing the Kingdom. There is often little reward in this life but when our Master comes, when the Kings returns for us then we will be rewarded and we will rule with Him.

.

"Honk if you love Jesus"

text while driving if you want to meet Him immediately"

Chapter 13

What is the Gospel of the Kingdom?

◆

Turn with me if you would in your Bible to the Gospel of Mark Chapter 4. As you do that I'd like, if you don't mind, to provoke your grey matter a bit. If I were to ask you the question; why did Jesus die on the Cross? How would you answer that? It's pivotal to our faith. We believe that God took on the form of man, lived a perfect life, died on a cross for our sins, was buried and rose again, – why? Because He loved us, yes He truly did. – But why? To redeem us, yes very good, but again why? Why would He want to redeem us? Because He loved us so much, so we can have a place in heaven, so we can be reconciled with God, to cleanse us from our sin. It's interesting that everything I've just listed is true but it's not the reason. Those are all parts of the work of the Cross, of our salvation, of our redemption and our reconciliation back to God. Heaven is our home. These are all truths to allow us to be conformed to the image of His Holy Son. All those things are true but it's not 'the truth'. That's possibly why the Church is so weak. That's possibly why the zeal and the passion that the early Christians had, has waned. – Because we have substituted, 'The' gospel for another gospel. The real question is; why did God send His Son?

Let's look as Mark Chapter 4, reading from verse 10. "*But when He was alone,*" speaking of the Lord, "*those around Him with the twelve asked Him about the parable.* (The parable of the sower) *And He said to them, "To you it has been given to know the mystery of the kingdom of God; but to those who are outside, all things come in parables, so that 'Seeing they may see and not perceive, And hearing they may hear and not understand; Lest they should turn, And their sins be forgiven them.'*" [Emphasis added] To the apostles and those who follow Jesus it was given to them to know the mysteries of the Kingdom. In the last days Jesus said that there will be a renewed thrust of the proclamation of the gospel of the Kingdom. In Matthew 24 verse 14 Jesus says, *"And this gospel of the kingdom will be preached in all the world as a witness to all the nations, and then the end will come."* But surely, that's what the Church has been on about? Haven't we been preaching the gospel of the Kingdom for the last 2,000 years? Well the reality is, no. We've been preaching the gospel of Jesus, the gospel of salvation, and we've even been preaching the gospel of our Church or our denomination. I've noticed on the stained-glass windows just above where I'm standing right now. It says that these windows have been donated for the adornment of the house of God. This is not the house of God. This is a brick and mortar building. The house of God, are the Saints. Peter says so in 1 Peter Chapter 2 verse 5, that we the Saints, we who are born-again, who are living stones, *"are being built up a spiritual house, a holy priesthood, to offer up spiritual sacrifices acceptable to God through Jesus Christ."* The gospel of the Church is not the gospel of the Kingdom. The gospel of the Church speaks about man's religion. We no longer hear about the gospel Kingdom today.

Jesus came to earth so that those who would believe on Him could receive His Kingdom. What did Jesus say to Nicodemus in John Chapter 3, verse 3? Unless a man is born-again he will not see the Church? He will not see heaven? Notice he doesn't say unless a man is born-again he won't see heaven, he says *"Most assuredly, I say to you, unless one is born-again, he cannot see **the kingdom of God**."* {Emphasis added] The Bible is written to account God's single purpose which is to restore a Kingdom, or I should say, reveal His plan of redemption so that as many who believed could inherit a Kingdom. This is a mystery.

There are many mysteries in the New Testament. Things that were in the Old Testament – they were there but you could only observe them through the lens of Jesus. – Clearly hidden in plain sight there, but not understood until the Messiah would come and redeem mankind. Only then, when we look back, do we see this incredible mystery revealed. The New Testament is not a book written about the gospel of salvation, it is written to expound upon the gospel of the Kingdom.

Unless we understand the Kingdom, we will not be able to stand. After His resurrection, just before His ascension, His own apostles, His own disciples asked Him in Acts Chapter 1, verse 6, *"Lord, will*

You at this time restore the kingdom to Israel?" See, the Jews had always been waiting for 'the Kingdom'. The early disciples were waiting for 'the Kingdom'. The Gentile Church is not waiting for the Kingdom. That's why the zeal and the passion for the things of God, has waned dramatically. Jesus says in Mark Chapter 4 and verse 11 that *"To you"* – to those who would believe on the Lordship of Jesus Christ. To those who would embrace Him as Saviour. *"To you it has been given to know the mystery of the kingdom of God;"* Do you want to know the mystery? Do you want to know something about this Kingdom? Do you want to understand what God is trying to do in your life? Unless we understand the Kingdom we won't understand what God is busy with in our lives. God is trying to conform us into the image of Jesus so that we can be citizens of His Kingdom.

In the 12th verse of Mark Chapter 4 Jesus quotes from Isaiah Chapter 6 verses 9 and 10. I would encourage you to follow this in your Bibles, as I said often, "Never trust a preacher; search things out for yourself." Don't take my word for it; take God's Word. Isaiah, like Jeremiah and Ezekiel were called to be prophets to the Nation of Israel. They had a wonderful ministry and God gave them an insight into their ministry. On the day He calls them He says "I've called you to be prophets to the nation but they won't hear you, they won't listen to you." In verse 9 of Isaiah Chapter 6 God says to Isaiah, *"Go, and tell this people: 'Keep on hearing, but do not understand; Keep on seeing, but do not perceive.' "Make the heart of this people dull, And their ears heavy, And shut their eyes; Lest they see with their eyes, And hear with their ears, And understand with their heart, And return and be healed."* Israel, as a nation, came to a place in their relationship with God where they no longer wanted to hear God. There was a very small remnant of God-fearing, law-observing Jews but as a nation they had rejected God.

Therefore, the Lord says to Isaiah that *"hearing, but do not understand."* This Hebrew word for 'hearing' or 'to hear' is very different from the Greek word. The Greek word to hear is 'akouó'. It means to give audience. That's what you doing to me right now, you're listening. But if you were Hebrew speaking and I said to you 'shama', which is the Hebrew word translated hearing in Isaiah, the meaning would be quite different to what an English speaker might understand. The word 'shama' carries far more weight than the Greek akouó or the English 'to listen.' Shama in Hebrew means to intelligently pay attention and immediately obey what you've heard. The Hebrew word to hear, doesn't give you a choice – it's not a suggestion nor does it mean to give audience, listen and make up your own mind. The Hebrew word is more of a command; pay intelligent attention to what is being said and immediately obey. Therefore, when you read the Hebrew Scriptures and you read God saying, *"hear oh Israel,"*- He's saying; "Listen intelligently, pay attention and you better do what I'm going to tell you." Very different from the English, isn't it?

Here in Isaiah the Hebrew is written like this; "shama, shama my law." By hearing intelligently and paying attention with the motive to obey, they will hear intelligently and pay attention but not obey. There's a big difference. It's not that they didn't understand it's that they refused to hear. In the New Testament then, when Jesus says, "He that has an ear to hear let him hear." He's speaking to a Jewish congregation in-keeping with this sense. They understood what He was saying. He wasn't 'asking' them to believe, He was 'commanding' them 'to believe and obey'. Do you see the subtle difference?

We read about the prayer of Solomon when he's inaugurated as King, in 1 Kings, Chapter 3 and verse 5. *"The Lord appeared to Solomon in a dream by night; and God said, "Ask! What shall I give you?"* – Basically, anything that you wish. What is Solomon's request? – He prays for wisdom. In the Hebrew however, it's very different. I just want to give you just a little insight into this because the English very often obscures the true depth of Scripture. In 1 Kings Chapter 3, verse 9, *"Therefore give to Your servant an understanding heart to judge Your people, that I may discern between good and evil. For who is able to judge this great people of Yours?"* That word understanding; *"give to Your servant an 'understanding' heart"* is interesting because it's the Hebrew word shama. So, Solomon in his prayer is actually crying to God saying, "God, give to me a heart that intelligently pay attention to your word and immediately obeys." Do you see the difference? He doesn't want to just understand, he wants to hear God intelligently, to fully understand all that God is saying and to passionately desire to obey. That's the heart of a Christian. The true heart of a believer is to lay aside our thoughts, to lay aside our opinions and to intently and intelligently listen to God and say; "Lord, I will obey, no matter how hard it is for me, I yearn to obey."

Do you want to know about the mysteries of the Kingdom? What is this Kingdom? Turn with me to Luke Chapter 12. It's a well-known portion of Scripture and the same theme is taught in Matthew's Gospel Chapter 6. Let's read Luke Chapter 12, from verse 22 to verse 32. *"Then He said to His disciples, "Therefore I say to you, do not worry about your life, what you will eat; nor about the body, what you will put on. Life is more than food, and the body is more than clothing. Consider the ravens, for they neither sow nor reap, which have neither storehouse nor barn; and God feeds them. Of how much more value are you than the birds? And which of you by worrying can add one cubit to his stature? If you then are not able to do the least, why are you anxious for the rest? Consider the lilies, how they grow: they neither toil nor spin; and yet I say to you, even Solomon in all his glory was not arrayed like one of these. If then God so clothes the grass, which today is in the field and tomorrow is thrown into the oven, how much more will He clothe you, O you of little faith? And do not seek what you should eat or what you should drink, nor have an anxious mind. For all these things the nations of the world seek after, and your Father knows that you need these things. But seek the kingdom of God, and all these things shall be added to you."* Now comes the really interesting part. *"Do not fear, little flock, for it is your Father's good pleasure to give you the kingdom."*

"It is your Father's good pleasure to give you the kingdom." Let's just pause there. This portion of scripture is so important. Christians tend to be great worriers. We have very few prayer warriors but we have a lot of anxious Christians. Jesus makes this statement, "He says you're not like the nations". The word translated nations, in Hebrews is the word 'goiim.' It means those who are outside of covenant. This is profound. Now I'm one of those ministers who do not believe in tithing – at all, at all, or at all. I'm vehemently opposed to tithing, it's Old Testament and I hate it in the Church. Do you want to give a tenth? give a tenth. If you want to give a tenth under the law, then I have an issue with you. Do you think you're going to get blessed by God because you give ten per cent? Show me that Christian who has been. I challenge you to show me one person whose barns have been overflowing and they're pleading with God to stop the blessing? If you can show me that Christian, I will repent and I will leave the ministry forever.

However, God has made a covenant with His people. If we will put Him first, He will take care of us. This is a phenomenal covenant and it's the Covenant that I live under. My children know what my income is and my son is studying actuarial science so he understands mathematics, quite complicated mathematics at that and he can't work out how my salary allows us to live our lifestyle. In other words, I have two children at university, living in a different city but he's coming to understand the reality of putting God first. You're not like the nations. You're not like those who are outside of Covenant. God makes a difference between those who are His and those who are not His. You and I should not be worrying about anything, if we put God first and if we truly seek His Kingdom. Matthew says in Matthew 6, actually it's the same, the same sermon that this was recorded in Luke 13. Matthew 6:33 Jesus says, *"But seek first the kingdom of God and His righteousness, and all these things shall be added to you."* The things of this life; food, clothing, a roof over your head, all these things will be provided.

Jesus goes on to focus on the gist of His message. He's saying in this life, whilst treading on this earth, put God first, and seek God with all your heart then He'll take care of you. But that's not the full story. Whilst on this earth, in this temporary life which is like a vapour, like the grass of the field which today is and tomorrow is burnt-up. He's saying the real essence of your faith and the real purpose that He came to earth is that *"It is your Father's good pleasure to give you the kingdom."*

Let me try to illustrate this for you. There was a period before time. The Father, the Son and the Holy Spirit were there of course, but there was no universe, there's no physical world, there were no angels. *"In the beginning was the Word"* – was Jesus. Jesus was with God, He was with the Father, He was with the Spirit and He was equal to the Father. It's all there in John Chapter 1. But it was in the heart of the Father to have a being that could respond to God's love. A being with intelligence, a being with the emotion that could grasp something of the person of God, and then respond to God. God the Father simply wanted to be a Father. Does that make sense? Therefore, in order to create this being, He had to create a universe. – A universe with solar systems, galaxies and planets so that a planet could contain life. So, the Lord stepped out from the eternity, in which he dwelt, and spoke out the words, "Let there be light." The

185

instant He did that matter was created. Not light as in the sun or the moon but the physics that would allow God then to create the tangible universe. At that exact moment, when matter and space coexisted, time began.

Those of you who are physicists know that space and matter creates time. Immediately that the scale of time was created, at that exact moment God saw everything. He saw the future before the second day, before God create another thing, He knew that this species, this man that He would make would willingly betray God. He knew that this creation of His would willingly bow down to an angel who would tempt him. Right at that moment God had to make a decision; do I continue, do we go to the second day, do I continue with this creation. The Bible says in the book of Revelation that Jesus Christ is *"the Lamb slain from the foundation of the world."* Before the earth was even created, before the planet was created, Jesus said I will pay the price so that Your will, Father, will be done. You will have a people to occupy your Kingdom. This is the heart of God; this is the purpose of God. He so loves us. His heart's desire from before the creation of the universe was to create man. A being like Him, in many respects: – eternal, with intelligence, with emotion, free will. That could, of their own volition, respond to God in love. Gods desires to give to as many of us that would bow the knee to the Lordship of Jesus Christ, He wants to willingly give to them a Kingdom. It was His heart's desire for Israel. As a nation they rejected it but He still cries out, "Will you come, will you believe, and will you bow down."

Unless you're born-again you will not see the Kingdom. This is what the Bible is about. It's about God desiring to bestow upon those who would embrace Him as God, as Lord and as Saviour. He wants to give you a Kingdom. Heaven is just a city; it's not the Kingdom. London is not England, do you know that? If you're Scottish, you say Amen! London is not England. London is merely where the Parliament sits, where the government is seated. Heaven is merely the capital of the Kingdom it's not the Kingdom. How's that for a bit of a mind bender. Have you learned anything yet? Has your understanding of Jesus just gone from narrow, to what on earth awaits us? – The Kingdom of God, the mystery of the Kingdom. *"It is your Father's good pleasure to give you the kingdom."*

Luke Chapter 22 verses 28 and 30 convey the same thought. Jesus says, *"But you are those who have continued with Me in My trials. And I bestow upon you a kingdom,"* notice that Jesus never promises us heaven. Have you noticed that? "You who believe me will go to heaven." That's a Church thing, that's a Church doctrine. It's not the gospel of the Kingdom. We're so focused on going to heaven. I often pose the question to Christians, "Why did Jesus die?" And many reply, "So I could go to be with Him in heaven." I then pose another, "What are we going to do in heaven?" Have you thought about heaven? Many have the view that we're suddenly going to be reduced to some fat chubby infant clothed with a loin cloth or a piece of linen, sitting on a cloud playing a harp. I say to many Christians, "Tell me about heaven?" They'll say, "Well, you know. It's got streets of gold and it's got these gigantic pearl gates and God's glory is there and we're going to be worshipping God. We'll be really worshipping God, and the streets are gold and there are big pearl gates. We'll be there for eternity, there will be no sorrow and we'll be worshiping God in the streets of gold and there's a big pearl gate!" Then I say, "Yes and…" They look at me and wonder if perhaps I'm a moron, that somehow I'm crazy.

And? – "Yes all that you've said is true, but is that heaven?" Forgive me but after a few billion years I might just get bored. I love worshiping God but, you know, sometimes I just need to go have a sleep or have something to eat. Worshiping God is an absolutely glorious thing but is that what heaven is about? The answer is, no. But there is a Kingdom. We, the Church, need to firstly understand that there is a Kingdom and that God is preparing you and me for that Kingdom. Then we need to understand, what it is we are going to be doing in that Kingdom. Would you like to know the answer to that?

You and I are not saved sinners. First and foremost, get that out of your head! The Bible says that we are the sons and the daughters of the Living God. The Bible says in the book of Romans Chapter 8, verse 15, *"For you did not receive the spirit of bondage again to fear, but you received the Spirit of adoption by whom we cry out, "Abba, Father." The Spirit Himself bears witness with our spirit that we are children of God,"* The Spirit of God in us cries out "Abba Father." The Holy Spirit is trying to convey to us our identity. When we pray, do we just recite the Lord's Prayer? "Our merciful redeemer that art in heaven, hallowed be thy name?" No, we call him Abba, Father, Dad.

That's family talk. You and I have been redeemed. The word redeemed means to be restored to a previous position. Therefore, we have been redeemed back to the position that Adam enjoyed with the Lord. Actually, we've been redeemed to a much greater position than what Adam had. But let's be clear, you and I are not sinners, saved. We certainly were sinners that have been saved but our position is now sons and daughters of God who unfortunately still do sin. Did you see the difference, the subtle difference? So many Christians relate to the Father as, "I'm a worm, I'm no good, and I shouldn't even come into your presence." And yes that is true. In my Church I tend to be very forthright; I'm toning it down. I'm in England, you are very polite, and you're not wild South Africans. We are hooligans so I've toned it down but in my Church, I say to people, "You are worms, none of you deserve to be in the presence of God, and just like me you're all pathetic." But just get over it, because God loves you." That's the reality. God loves you; God embraces you as sons and daughters. That's who you are now.

When you offer to surrender your life to the Lord Jesus Christ, as Paul writes to the Colossians in Chapter 1, verse 13. *"He has delivered us from the power of darkness and conveyed us into the kingdom of the Son of His love."* You've been taken out of one kingdom, the kingdom of Satan, the kingdom of this world. You are now, as he writes in Ephesians Chapter 2, verse 6, *"Made us sit together in the heavenly places in Christ Jesus."* Therefore, although you may be sitting here, in this Chapel today, your spiritual position is "a son or a daughter, seated in heavenly places, in Christ Jesus." You are not a saved sinner. You were a sinner but you got saved and have been adopted. You are part of the family of God. You are an adopted son or daughter and God wants you to respond to Him as such.

This requires the renewing of your mind. Do I deserve to have the title "Son?" No, no, none of us do. It's only because of God's grace and His love that allows me to say to Him Abba. Are you understanding this? You are His son or His daughter, if indeed Jesus is the Lord of your life. If indeed your heart's desire is to yield to Him and obey Him. If you truly have given yourself to Him then He is Father. He wants you to relate to Him as Father. How on earth do you expect God to answer your prayers when you come to Him with such doubt as to your own forgiveness? The Bible says in the book of Hebrews Chapter 11, verse 6 *"But without faith it is impossible to please Him, for he who comes to God must believe that He is."* That word 'is' doesn't mean that He exists, it means that He is who He says He is and that He will do what He says He'll do. How do we come to God with boldness if I think of myself as a worm that shouldn't even be using the name of Jesus? Then we wonder why our prayers aren't answered. It's because there's no faith.

Now we don't have to talk about faith because then we think of all the charismatic over-the-top tele-evangelists and we don't like to use that faith. So, what we do is that we just take that part and you rip it out our Bible because, you know, there are certain men who use the same Scripture wrongly so we just take it out, don't we? We don't talk about faith and we think that we've been pious and righteous and religious. No, we're being rebellious and disobedient. We're not 'shama,' we're not hearing God. You are not being a son or a daughter.

You might say I don't feel like a son or daughter. That's ok, that's fine. There are many things I don't feel but we don't walk by feelings, we walk by the faith. We are a son or daughter because God calls us sons or daughters. If your heart hungers for God and your heart is in right-standing with the Lord, then you are a son or a daughter irrespective of how you feel. Faith transcends feelings. Do you need more scriptures which talk to you about being a son or daughter? You've read the New Testament, it's there don't you agree? Praise God. Let's move on. I don't want to linger on things that you should already know.

What is this Kingdom and when are we going to receive this Kingdom? This is important because there are those who are teaching a doctrine called dominionism. They are saying that, the Church will inherit this world and that all the governments of the nations will fall into Christian hands. That the big corporations will all be run by Christians and that we will slowly and systematically take over the world. The Lord never promised us this fallen world.

When will this Kingdom come? When will this Kingdom come to earth? Well the Lord showed all that to a pagan King by the name of Nebuchadnezzar in Daniel Chapter 2. Nebuchadnezzar had a dream and he saw in his dream a vast statue. The statue is then struck by a little stone that is carved, without hands, out of a mountain and the statue is completely obliterated so that no trace of it remains. This little stone grows and grows until it eventually covers the whole earth. But none of the magicians, nor the wise men of the Chaldeans, could interpret the dream until Daniel comes. Daniel interprets the dream and declares that the statue and the various metals and elements that comprise the statue are synonymous of Kingdoms. That the top of the statue made of gold was the Babylonian Kingdom. The breast was representative of the Medo-Persian Empire. The waist was the Greeks and then the legs of iron and clay represented the Roman Empire. The interpretation, as you can read for yourself in Chapter 2, is that at the time of the final Empire, God will begin His Kingdom. His Kingdom will decimate all the kingdoms of men so that there will be no more kingdoms of men. There will be no more government of man. Think about that.

When the Lord sets up His Kingdom, no human being who is not born-again will rule in that Kingdom. There will not be any person in any form of power or authority that is not a blood-washed son or daughter of the Most High God. It's exciting isn't it? When does His Kingdom come? This Kingdom comes when the kingdoms of men are stripped of all their power, when man no longer has any authority on this earth. The Kingdom will come when Jesus comes and He sets up His Kingdom. When Jesus comes and reigns from Jerusalem for a thousand years. That's when the Kingdom will begin. It goes way past the millennium reign of Jesus Christ. Who will inherit the Kingdom? – Those who are born-again, those who 'shama', those who hear.

Unfortunately, in many of our Churches today, we have cheap grace. We have a gospel message that says, "Come to Jesus, just as you are and ask Jesus to come into your heart and He will give you the things you have needed, He'll give you a peaceful life, He'll give you healing. Come as you are." On the other hand, the gospel of the Kingdom says, "Unless you die, unless you lay down your life, and unless you surrender all, you are not worthy. Not even worthy to call on My name. Do you see the difference? We have a Church full of people who have added Jesus to their daily life. Jesus is an addition; He's an annex to their lives. But they still live like the world and they think like the world. However, they go to Church because they've said a prayer and now they're saved. As we say in South Africa, "You can sleep in your garage but it won't turn you into motorcar." Christianity doesn't happen by osmosis. You don't morph into a Christian. Christianity is a very specific decision that one makes to surrender to

His Lordship. The sons and the daughters of the Kingdom are those who have willingly surrendered their lives over, who understand the cost. To truly be a son or daughter of the Kingdom you have to give up everything, you have to surrender everything to His Lordship. And here is just the awesomeness of God because in surrendering everything, you lose nothing because the pitiable things that you have surrendered cannot compare with the glory that awaits.

So, do you want to know what you'll be doing in the Kingdom? Are you interested? All right I shall tell you. Let's go to the book of Revelation Chapter 20. You know this, but you don't know this. You have gnosis of this. Greek is a wonderful language; it's almost as good as Hebrew. In Greek there are different words for knowledge. We have the word 'gnosis' which means the knowledge of things. I have knowledge of South African history. In 1652 a Dutchman from the Dutch East Indian company named Jan van Riebeeck. Normally I'll say this with our homeland Dutch accent because it sounds better. But in 1652 young Jan van Riebeeck arrives at the Cape of Good Hope with three ships the Drommedaris, the Reijger and De Goede Hoop and there they established a halfway station. Did I ever meet Jan van Riebeeck? No. I have knowledge of him, but I do not have epignosis. I have 'gnosis' but not 'epignosis'. Epignosis is to know the man intimately, to understand the way he thinks so that I understand why he behaved the way he did. We have knowledge about Scripture but we do not have revelation, 'the epignosis,' the absolute understanding. God wants us to know, that we know, that we know, what His word says.

Paul's prayer to the Ephesians in Chapter 1 verse 17 was: *"That the God of our Lord Jesus Christ, the Father of glory, may give to you the **spirit of wisdom and revelation in the knowledge of Him.**"* [Emphasis added] Paul prayed that God would give them revelation. Only God can give us revelation. What I'm sharing today, if I share it in my own humanity and you receive it as one man talking to another, it's not going to take root in your heart. But if the Spirit of God carries what I'm saying to your heart, which happens to be receptive, then you'll get a revelation. God will do something inside you that will change the way you understand your Christian walk and your relationship with God.

You know that you're going to rule and reign with Jesus for a thousand years, do you not? You know that, right? That is exactly what Revelation 20, verse four says. *"And I saw thrones, and they sat on them, and judgment was committed to them. Then I saw the souls of those who had been beheaded for their witness to Jesus and for the word of God, who had not worshiped the beast or his image, and had not received his mark on their foreheads or on their hands. And they lived and reigned with Christ for a thousand years."* Praise God. That's what we're going to be doing in eternity, ruling and reigning. That's the theme of the New Testament. Now that's unsettling. If we understand Kingdom and you folks in England should, because until the last century this nation was ruled over by the monarchy. Nowadays you have a constitutional monarchy. You still have the monarchy but it has limited powers. But the history of this nation was of a people ruled over by monarchy. The King would give authority to his lords and to those who were his allies. They would be given authority over counties and towns. Were commoners allowed to be part of the Kingdom? Not a chance. No, you had to be connected to the king.

Hold that thought in your mind and let's go to the parable of the minas. The parable of the minas is recorded in Luke Chapter 19. In Matthew 25 the words of Jesus are recorded as He talks about the rich man who goes on a journey and gives talents to his servants. But Luke's account is considerably different in many respects and I want us to look at it. Luke Chapter 19 reading from verse 11, *"Now as they heard these things, He spoke another parable, because He was near Jerusalem and because they thought the kingdom of God would appear immediately."* Interesting! Let's change our mind-set; it's not about the Church. The Church is simply the blood washed Saints who come together in worship and service to the King of the Kingdom. That's what the Church is. The Church is not the Kingdom. The Church is composed of princes and princesses in training, that's all we are.

So, in this parable, they're approaching Jerusalem. The Jews are anticipating the Kingdom. This is the promise of the Old Testament and you know that there are hundreds and hundreds of verses of Scripture that prophesy about a messianic age. That is why His disciples were always on about the Kingdom. They were always asking about the Kingdom, they never asked Him about heaven, they always asked about the Kingdom. Their prophets of old had spoken continuously about this Kingdom, this incredible age when God's anointed, the Mashiach, in Hebrew, the Messiah would come. When Israel would be the chief nation of all the nations of the world and God would reign from Jerusalem in a rebuilt temple. When God's glory would be seen and the nations would come up to Jerusalem on the appointed feast days to worship God and they would come under the Mosaic Law. Do you know that that is what the Old Testament foretells? That in the reign of Messiah, when he sets up His Kingdom the whole world will be under Mosaic Law. He doesn't talk about grace. There's no grace mentioned, it's all law, law and one more law. Read it yourself in Ezekiel Chapter 14 then Chapters 40, 41, 42, 43, 44, 45 and 46. These talk about the new Temple in Jerusalem and the daily sacrifice and the sin offering and the trespass offering and the animals that are slaughtered. Does that sound like the Church? Does that sound like grace? No. When the Lord returns the dispensation of grace is over forever. Never again will anybody be born-again. When the Lord returns for His Church never again will anyone be born-again. That understandably triggers a whole lot of questions in your mind about what happens to the people alive on the earth during the Millennium. That is a good question but we're not going to answer it right now, however, we will answer it. Am I shaking up some of your theology a little? Praise the Lord, that's my job.

Back to verse 12 of our parable in Luke Chapter 19. *"Therefore He said: "A certain nobleman went into a far country to receive for himself a kingdom and to return."* The nobleman, Jesus, goes to a far country – back to the Father. – To do what? – To await a Kingdom. When He receives the Kingdom, He does what? He returns. Why does He return? He returns to share the Kingdom with His subjects. See how clear that is? The nobleman is Jesus. He goes off to a far country, to the throne of His Father, to receive for Himself a Kingdom and then He returns or will return.

To cut a long story short, because of time, He calls His three servants. To the one He gives ten minas, a Greek coin, to another five and to another just the one. Is that right? Okay, good. Then He returns and we take up from verse 16 because what I really want to focus on is the reward. How does Jesus reward these faithful servants? In Matthews account He doubles their money. – Matthew is Jewish, so he's writing to the Jews. Luke is more Greek so – I'm just kidding. All right, please don't say that I've just made a theological statement! Verse 16 of Luke 19; *"Then came the first,"* and this is at the Lord's return so he now gives account of his dealings, *"And he said to him, 'Well done, good servant; because you were faithful in a very little, have authority over"* – just read that aloud for me, just to be sure that your Bibles says the same as mine – *"have authority over,"* over what? – *"ten cities,"* interesting isn't it. Let's move down to verse 19 and then the second, he comes before the Lord and his mina had earned five minas. Verse 19, *"Likewise he said to him, 'You also be over five cities.'"* What is the reward for faithfulness? Cities; ruling over cities. Now is this doctrinally sound? This is very unsettling, very uncomfortable, "I just want to get to heaven Lord. I just want to get there; I just want to make it out of this Earth. Please don't give me authority; I can barely cope with my household budget. Now you want me to rule over a city!" Oh Christian, that is why we are so weak and pitiful. Because we don't understand God's purpose and we are not readying ourselves for His purpose.

I want to confirm from the scripture that this parable of the minas is not just an isolated account. That it's not just mentioned only this once and it's not a confirmed doctrine of the New Testament. In Revelation Chapter 2 reading verses 26 and 27, Jesus rebukes the Church of Thyatira for their compromise in allowing Jezebel into their midst. But then He says this, in verse 26, *"And he who overcomes,"* – to those who do not go into false doctrine, to those who do not forsake Jesus, so those who remain faithful in a depraved Church, He says, *"And he who overcomes, and keeps My works until the end, to him I will give power over the nations—*"What nations, which nations, whose nations? We're coming back with Jesus when He sets up His Kingdom for a thousand years and He's going to rule the nations with a rod of iron. Who's going to rule with Him? – Yep, you and me.

Why is this important? Why is this important to understand? Doesn't that intimidate you? Doesn't that make you feel over-awed? How am I going to rule? I can barely serve God properly now. Saints, when you know what God's will is for your life, when you know what God is trying to mould you into, then you begin to cooperate. You see, too many Christians are just trying to make it to heaven and not enough Christians are trying to get prepared for the Kingdom. When I read this I say, "Dear God, have mercy. I want to be a man that will rule, as you'd have me to rule." You see God is trying to conform us into the image of Jesus. This is God's plan with you. You are going to inherit a Kingdom. The Bible says when He returns, *"When He is revealed, we shall be like Him,"* we will have His character, but of course, not His deity. God's plan with your life is to conform you into the image of Jesus Christ so that when He sets up His Kingdom you will reign with the same virtue, with the same wisdom and with His character.

I want to close with Romans Chapter 8, a wonderful, wonderful portion of Scripture. Romans Chapter 8, verse 29 and 30, *"For whom He foreknew, He also predestined to be conformed to the image of His Son, that He might be the firstborn among many brethren."* Whom God foreknew, whom God knew would bow their knee to Jesus. You see Calvinists, now I'm not against Calvinists per se, I heard Calvin's commentaries on Daniel where he calls Jesus the Antichrist; I mean yeah, I don't think Calvin was a very good theologian. He was an appalling Governor as well; he just murdered everybody that didn't believe as he believed. So yeah, he's the epitome of a good Christian! If you're a Calvinist repent, God will forgive you and you'll become a Christian. All right, moving along; some of these things need to be said; really they need to be said. Calvinism, what I cannot tolerate and I need to say this because it's going to be recorded. What I cannot tolerate is Christians leaving word-of-faith hyper-charismatic Churches then they go to a Baptist Church that is hyper-reformed and say, "Oh praise God, I'm safe now." Really, that's like going from the frying pan into the fire. If you think that you're in a hyper-Calvinistic Church that believes in predestination and the cessation of the gifts of the Spirit and you think that you're in a good sound Church – are you serious? Alright, Praise God; this message was brought to you by the Apostles of the New Testament.

"For whom He foreknew, He also predestined to be conformed to the image of His Son," Foreknowledge, in this case, is what I explained earlier. The second God said, "Let there be light," time began. God knows all who will bow the knee of Jesus. This is the foreknowledge that Paul is talking about. He's not talking about the preordained selection of certain individuals to salvation to the exclusion of others. That would mean God is partial. Which if He did it would make Him a liar because His word says He does not show partiality. If you can possibly believe in a God who is partial then burn this book because the author of it is a liar. He either shows

partiality or He doesn't. Either salvation is for all, or it is for some, – both cannot be true.

God has purposed that everybody who will embrace Christ as Lord and Saviour, He has purposed for them to be conformed, moulded, changed and transformed into the image of His Son. So that His Son might be the firstborn among many brethren. What is God busy with in your life? He's conforming you into Jesus's image. He's not interested in your comfort; He's interested your character. When you submit your life to Him and say, "Father, whatever it takes conform me, take out everything in me that displeases you." When you are serious in saying that, then God nurtures you, but until that time you are never going to leave the wilderness. You are going to be in a very dry place. God wants us to surrender to His purpose. There is a Kingdom. Saints of the Most High will inherit that Kingdom but it requires that we reflect Jesus, so that we will rule as He would have us rule.

Jesus Christ died so that those who believe and are born-again may receive a Kingdom. The Kingdom will reign over all the earth for a thousand years and into eternity. But that's a different subject. You and I who are blood washed, born-again and remain faithful will be co-heirs of that Kingdom. God is working on our character so that we can govern as His Government. Set your mind on the things that are above. It's not about your salvation anymore it's about your transformation into His image

"Without the Bread of Life

you are toast"

Chapter 14

The Gospel of the Kingdom of Heaven

◆

M atthew 24:14 states; "And this gospel of the kingdom will be preached in all the world as a witness to all the nations, and then the end will come."

The following is that gospel. Preach it throughout the whole world. Go out into the highways and hedges, and compel them to come in, that the Father's house will be filled.

The King is coming. A Mighty King is coming to reign over all the nations of this earth. All other power and authority on this earth will be instantly annulled and cease. Every person alive in the world today is faced with a decision. This coming Kingdom is absolutely certain; therefore, you must answer this question. "What is your position going to be in this Kingdom?"

1. Will you be a citizen and reign with the King?
2. Will you attempt rebellion against the King?
3. Or will you risk to somehow remaining alive with your only hope, a subject without rights in this Kingdom while you await judgement?

The choice is yours but it can only be made now before the King appears. The time is very short.

Who then is the King and why should you prepare for Him?

It is recorded in the annals of history that 2,000 years ago Jesus came to this earth as the suffering Messiah and lived here as a man for about 33 years before His gruesome death followed by His resurrection three days later. Before returning to Heaven Jesus told His followers plainly that He would be back. There were hundreds of recorded prophesies spoken by many different men of God relating to the birth, life, death and resurrection of Jesus and every one of them was fulfilled exactly. Many of these same prophets unambiguously describe the return of Jesus to triumphantly take up His Kingdom and rule over all the nations of this earth in great power. The King is Jesus – Messiah son of David.

Considering the proven track record of the prophets when heralding the first coming of Jesus it is imperative that every living soul urgently takes heed to be ready for His imminent second coming.

You may declare, "I don't believe in God. Such talk of a superior being to whom I must submit is an imaginary invention of generations past with no relevance to modern enlightened understanding." That of course is your choice; God did give you free-will – an undeniable fact. However, before you dismiss this out of hand let's consider many very precise Biblical predictions relating to the return of Jesus that have been fulfilled already in recent history. It's reported that a Russian leader once asked an advisor to prove the existence of God. The man answered in one word - Israel! The Jewish people were scattered to all corners of the globe following the sacking of Jerusalem in 70 AD and the Nation of Israel ceased to exist. However, the Bible foretold that at the end of time the Nation of Israel would be reborn and would again become a strong and prosperous people. Dozens of very clear prophecies given thousands of years ago came to pass exactly as they were described during the re-birthing of this Nation in 1948 and since. This Nation is an indisputable banner to the world in recent living history that God is who the Bible says He is. Regardless of your belief however, Jesus IS coming back and He IS coming back as King to rule over all the nations of this earth in great power.

However, just believing in His return is not the critical issue. The important question is what will your position be in this Kingdom? A ruler with the King, a subject without rights, awaiting judgement or a rebel that will be instantly destroyed by the power of His arrival. The choice is yours and only yours. Furthermore, that choice can only be made now, before He appears. Choose life today.

In the beginning, God created mankind because He wanted to enjoy a close interpersonal relationship for the benefit of both God and Man. However, following the sin of Adam, mankind fell into rebellion against the Almighty God. Every man or women born since Adam has inherit his same rebellious nature. Every person is born separated from God, controlled by a soul capable of only increasing that separation. All mankind is immersed in rebellion against God and regardless of the works of our life, that rebellion cannot be breached.

God's love and longing for a responsive rapport with mankind remained and God yearned for a way to restore that relationship. However, the rebellion of mankind was so repugnant to God that the only way to remove the stain of it was through death. God's righteousness decrees that it is appointed for man to die once, but after this the judgment. Mankind was in an impossible situation with no means to pay the penalty for the rebellion and only judgement when he died. Because of God's great love however, He sent Jesus, born not of the seed of Mankind but of the full and exact essence of the divine nature and character of God – born of a virgin. Jesus lived a perfect life on this earth and when He died, that factual death on the Roman cross, God the Father laid upon Him the sin of all mankind. Jesus shed His blood and gave His life to pay the required price for the redemption of your life and that of all mankind. He paid the full penalty of the sin that separated man from God. Why? Because of God's great love for you. The proof that God accepted this payment for the sin of mankind is that He raised Jesus from the dead. It is well documented that hundreds of people, sceptics included, saw, spoke and ate with Jesus during a period of 40 days before He ascended to heaven. Jesus is a real person who at this very moment is physically seated in heaven at the right hand of God until the time that is decreed for His return to this earth to set up His Kingdom. His return is imminent.

Jesus said, *"For God so loved the world that He gave His only begotten Son, so that whoever believed in Him* (in Jesus) *would not perish but have everlasting life."* He also said that He came to earth and died so that *"they may have life, and that they may have it more abundantly"*. The death of Jesus did not just eliminate the separation between Man and God. The love of God was so great towards mankind that He declared that those redeemed through the selfless sacrifice of the blood offering of Jesus should be;

Joint heirs with Jesus.

They would be adopted as sons or daughters of God.

They would be blessed us with every spiritual blessing in the heavenly places.

They would inherit the Kingdom with Jesus. Jesus told His disciples, *"It is your Father's good pleasure to give you the Kingdom."*

An incredible inheritance with a marvellous eternal life awaits all those who accept Jesus as their Lord and Saviour - to rule and reign forever with Jesus in His Eternal Kingdom.

The key to receiving our God ordained inheritance is to accept Jesus as your Lord and Saviour. Jesus said *"I am the way, the truth, and the life. No one comes to the Father except through Me."* Why?

- Jesus is the only one who has ever lived a perfect life.
- Jesus is the only one who made His life an offering for the sin of all mankind.
- The life blood of Jesus was the only offering that God has, and will, ever accept for mankind's sin.

There is no other way to enter eternal life than through Jesus. The Bible states; *"Nor is there salvation in any other, for there is no other name under heaven given among men by which we must be saved."* It is impossible to achieve a position in the Kingdom by human endeavours or faith and trust in others. The Bible describes man's very best efforts as but filthy rags, – totally unacceptable to God.

The only way to obtain eternal life and to be a part of this Kingdom is to completely surrender your life to the Lordship of Jesus Christ. Acknowledge that in your natural, sinful state, you are blocked from the presence of God, deserving only eternal death and torment. Earnestly cry out to Jesus in repentance, turning from your current sinful life, and ask Jesus to be the Lord of your life. If you genuinely call out to Jesus in this way, truthfully accepting all that He has done for you, then He will instantly redeem your soul and restore it to the relationship God intended at creation. You will become fully born-again. Accepting the sacrifice of Jesus will make you completely righteous, placing you in perfect right standing with God for all eternity. You will be spared from the wrath of God that is soon coming upon this earth and you will be rewarded with eternal life, living and reigning with Jesus for ever and be blessed with every spiritual blessing in the heavenly places, in Christ. What amazing grace – unmerited, undeserving, but incredible favour from a God who loves you extravagantly?

That is the Gospel of the Kingdom. All those who receive this gospel and fully submit to the King of the Kingdom will immediately, during this earthly life, become citizens of Heaven and will reign with Jesus, King of Kings and Lord of lords, for all eternity. Once you're born-again God the Father will embed His Holy Spirit within you, which will enable you to live out your time on this earth in service to the coming King, advancing the Kingdom of Heaven.

All those who eagerly wait for Him to appear a second time, living apart from sin, will receive eternal salvation and inherit the Kingdom with Jesus. Jesus Christ is returning physically very soon to snatch away all those that are true to Him while God pours out His wrath on the unrighteous remaining on this earth. At that point the period of grace and salvation ends. After that there is only judgement. Choose life today because the King is coming and with Him will be all of the redeemed sons and daughters of His Kingdom.

Perhaps you've never actually accepted Jesus as your Lord and Saviour and don't like the sound of being subjected to God's eternal wrath, especially when the alternative is not at all onerous. If that's you I would strongly urge you to cry out immediately, right now, to Jesus. He is real and currently living in heaven. He is God who hears and sees all things. Tell Him you don't want to be separated from God for a moment longer. Freely admit to Him that you are a sinner. Ask Him to cleanse you and help you turn away from your past sinful life. Genuinely submit to Jesus and declare that He is now the Lord, the King, and the Boss of your life. That is all God requires of you to be saved. It is not difficult – repent now, do it today.

God bless you if you have just genuinely cried out to Jesus like that. You have just begun your journey with God. By truly making Jesus the Lord of your life you become born-again, you will receive eternal life and you will inherit the Kingdom. If you continue under His Lordship, you are guaranteed to be spared from God's imminent judgement.

As a born-again son or daughter of God I recommend you join other believers to meet together, to praise our Lord and Saviour and study the Bible – His Word. Speak regularly with God the Father in prayer and, if you can obtain a Bible, read it every day and ask a fellow Christian to baptise you in water.

Praise the Lord!

About the Author

Robert Cottle

Robert (Bob) Cottle has been a scholar of the Bible for over 50 years having read, studied and analysed God's word extensively during his lifetimes' walk with the Lord. The discipline of reading his Bible was instilled upon him at a very young age. At first, this was a burdensome chore but later it developed into a perfunctory habit progressing on to a pleasurable pastime of exploring, in amazement, the detail of the God he loves and serves.

Bob has been actively involved in Church life from a young age and served as a lay preacher for a number of years as well as a Church elder.

Married for 37 years, Bob and his wife Julie live in Nelson, New Zealand, and have three adult children and one grandchild – to date. In his secular life, Bob trained and worked in professional engineering then later in senior business management but is now retired from full-time employment and enjoys writing Christian books.

Blessed with an aptitude to portray verbal and/or written word pictures Bob has focused his abundant free time in retirement to the study and understanding of God's Word – the Bible. Bob is confident with the subject matter of this book given his extensive knowledge of the Bible and the guidance of the Holy Spirit. His desire is to pass on a little of this understanding to aid fellow Christians in the furtherance of God's work.

This is his third book to be commercially published,

Feel free to follow or contact Robert (Bob) on;

Robert J Cottle Author,

@bobcottle,

robertjcottle@gmail.com

If you have been helped by the teachings of this book or have recently become born-again please drop Robert an email and let us know as it's encouraging to hear of God's work in others.

About David Nathan

David was born into an orthodox Jewish family and for the first twenty plus years of his life he studied the Torah and lived as an Israelite knowing only the Law of Moses. God, however, had other plans and, in 1986, David came to faith in Yeshua Ha'Mashiach, Jesus the Messiah. He entered full time ministry in 1992. Since then, he has been involved in many diverse ministries, from evangelism to messianic pastor, training leaders and church planting. David lives in Johannesburg, South Africa and is married to Jacqui. They have two adult children, Jonathan and Jessica.

David is the Lead Elder of Bread of Life Ministries based in Gauteng, South Africa. Bread of Life Ministries seeks to portray a Biblical embodiment of a New Testament Church with a robust sense of community. Doctrine and fellowship are based on the apostolic teachings of the Scriptures together with a Hebraic understanding of family and discipleship. It is of great encouragement to David that, in accordance with the Scriptures, the Lord will perfect His Bride, the Church, before His return. In order for this to happen, there needs to be the restoration of sound Biblical truth in the Body as well as a genuine move of the Holy Spirit to empower believers to preach the gospel of His Kingdom and salvation to all nations, as spoken by Jesus in Matthew 24:14.

The foundation scripture that inspires Bread of Life Ministries is found in John 8:32 *"Then you will know the truth, and the truth will set you free."* David has a passion for Biblical teaching of truth and while he is not a natural teacher, the Lord has blessed him with an outstanding spiritual gift to teach. David teaches on numerous relevant subjects, those essential to a Godly Christian walk and development. He has a YouTube channel that contains a substantial library.

Feel free to follow David on:

YouTube: https://www.youtube.com/user/HighlandWayWhisky

Or contact via Bread of Life Ministries: https://www.bolm.co.za/

Other books by Robert J Cottle

Fifty Shades of White

ONE MAN'S QUEST FOR RIGHTEOUSNESS

ROBERT J. COTTLE

THE

Bible

TRUE, RELEVANT OR
A FAIRY TALE?

ROBERT J COTTLE

Ingram Content Group UK Ltd.
Milton Keynes UK
UKHW012201200323
418888UK00011B/316

9 781087 821948